TERRY SANDS was born in the USA, studied there, served as an army officer, practised law in his own firm, qualified as a Yoga teacher, then moved to New Zealand. He has travelled widely, thoroughly researching existing spiritual paths and has undertaken spiritual training in India and elsewhere.

He is a registered psychologist and psychotherapist, specialising in personal development and spiritual psychology. He has numerous educational qualifications and degrees. Terry currently lives with his family in Canberra, Australia.

Our New Human Consciousness
A Blueprint for our Future

Our New Human Consciousness
A Blueprint for our Future

Dr Terry Sands

ATHENA PRESS
LONDON

Our New Human Consciousness
A Blueprint for our Future
Copyright © Dr Terry Sands 2008

All rights reserved

No Part of this book may be reproduced in any form
by photocopying or by any electronic or mechanical means
including information storage or retrieval systems
without permission in writing from both the copyright
owner and the publisher of this book.

ISBN 10-digit: 1 84748 187 6
ISBN 13-digit: 978 1 84748 187 0

First published 2008
ATHENA PRESS
Queen's House, 2 Holly Road
Twickenham TW1 4EG
United Kingdom

Printed for Athena Press

TESTIMONIALS

'I encountered this Material in 1980 and it literally saved my life. It was what I had been searching everywhere for, and had almost given up hope of finding – clear, pure Truth, a reason for my existence, a connection to something I had sensed, and a subtle map for navigating these interesting, turbulent times we live in. This assistance has been priceless.'

Ms L W (Canberra, Australia)

'Terry Sands' Material has endured the test of time. Twenty-two years of exploring it has given me a different, richer perspective on life. Dr Sands' Material is the only work that I know of that contains practical suggestions of how to mitigate the effects of the current speed of change as well as offering alternatives of how to deal with oncoming issues related to those changes. This Material has helped me deal with the issues that are common to all in the challenging times that we are living. It offers powerful tools to navigate the huge change currently in process and how it can be dealt without fear.'

Mr H S (Melbourne, Australia)

My Copyright and Service Policy

Copyright

This Material is subject to copyright, and I reserve all rights to editing, publication, and distribution. Except with my express permission, no part of my Material shall be published, reproduced, stored in a retrieval system, or transmitted by any other means, electronic, mechanical, photocopying, recording, or otherwise.

I am not aligned with any organisation, religion, cult, or political party.

Service

I am the sole author of this Material. Anyone who receives this Material and wishes to offer feedback or ask questions may contact me directly. I will respond to all sincere overtures.

Cost

The proceeds from the sale and distribution of this Material go to an educational trust to support my work. If you wish to make a contribution to further this work beyond the cost of the books and soundtracks, please contact me.

Contact Details:
Dr Terry Sands
Email: terry@terrysands.com
Web: www.terrysands.com

Contents

Foreword		11
'Who am I, and Why am I Here?'		13
Our Opening of Awareness		21
An Overview		23
1	A Change of Consciousness	26
2	Opening of Awareness	32
3	Inevitable Consequences	37
4	The Activities of Healing	43
5	Avenues and Attractions	49
6	The Attraction of Yoga	55
7	Beyond Yoga	60
8	The Avenue of Devotion	66
9	Transcending the Past	71
10	A Reorientation	77
11	Being and Seeing	83
12	First Steps: New Decisions	89
Our Path of Self-discovery		95
An Overview		97
13	The Path of Self-discovery	100
14	Guidelines on The Path of Self-discovery	107
15	The Way Things Are	110
16	Beginning Discrimination	116
17	Keeping a Balance	122
18	Making the Shift	128
19	A Consequence of Seeing	133
20	Aspiration and Inspiration	139
21	From the Inside Out	145
22	The Dawning of an Inner Discipline	151

| 23 | Self-transformation of the Ego | 155 |
| 24 | Self-reflection and Self-discovery | 160 |

Our Awareness in Transition — 163

An Overview — 165

25	Our Awareness in Transition	169
26	Discrimination in Action	175
27	Accepting True Responsibility	179
28	Shifting the Onus	185
29	Making the Commitment	188
30	Refining the Communication	193
31	Resolving the Dilemma	199
32	Recognising Inner Discipline	206
33	Developing Inner Discipline	212
34	Access	219
35	Attitude and Understanding	226
36	Effort and Action	229

Our Process of Self-determination — 237

An Overview — 239

37	Self-determination	242
38	Reducing Dependency	248
39	Consequences, Ignorance, Action and Destiny	254
40	Relating to the Aphenomenal	259
41	Educating the Life Vehicles	264
42	Facing an Alternative Reality	269
43	Manifesting a New Personal Reality	274
44	Rejecting, Dismantling and Discarding the Old	279
45	Attitude in Transition	284
46	Dismantling an Obsolete Belief System	290
47	Questioning the Basic Assumption	295
48	It's Time for a Change	301

Last Times, First Times: The Work of the Pathfinder — 307

Epilogue: 'Why Me, and What Should I Do?' — 317

THE *TERRY SANDS* MATERIAL

Foreword

I offer this book as an introduction to Our New Human Consciousness which is evolutionarily imminent for humankind on this planet, and I offer a description of some practical steps that we can take towards the creative assimilation of Our New Human Consciousness.

First, we discuss some of the unique characteristics of Our Opening of Awareness that are now being experienced by many in the Western world during this transitory time, and the changes it is bringing. Then we look at Our Path of Self-discovery which is opening up for the Western world. We then discuss Our Awareness in Transition and how we could move into a new consciousness. Our Process of Self-determination describes the steps you can take to develop a new approach to intellectual, emotional, and spiritual growth. Finally, we discuss the Work of the Pathfinder and what you can do to help implement this new consciousness.

Please note: You may find that reading this book is not like reading other books. You might not be able to read a whole chapter or many pages all at once. You might become tired or restless. This is natural. I recommend that should you experience any of these responses, you set the book aside for a time to allow this Material to be gently integrated into your psyche.

As you read, there will be passages which appear to be repetitious. This is intentional. If you consider this book a 'training manual', you will see that certain concepts are introduced early on and then summarised and then expanded in later parts of the book.

The companion volume to this work is:
Our New Human Mind
Leading Edge Mental Technology for

Our New Human Consciousness.

It is available on my website:

www.terrysands.com

Dr Terry Sands

Our New Human Consciousness

'Who am I, and Why am I Here?'

'Who am I, and why am I here?'

This question is perhaps the only thought that occurs to every one of us at some time during our life. There is only one answer to this question, but that answer manifests in a unique way to each culture and to each of us individually.

For some, this question is merely a passing thought; for others, the question is answered by religious teachings; for still others, the question is so serious that it prompts a search of paramount importance and becomes the all-consuming purpose in their life.

As each of us asks this question, so does the voice of our culture rise above the day-to-day struggle and call for an answer of its own. We are calling for a way, a path, and a metaphor to help us understand the nature of our identity and the meaning of our life.

What happens when you ask this question?

If you have asked this question with more than a passing interest, you have probably explored various avenues that appeared to offer any semblance of an answer. You may have looked at various religions; you may have read the odd treatise or book about various spiritual paths now in existence; you may have journeyed to far-off lands and partaken of the answer of a foreign culture; and you may have been attracted to various forms of so-called 'New Age' philosophies. Most of us have read a book or an article or seen a programme about some of the modern gurus and cults that claim to give an answer to those who will follow their teachings. Some of us have even followed one or two of them.

Many of us have all but exhausted the various avenues and attractions that offer an answer and have found the answers wanting. Certainly, many of those paths contain some truth, and many of them are genuine. That is not the question which remains when they have been sampled or explored. The emptiness that hangs in the mind seems to ask for something to fill the void that makes that truth apply to *'me'*. It may say, *'This path may be fine for you, but what about me? Where is the answer that makes my heart sing?'*

We may have explored the history and nature of the paths of other cultures and the reasons why they may not work for those of our new culture who harbour a 'neo-sophistication'. We are different. The philosophy of our culture was born with us. It lay dormant for many hundreds of years, but it was there. As with all cultures, the initial concerns were with a homeland and a home, food and sustenance, propagating our cultural family.

What is a 'culture'?

In this context, a 'culture' is the evolutionary appearance of an old tribe of souls that manifests to occupy once again a time–space spectrum on this planet, or it is the evolutionary appearance of a new tribe that manifests for the first time on the planet in the initial stages of its collective search for development and truth.

The process is ongoing, and, indeed, eternal. A culture may occupy the earth for hundreds or thousands of years before it lifts away for a period of evolutionary development on another plane or level, making way for another tribe or culture to sweep down and spend some time on earth.

Likewise, there comes a time when the individuals of a culture begin to find a way to seek the truth that is timely for them, and hence the culture itself begins to manifest its own form of The Answer. At first, this Answer will be a path to spiritual truth and enlightenment. As the years go by, the Answer codifies and solidifies into religion – a reflection of the Answer that those early seekers worked so hard to find. Also, in the early days, a culture may borrow a religion or a path from another culture or tribe that occupies the earth at the same time. This is especially true when the new culture has not had time enough yet or is not mature enough yet to begin to develop its own path.

What is the new evolutionary path?

The time comes, though, when the new culture must develop and manifest its own evolutionary path.

The new path that is emerging for our culture differs from the old or borrowed paths. For a start, it begins evolutionarily ahead of where the path or religion of the old culture was when the new culture borrowed it. Let's look at our scenario.

Those who are of this new culture know who they are, and they recognise one another. They may have been born to parents of a long line of physical ancestors, but the soul of the culture and the soul of each individual is different: both start with an expanded awareness and a rejection of the old ways.

A new culture is the next stage of the evolution of our human family. Most often, when it is time for a new culture to manifest, it first takes birth in an existing culture, and then breaks away with its own beliefs and values, and it then begins to develop its own spiritual path. Until it is time for the new culture to break away, it follows the ways of its parent culture, and it accepts the ways of that parent culture including the religions of that older culture.

Our new culture has been growing for a few hundred years now – a relatively short time as cultures go. It has been following the religions it inherited from its parent culture. The new culture now comprises an aggregation of souls from many parent cultures and a confluence of many existing religions. The new culture has carried mainly the Judaeo–Christian religious heritage – in many various forms – forth to the present day. This religious heritage was based originally on a real spiritual path. Other cultures have developed their own path, often based on the revelations of a spiritual leader. Each of these religions has developed a higher or hidden (occult) side of the teachings.

Often, a person in a new culture who feels the longing for spiritual growth will find their way to the *occult teachings* of an older culture. Some such persons may have even migrated from the older culture and incarnated to help the new culture.

How will our culture manifest its own path?

The emerging spiritual path of our culture is distinguished from the early spiritual paths of old in one very important aspect: *it will not be manifested by a single teacher*. This new path will manifest from the Spiritual Self of each individual.

This means that the point of manifestation will be a bit higher than it has been for some cultures. When the truth manifests to a culture, the way that truth manifests will depend largely on the state of evolutionary development of the culture. A culture of less evolutionary development will need a more tangible manifestation of the truth: it may need a real person in the flesh who is much more evolutionarily advanced than the others to come among them and tell them how it is.

A culture that is more evolutionarily advanced can become eligible to raise its point of manifestation. This means that it may essentially say, 'All enduring teachings tell us that the Truth is Within.' So, can we find it within? ***Can we do it this time without a guru, a messiah, an avatar, or a master?***

This is an important decision for a culture to make: it is a hard decision, and it is a hard path. It hasn't been done in our culture for a long time, if ever.

How does this new path differ from other paths?

The first thing that is new about this new path is that the truth is going to come from within each one of us: we don't have the luxury of someone coming down from the mountain with the truth in their hand and doling it out to us in scriptures, platitudes, or parables.

There is another characteristic of this new path that distinguishes it from the way previous cultures have manifested their search for truth and enlightenment. We know from the teachings of our religions that periodically there have been natural disasters that essentially wiped out life as it was then known: fire, flood, or other natural cataclysms. This has happened mostly when the situation here got so bad that it could not be corrected except with such a drastic house cleaning. These disasters happened, obviously, at the physical level; we were almost wiped out as a race, at least for a while. And when we woke up from the disaster and started again, we had virtually forgotten the problems of the past. In many ways, these disasters were a luxury for the human race, in that they cleaned out the house very quickly so we could make a fresh start. Some of the instances of this have been lost to our history: for instance, the fate that befell our early brethren in Atlantis and Sumeria.

Now we have to *go through* the cathartic process of cleaning up our own house. In some ways, this is related to our decision as a culture to manifest our own path towards truth from within ourselves. We have decided *not* to have a physical teacher, and we have decided *not* to have a physical disaster.

'Great,' someone says. *'So that means that we're not sentenced to death.'*

'Right,' comes the reply, *'we are sentenced to life.'*

The good news is that we each get to see the truth for ourselves; the bad news is that we have to be able to handle what we see in our truth. It would probably be easier to die and come back again after things are cleaned up than to go through the psychological and spiritual catharsis that we now face. *The fact may be that the salvation from the ravages of the former is inherent in the development of the latter.*

In other words, if we can develop a way – a path – to see the truth (and there is some urgency), and if we can work out a way to apply the truth to ourselves in each of our lives, we can avoid – or minimise – much of the pain that we will have to endure in the transition period while all of the aspects of our new culture emerge.

When will this path emerge, and who will manifest it?

This path is already emerging. There are many who are taking it upon themselves to manifest parts of this new path and *our new consciousness* that comes with it.

These pathfinders who are working with this new way of unfolding the truth within themselves – *Our Path of Self-discovery* – are ordinary people like you and me.

Hundreds, maybe thousands, of such people are accepting the responsibility to experience and document what they know and see so they can add their own unique contribution to this new path.

I have a contribution to make, and I will share it with you.

Part of my contribution has been to search out and document what has been available in some of the other established paths and to help decide what we can use in our new search. This I have done to the best of my ability.

Another part of my work is to take what I know *within* and work out how it can be used to help us find truth. I do not claim to have all of the answers, but I have found some of the questions, and I have worked out some of the answers.

So, who am I, and why am I here?

This question, 'Who am I and why am I here?' is one that each of us must ask ourselves. The answer can come from within you for application in your own life. But the answer to this question alone does not really help us deal with the fearsome prospect of going through the next few years – or even the next few days, or the next few hours – if we cannot apply it in our life. We must develop a way to put this awesome knowledge into practice, else we will go through our own personal cataclysmic disaster, notwithstanding that we as a culture will probably survive physically intact the traumatic transitional time we are entering. The question is whether we will survive psychologically.

I have searched long and hard to discover my share of the aspects about this new path. I am opening some of these findings in this book. They may help you develop a way to find the truth within yourself, and they may help you apply that truth in your everyday life. What you do with this information is your business and your responsibility, for you will create your own consequences, just as I create mine.

To make sure you don't burn yourself up in the process – and have to start all over again – it helps to understand that manifesting this process takes some time and that you will encounter some resistance from your life vehicles – your mind, emotions and body – as you go. If you will take some time to work through the Material in this book, you may find that it works for you.

How will this affect our culture?

Not only are we manifesting a new path of personal enlightenment and truth, we are manifesting a new step in human evolution. This is part of the deal: if we agree to help manifest a new way of life for our human family, we get a new way of life for ourselves: we get to see some truth, and, depending on our own resolve, dedication, discipline, and commitment, we can each move through many lifetimes of our own evolutionary development in a very short time.

Where do we find the strength and inspiration to do this?

To do this, we must first access a new source of Light: **a Positive Presence**. The access point of this new source is at the Point of Becoming just above the top of the head. By 'Point of Becoming' I refer to the point where your Spiritual Self focuses within the soul to manifest into a human being. The planes above the Point of Becoming are spiritual – the Positive realm, the *aphenomenal* realm, the planes of that which is yet to be manifested.

The physical world below that Point of Becoming is the world of *phenomena*: the *phenomenal* realm – the negative realm – the *reactive world*. This is the world we live in: the world in which we play out the inevitable consequences we have created by our actions, thoughts, words, deeds, wishes, fears, hopes, desires, and beliefs. As you tap the opening at the Point of Becoming and open it to an increased flow of Light of the Positive Presence, that light from your own *Light Source* will begin to transform the circuits of your life vehicles: mind, emotion, and body. If you open to it long and strong enough, it will subsume you, and you will become a complete expression of the Spiritual Self: the 'I'.

When you know who that *'I'* Is, you will *know* who you are; you will know more of the truth than you do now. But even if you know who you are, that is not enough: you are only part way there! It is not enough to *know* who you are; you must *become who you are*. When you *are* who you are, then **I am that I am**.

I'll see you there!

Our New Human Consciousness

Our Opening of Awareness

An Overview

When the awareness begins to open, it can herald a time for a personal **Change of Consciousness**. This change of consciousness is that change which is evolutionarily next for humankind. This chapter examines how consciousness works. Then we look at the **Opening of Awareness**. An Opening of Awareness enables one to become aware of being conscious, and this opening is dependent upon a certain degree of evolutionary maturity. When this opening occurs in one who has been completely enmeshed in worldly or secular life and in material pursuits, the opening can be traumatic and dynamic.

It helps if one is acquainted with the concept of **Inevitable Consequences**, the workings of karma. Each lifetime is but a day in a lifetime of lifetimes. As the course of one's lifetime is shaped in this manner described above, so is the course shaped of one's lifetime of lifetimes. As one begins to open, one may become interested in **The Activities of Healing**. In our world at present, there seems to be an obsession with healing, but before one embarks on the 'healing path', it is best to acquaint oneself with some of the consequences of healing and how it works.

Then we look at some of the **Avenues and Attractions** that may appear interesting as one opens. These include astrology, spiritualism, and meditation. But one of the most popular attractions is **The Attraction of Yoga**. Here we discuss the various forms and purposes of yoga, including the benefits and the pitfalls of which one needs to be aware – especially working with the *kundalini* and why these activities are not suited to the present Western culture and certain schools of yoga imported from the East.

Our change of consciousness will herald a new approach to spirituality which will go **Beyond Yoga**. Although we have experienced a great interest in Eastern disciplines such as yoga in the recent past, we will now move into the creation of a special path tailored to the needs of the Western world. We will see that the point of destination of the practices of old is the point of beginning of the practices of the new which will emerge from a change of consciousness: **the new starts where the old finishes, and one who attempts to follow imported disciplines from other times and cultures may face the daunting realisation that the cause for which one has fought and struggled is now obsolete.**

Another path which we have inherited from cultures of old is **The Avenue of Devotion**. In the past, the application of devotion was on the part of a devotee, or a disciple, and, in the first instance, it meant devotion to the guru: 'the one who waits'. The new path will be based more on a path of enquiry rather than on devotion to a guru. One who is opening starts with a 'knowingness' within; and that knowingness, while yet to be fulfilled, leads one on a path of enquiry into truth. There are very few of the trappings of the old path in the new one. We are truly faced with the task of **Transcending the Past**. We will work with a new mental operating system to develop *Our New Human Mind*, we are dealing with new energies becoming evolutionarily available to us, and we are manifesting a new path of self-discovery which emanates from within the Spiritual Self of each of us.

To place one's foot on *Our Path of Self-discovery* requires **A Reorientation**. It is an evolutionary fact that if one is incarnated at this time on this planet in the condition that the planet is in, one is now facing not only one's own trove of personal evolutionary inevitable consequences, but also facing, in some part, the consequences which the planet must inevitably face as a whole, as individual tribes, and as a collection of tribes and nations. Thus, by one's presence on this planet at this time, one is, by definition, involved in this present state of affairs and in the changes which are now taking place.

There is a very basic difference between the old approach and the new approach.

> **The difference in approaches is so basic as to be foundational: it involves the difference between concentration and non-concentration; the difference between placing *energy* into a place, spot, or point where it is *concentrated* and the placing of *awareness* so that it is present and *concentred*, but not *concentrated*.**

This new approach will go about things in a way which is almost certain to be almost completely in opposition or contravention to that which one has been developing and employing in one's practices, techniques, and thoughts.

The key words for this new approach are **Being and Seeing**. For starters, memories just aren't what they used to be. One opening now in this time of transition may find that the recall process, or the circuit memory, of even a short time past is becoming less effectual. One may also perceive that the items recalled, the memories themselves, carry less and less significance. This can be very disconcerting, and we now have many walking the earth who have become disoriented, confused, and depressed. This is a characteristic of *Our Awareness in Transition*.

As we develop a new mental operating system, we take the **First Steps: New Decisions**.

Today humankind in the Western world is reaching the point where even the most outlandish desires are within easy reach. Now where does this leave humankind? With a new hunger. It leaves us with new needs – *really new needs* – from projects which we have manifested into thought-form and further into the form of desire-plan. But it also leaves us with a mentation process which is ill-equipped to deal with even a fraction of the intricacies, details, and creation of the articles of fulfilment of these new plans and intentions. **We are left with the massive problem of how to meet the consequences of desires and actions, let alone the incomprehensible consequences of the gargantuan proportions to which the individual – as well as the collective ego – will expand as a result of the accomplishments and the pride taken therein.** One who is opening to that which is known within will recognise that which is being described here.

How then is one to dismantle this self-limiting syndrome? There are two basic simple steps which one can take. The first involves the approach to that which arises from within the Self in the nature of a prompting – a 'knowingness' that one is about to be called upon to do something or take some action, the nature of which, at least at first blush, is unsupported by any 'logical' purpose. The second step involves the development of the ability to move to the action to be taken after perceiving only the initial action to be taken. This comes without knowing or being able to perceive the actions which will then follow, or even the reason for the first part of the action to be taken, let alone the entire operation. One who can begin to work with what is described herein will be ready for the Material which will follow this book.

1 A Change of Consciousness

When the awareness begins to open, it can herald a time for a personal change of consciousness. But before we can see how consciousness changes, we must first examine how consciousness works.

For the purposes of this discussion, we will accept that *consciousness is*. Consciousness exists.

If so viewed, it could be said that consciousness does not change.

Consciousness projects: into matter.

In its projection, consciousness amalgamates or fuses with matter.

Matter is constantly changing.

Matter changes according to its own laws, and consciousness, below its point of projection, and in its matter-fused state, is subject to those laws of matter.

Changes in matter are not necessarily changes of consciousness.

Changes in matter are rearrangements of matter according to the laws of matter and are largely reactionary in nature.

The laws of matter are a reflection of the laws of evolution.

Consciousness in matter changes according to the laws of evolution.

A change of consciousness is a transformation rather than a rearrangement, and it precipitates a change in the laws of matter.

Consciousness exists in matter regardless of the evolutionary maturity of matter.

Matter, once it has reached a certain evolutionary maturity, has the potential capacity to become aware of itself.

Once matter begins to become aware of itself, it begins to become aware of being conscious.

An opening of awareness enables one to become aware of being conscious, and this opening is dependent upon a certain degree of evolutionary maturity.

The change of consciousness referred to here is precipitated by an evolutionary necessity, according to evolutionary laws, for those on this planet to become aware, to become aware of the need for change, and to change.

A change of consciousness is something in and of itself. Its nature is something new and different. Although it will borrow from the old in some ways, it is more than a mere rearrangement of the old ways.

The change of consciousness will be a true change: that is, it will be a metamorphosis, wherein that which is now one thing will become something else, retaining only the slightest hint of a resemblance to what has gone before.

The events of the past several decades, and even the events of the past several hundred years, have been merely manifestations of that which can be and has been created by an obsolescent consciousness on the part of humankind.

Anyone who views only the outer manifestation of creation, that is the phenomenal proliferation, ignoring the deeper aspects of humankind's nature, may believe that these events in history are the cause of that which is coming. These events are, in fact, neither the cause of the change of consciousness nor even an indication of the need for change.

Rather, the change of consciousness is that change which is evolutionarily next for humankind. 'Change of Consciousness' in this Material does not refer to the changes which humankind must make to enable it to accept the change of consciousness. Those changes which humankind must make are changes in lifestyle, thought style, relationship, and attitude, and they are preliminary to the creative implementation of the change of consciousness.

It is not implied nor to be inferred nor assumed that humankind's ability or inability to make these changes will determine whether or when the change of consciousness occurs; rather, the change of consciousness *is* inevitably next. It is the next evolutionary transformation of humankind's nature.

The comments in this book offer a way for one opening in awareness to assimilate creatively the change of consciousness through one's individual life, and hence into the collective consciousness, for that which one does affects all. What one does in one's own life can and does, even in some small way, affect the evolutionary state of all.

The *opening* to which reference is made here is an opening to another part of one's whole being.

In the beginning, when one first begins to notice that something is happening, it may appear as a very private sensation deep within. This sensation will be only a hint at first, and it will most likely be ignored by one who is feeling it. There is a way to become receptive to it, but before one can become receptive to it, one must take notice of it: that is, one must acknowledge that it is there.

When the possibility begins to dawn that something is happening within, one may feel some apprehension, and this will probably be a time when one attempts to pursue activities which will divert the attention so that one will not have to take notice of these new and strange sensations. The activities in which one will engage will be as intentional distractions. And they will work for a while until the sensation begins to grow and until it cannot be ignored any longer.

That which is happening is a natural phenomenon which, if approached correctly, will occur naturally, as it is meant to do. This is an 'opening'. This opening can occur within anyone, regardless of where one finds one's self in life, regardless of one's physical age, and regardless of how open one believes one's self to be already. This opening occurs so that one can become changed.

There is a basic opening of awareness which occurs when one first begins to open, and there are further openings or what becomes one continuous opening as one adapts to and moves with the changes in one's expanded awareness.

When this opening occurs in one who has been completely enmeshed in worldly or secular life and in material pursuits, the opening can be very forceful and traumatic. It will probably shake the very foundations on which one's concept of reality rests, and there will be little that one opening can do about it. There will probably be no one, at least no one of whom one knows at that time, to whom one can turn for help. If one turns to one similarly enmeshed in the material world, that person to whom one turns will not understand, unless he or she has also experienced the opening to some degree. There may not be anyone or anything which would seem to be of help.

This book describes what one may feel as the opening of awareness begins. It discusses some of the avenues and attractions already in existence to which one may be drawn in the early stages of the opening. It provides a perspective which the one opening may be unable to provide for one's self in this time of transition. Finally, it suggests the emerging outlines of a way – a different approach – by which one can maintain a state of personal balance as one enters a time of the opening of our Awareness in Transition.

This book is an introduction to the concepts presented, and other books that follow this will present increasingly specific and detailed discussions of various aspects of those concepts.

One who is opening in awareness and is first affected by this change of consciousness may begin to become aware of what appear to be hints, promptings, nudges or suggestions, from within or without. These suggestions are coming from the part of one's self to which one is opening, and one of the purposes of this book is to help one to become more open to these suggestions.

If one senses that one has detected a suggestion from within or without – a hint that 'something is happening' – one can begin to work with such a sensing by first recognising that a change, or part of a change, can first signal itself from within one's self. One needs then to recognise that a change which is signalling itself first within one may be an aspect of a change which is signalling itself simultaneously within others, and which will, in time, manifest externally.

As a change becomes more manifest or phenomenal, it will in time be signalled also from without either by imposition, unrest, or change of custom. There is a suggestion here that something can have credibility and authenticity while still known only within the self, even before there is any hint of external

Our Opening of Awareness

confirmation; and one who is opening will find the hint of this possibility very significant as one's opening unfolds.

One may first recognise that a coming change can be sensed by one, within, here and now:

- before it is sensed or seen by others;

- before one hears about the change from another source outside the self;

- before one is forced to accept a change due to an event in one's life illustrating the change;

- before a series of collective successive events culminates in forcing one to draw the conclusion, intellectually, that one must make a change; and

- before the change is recognised by one's peers, or society, and imposed by a change of societal custom or law.

If one can recognise early on that there exists at least a possibility that one can sense, that is, that one has the capacity to sense, *at all*, from within, it will greatly increase one's receptivity to one's internal sensory system. As one opens, the sensings will become so strong that one will no longer be able to ignore that this internal sensing system exists. One will naturally wish to place into action what is needed for one to avail oneself more and more of these vital suggestions.

It is at this point that one will follow one of two approaches:

1. one will either move with one of the sensings and thence develop some trust, or

2. one will trust a sensing and move with it, even though one does not understand that with which one has resolved to move.

A result will ensue.
One will mentally assess this result by two sets of criteria:

- **Firstly**, it will be assessed to be personally either right or wrong;
- **and secondly**, it will be assessed to be personally either painful or pleasurable.

Following the first approach described above, that is, moving with a sensing in order to decide whether or not one can trust it, one will, invariably, base one's assessment of the result on the second set of criteria, that is, the resulting pleasure or pain, and one will probably react and plan future action accordingly.

If, however, one employs the second approach, that is, to first trust the sensing and move with it even though one does not understand that with which one has resolved to move, then one will be more likely to base one's assessment of the result on the first set of criteria – that is, whether the result is personally right or wrong.

One who is experiencing a dawning detachment may then, with some effort, perceive that a result can be personally right although painful, or personally wrong although pleasurable. At this juncture, one will become more capable of creating an attitudinal environment in which the sensing system can be utilised and expanded fully and intentionally.

One can be more receptive to this sensing system if one can conceptualise what one formerly believed to be the first indication of change is now really the last indication of change: that is, the final manifestation of a change which one perhaps earlier first saw within oneself. If one continues to wait for the last or final indication of change, that is, if one delays recognition of the change until it is imposed from without, one invites trauma in reaction and adaptation.

If one can begin to recognise the possibility that change can happen from within outward rather than from outside inward, then one can begin to sense changes coming before they are imposed from without. This is a branching out in a new direction not only for a fresh culture but also a branching from the disciplines which have existed before now in other cultures. It is a new direction and it requires a different approach.

However, before discussing a new approach, it will be useful to discuss the teachings and disciplines that are already in existence. We will present an in-depth discussion of just how these disciplines and teachings have served in the past, what they teach, and what there is in them which may be carried forth towards the implementation of a change of consciousness.

Then some of the later chapters offer an introductory description of some aspects of the 'different approach' which is now beginning to emerge and which concerns the changes which may come about mentally, emotionally, and physically in one who is opening.

It is intended that the Material contained in this book, and the books which will follow, will enable one to approach the changes which are occurring with lightness, joy, and a positive approach. There is a way to do this, but it must be practised to be experienced and seen.

However, these matters of which we speak here are only preliminary, and this chapter has been an introduction. It was placed here, in Chapter 1, because no one ever reads an introduction!

Here's wishing you a joyous opening!

2 Opening of Awareness

The opening of awareness to which reference is made here is occurring in large numbers of those in a fresh culture in the Western world, for which this Material is written, as that culture prepares for the assimilation of certain aspects of a change of consciousness.

There will be a necessity for the fresh culture to undergo certain changes in a relatively short time as the time approaches for the implementation of a change of consciousness.

As one's awareness begins to open, one's perspective will begin to change and one will begin to take a different view of life. There may be a feeling that one is no longer a part of the stream of activity in which one has previously engaged. A certain 'awareness' will begin to emerge.

In some, it will engender a feeling of personal urgency. In others, there may be a compulsion to seek out information which previously held little interest. In all, there will be a turning from one pursuit to another. There will be a rearrangement of priorities in one's life.

As one begins to open in awareness, one will be affected in each of the three physical articles of expression – the life vehicles – that is, the physical body, the emotional body, and the mental body. What is happening at this time, to one feeling new and different sensations, is merely an opening to another part of the total being.

That to which one is opening is of a part of one's being which is not physical, not emotional, and it is not mental. The nature of this part of the being to which one is opening is unable to be grasped or comprehended by any of these life vehicles with the state of consciousness at the time of the initial opening.

The existence of this part of the total being is often dismissed because there is no adequate scientific, social, or religious explanation: it is outside of the intellect, and it is beyond the mind. It cannot be understood, but it is real, and the acknowledgement of its existence is the first positive step which one can take in the opening.

This acknowledgement is a natural and evolutionary step.

This acknowledgement of the existence of this non-phenomenal part of one's being will have profound effects on the physical bodies, that is the physical body, the emotional body, and the mental body. It will have profound effects on the way one views those bodies; and it will have profound effects on the way one relates to those bodies.

By taking this step of acknowledgement, one implicitly takes notice that things are not as one has believed them to be. This acknowledgement will shortly become more explicit and patent as it moves into the external awareness, for it will have consequences at all levels of one's existence.

Once one has made this acknowledgement, one has thus set in motion a process of finding out how things really are. It is then inevitable that one will find out how things are.

Having set in motion a process of finding out how things really are, one will begin to pursue some line of enquiry towards that end. For some, this acknowledgement will create an impetus to explore certain avenues and attractions which have previously held little or no interest. For others, perhaps already interested or involved in the investigation of these existing avenues and attractions, there will be a heightened sense of investigative purpose, and an interest in what lies beyond that to which they have already been exposed.

For some, the existing avenues and attractions will intuitively be found to be of little interest, for they will be drawn directly to metaphors of expression which are only now beginning to emerge, which are most suited to the needs of a freshly questioning generation, and which hold little relationship to those avenues and attractions that now exist.

The nature of this time of exploration will vary according to one's own individual evolutionary needs, and it is not to be assumed that each one opening will have the same range of experiences, or even the same experiences to the same depth or breadth. The depth and breadth of the experiences one will have and the activities in which one will engage will vary from one person to another.

There may be a curious admixture of these experiences and activities, for some of them come from the past and some from the future. Some come from the past of one's own evolutionary experience and will be determined by one's own inevitable consequences. Some will come from the opportunities which can or will open to one in one's future.

Some will draw from both of these as one faces an inevitable consequence which provides the back-pressure to bring forth whatever is needed for one to open to an opportunity.

On opening, one may have difficulty if one attempts to reconcile the experiences which one is having with one's present concept of reality, for one's perspective of reality is changing and one's perception and interpretation of one's experiences are, to say the least, then limited. As soon as possible after one begins to open, *and at appropriate times thereafter*, it is helpful on opening to acknowledge that something is happening or has happened in one's self, in one's life, and to acknowledge that at present it is inexplicable. This is most important!

There is interplay between intellect and emotion which may lend impetus to the tendency to attempt to explain that which one is as yet ill-equipped to understand oneself. As well, there may be pressure on one from others to attempt to explain that which one is experiencing.

The nature of the difference between the experiences of one who is opening and the experiences of someone not yet opening renders it impossible for this abyss (essentially a time differential) to be bridged by explanation or discussion. There is, at present, no intellectual structure which can span that gap.

When one comes into contact with any material which offers one some answers to the questions posed as one opens, there is an understandable elation at finding some answers. Unfortunately, it is the nature of the ego of the Western world to analyse that elation instead of simply experiencing and enjoying it.

There is an obsessive need to understand, understand, understand, and when one has grasped some understanding, or believes that such is the case, there is then an obsession with attempting to share that understanding with others, even if the others do not wish to be told.

Soon the introduction of the change of consciousness will move the collective ego of humankind of the Western world towards a time when the present concept of 'understanding' will be recognised as outmoded and obsolete. There will be a growing tendency towards an acceptance of another dimension of understanding and 'knowingness'.

One will be well advised to adopt an attitude of enquiring receptivity as one opens in awareness. Although there may be a beginning of a knowingness within, still one is ill-equipped to explain, even to one self, the full and exact nature of that which is happening within, and there is much yet to unfold within. Such an attitude of enquiring receptivity will enable one to experience the opening with the most ease.

Let us now consider this awakening or opening of awareness. Let us consider some of the experiences which one may have and some of the activities in which one may engage, from the time of the awakening to the time when one truly begins to experience a further unfoldment. That with which we are here concerned includes those matters which present themselves to one who is opening and which are presently outside their secular activities or lifestyle.

In the beginning there may be a dawning of an interest in such matters. They may be suggested by one's friends or acquaintances. They may continually appear in the books one picks up or the articles one reads. But they have this one thing in common: they are not included in the present secular activities of the one who is opening. Thus, they could be said to be personally 'asecular' or 'non-secular' activities.

In the discussion of the various avenues, attractions, and activities which follows, it is not suggested that one who is opening should follow or pursue any of the avenues or attractions here discussed. Nor is there any intention, insofar as possible, to place any judgement on the value of any of such approaches, for it is part of the nature of that which is emerging that every individual is to determine the length and breadth and depth and substance of their own enquiry.

Those avenues and attractions which are discussed herein have at least three things in common.

- **Firstly**, they are now in existence: that is, they have been manifested, they are established, and, in some cases, they are so established they have been crystallised. They are, in many cases, set in their ways.
- **Secondly**, the characteristic which they share is that they all, with few exceptions, were created to accomplish a rearrangement and are sustained by an energy which is employed in a concentrated manner.
- **Thirdly**, they are, for the most part, concerned with affecting the articles of expression, that is, all three of the physical bodies: the physical, fleshly body; the emotional or astral body; and the mental or intellectual body. They work and operate with the energies which operate in these bodies.

These points are mentioned here because the one who is opening and being approached by or attracted to these activities may find that there are sensings – within – which will affect the way in which one relates to these activities. That is, in contrast to being able to accept anything which is crystallised, on opening one is opening to activities which are characterised by a dynamic fluidity.

Further, the change of consciousness is characterised by true change, that is, change which is not a mere rearrangement of that which is already in existence, and it is manifested by a Presence rather than a concentrated energy.

Additionally, while the care and sustenance of the physical bodies is of major concern in the maturation and later transformation of the life vehicles, it is not to be considered to be an end in itself; and one who is opening will sense this fact. It will become clearly sensed, as one opens, that it is imperative to have clean and clear bodies in order to see and do that which one will be prompted to do from within, as one's own purpose begins later to make itself known.

The other one characteristic which must be mentioned here and now, but which must wait until later for expansion, is that the avenues and attractions to be discussed in their present form rely on a mentation process, a way of thinking, which is in itself crystallised and which is now obsolescent, if not fully obsolete.

One who is opening, also opens up to the introduction of a different mentation process: this is not just a different way of looking at things, but a different way of seeing things.

These various avenues and attractions to which one may be drawn are, however, useful, and, in some ways, necessary. They can, in some instances, open up vistas which were theretofore closed to or non-existent for the one who is opening.

Some of them are of a religious nature, that is, they are activities which are derived from spiritual teachings of the past and which are now crystallised in some form of teaching or dogma which is or has been useful for a culture and those who reside in a culture which required some form or framework within which to live: some dogma by which to make some order in life.

Religious activity, especially in the West, derived in the beginning from the manifestation and appearance of spiritual truths, but these truths were then formularised into precepts which actually appealed more to the intellect and the emotions rather than to that part which one who is opening will eventually come to know as the Spiritual Self.

Some of the avenues, attractions and activities dealt with in the chapters following the next chapter are discussed in varying detail for the purpose of enabling one who is opening to become familiar with them. It is not suggested that everyone opening will find an equal attraction to those approaches described; however, as we have stated earlier, familiarisation with them – to a greater or lesser degree – enables one who is opening, in this time of transition, to gain some appreciation of that which has been available in the past. It also gives one some basis for moving with that which is to be offered in the future.

Before moving to that discussion, however, it is important to explore the concept of Inevitable Consequences – the principle of karma. This is the subject of the next chapter.

3 Inevitable Consequences

For a soul taking birth repeatedly in the earth realm, there is a wheel, or a circle, upon which the soul is riding or around on which the soul is revolving. This is a cycle through which the soul is moving while it is evolving. During the revolutions of birth, death, and rebirth and re-death, the soul accumulates a storehouse of experiences. From these experiences arise desires for more experiences or desires to avoid certain other experiences.

Most of the experiences which one has are merely the result of other experiences through which one has gone and in which activity one has expressed a desire. Actually, these desires in themselves are enough to create certain consequences, but, together, the activity in which one engaged and the desire which one expressed create a new consequence that the soul must eventually and inevitably experience. If the particular experience is not encountered in the present lifetime, then, to undergo that experience, the soul must be born again and take on another set of integrated physical life vehicles.

During this cycle, the consequences which one creates could be said to be of three kinds:

- **Firstly**, there are the consequences that are being created by the actions, reactions, desires and thoughts. These are being 'put away' for the soul, and they will eventually and inevitably be brought forth for the soul to face and, as the case may be, either to enjoy or to endure;
- **Secondly**, there are the consequences which have been stored for some time, or times, and which are now in the trove of experiences which the soul is facing, enjoying, and enduring in the present incarnation; and
- **Thirdly**, there are consequences which are now in storage, as it were, and have been in storage since they were created by action, reaction, desire, or thought, and they will remain in 'storage' until they are brought forth to be faced in some future lifetime.

If these consequences are likened to seeds, they could be said to be first, the seeds which one is sowing (the creation of consequences); second, the seeds which are stored and quietly resting just below the surface and germinating in preparation for the time when they will sprout – that is, the seeds which are growing (consequences already created which are being stored for future experience); and, third the seeds which have sprouted and which one is now harvesting or mowing (those consequences which one is now facing and experiencing).

As mentioned, these consequences that must inevitably play themselves out arise as a result of previous activity by which they were created, and which activity was done by the one who must, inevitably, face the consequences. These consequences were probably created, for the most part, more by a reaction rather than an action. However, for the purposes of the creation of consequences – at least for our present purposes – they are essentially the same.

We will eventually see that a particular attitude and a particular kind of positive action, as opposed to reaction, can have an effect on the consequences which one creates; it also has an effect on what happens when these consequences are inevitably faced.

During the course of each day while one is occupying a physical body on the earth, one faces innumerable events and situations which elicit some kind of activity or reaction on one's part. These events and situations may appear as a stroke of good fortune; a temptation; a surge of anger; the appearance of some dis-ease; the flash of an idea; the receipt of some news, good or bad; an outpouring of love or compassion; the compulsion of some desire; or any of a host of other ways of inventive expression.

By the end of the day, only a few of the incalculable number of thoughts, desires, emotions and actions remain in the waking memory. By the following morning, even fewer of those events and their related activities remain in the waking memory. With the passage of more days, fewer yet appear in the waking memory, and only a minute number of them are recallable at will, in spite of one's continuous attempt to hold them available for consideration.

Yet, these events, the activity in which one engaged in relation to these events, and the activities in which one will, in some future day, engage in relation to these events, all remain deep within one: deep within a peculiar storage system. They cumulatively shape the events that one will face during the present, and they shape a behavioural repertoire that will in turn shape the activity in which one will engage in relation to those events which are faced during each day.

Although certain scientific approaches have attempted to postulate and theorise on the workings of this behavioural system, none has yet adequately explained it, for they pay attention only to the physical aspects and neglect certain other elements, the existence of which they have thus far refused to acknowledge.

The events themselves which one faces each day actually began as consequences from activity in which one engaged when faced with an event on a previous day. They now come forth to elicit some activity on one's part, and

Our Opening of Awareness

they then become embellished with the results of the present activity and speed forth to meet one on some future day in the form of yet another consequential event in a meeting which is, so to speak, cosmically inevitable.

Each lifetime is but a day in a lifetime of lifetimes. As the course of one's lifetime is shaped in this manner described above, so is the course shaped of one's lifetime of lifetimes. Just as the memory of the events and actions of each day fades with the end of each day, so does the memory of the events, actions, and activity of each lifetime fade with the termination of each lifetime, and the consequences being carried forth for one to meet them in the next day – or a later day – in the lifetime of lifetimes.

Just as at the beginning of each day one faces certain events, so at the beginning of each lifetime when the soul projects into an integrated set of life vehicles, there are certain events which are programmed by oneself, incidentally, for one to face during a lifetime. Some philosophies and teachings misinterpret this course of events as one to be lethargically and passively endured.

While it is true that one is, in the beginning, largely at the mercy of the events being faced, one can be in a position, with a certain attitude, to face and convert such events to opportunities. But more is needed than just a change of attitude.

In this era, on this level of creation, humankind is not generally sufficiently evolved for most of those taking birth to be able to remember, or to be able to recall from one day to the next, nor from one lifetime to the next, all of the events, activities and consequences which cumulatively shape one's course. Nor have we had, in the past the ability to perceive and interpret the connective interplay of these events, activities and consequences from past days and past lifetimes. This will soon change as well.

During the lifetimes when one has taken birth and occupied a set of physical life vehicles, one has also created behavioural patterns which are actually an automatic reaction system. This system was created by a summary of desires, fears, sympathies, antipathies, curiosities and wonderments. Whether one is externally aware of the automatic reaction patterns or not, these patterns are stored in one's circuits, carried with one from day to day and from lifetime to lifetime. When certain events transpire to stimulate them, these behavioural patterns pop forth, sometimes automatically, sometimes deliberately, and engage the life system in yet another reaction. One has almost no control over this system and the reactions it precipitates.

Whether one intends to express those reactions or not, they are just as effective for the purpose of creating further inevitable consequences as are those actions or reactions which one intends to express. The operation of this system of behavioural patterns, coupled with the immense trove of stored experiences, thus renders most of the activities in which one engages not to be actions at all. These activities in fact become mostly reactions, either intended or unintended, automatic or deliberate. Until one begins to transform one's vehicles towards gaining some ability to engage in creative action, the notion of free will remains a myth.

In addition to this almost endless trove of experiences and events, which will eventually come forth, and in addition to the system of automatic behaviour within each one, there is also an intricate and complex system of mentation: a method of thinking and making decisions. This complex thinking system has grown and developed in each individual consciousness and in the collective consciousness of most of the tribes which now inhabit the planet. This system attempts to anticipate present and future events mostly *by reference to past events*. It attempts to plan the reactions which one will put forth to meet those events by reference, once again, to past events. Such plans are further usually made in reference to past strategies. It is seen, then, that this complex system of mentation is not an objective, pure, creative system, but it is, in fact, crystallised and reactive in nature. This mentation system or decision-making process will also change and be replaced.

One who is facing the events which arise is also constantly faced with conflicting signals from the various levels of the integrated vehicles – signals of physical need, desire, reason or rationalisation – which attempt on occasion with varying success and un-success to override the competing needs and desires. The resolution of these conflicting signals, within, is one of the things of which personal evolution is made.

If one who has spent many days, or lifetimes, dealing with the conflicts of desire and reason, need and want, and one's awareness is now beginning to rise above the imbroglio of the lower levels of personal activity, one may speculate on the possibility of changing this procedure, and the system, at least within one's own life. Inherent in the coming change of consciousness is a way in which one may begin to institute, personally, this change of procedure. If one accepts this change and works with it, one will have the opportunity of engaging in some creative action.

One of the prerequisites to having such an opportunity, however, is the assumption of Accepting True Responsibility. One who is opening is cautioned against drawing any conclusion as to the definition of this term, because, as with many terms and concepts employed in this Material, this concept of responsibility may take on dimensions and meanings which one may not heretofore have considered, and of which one may not previously have been aware. Responsibility will be explored in depth throughout this Material.

The delusion under which much of humankind labours at this time seems to suggest that one is not responsible for events which occur in one's path, nor for the activity in which one engages in relation to those events. This delusion perpetuates superstition, belief in chance and luck, blind faith, fear, and a belief that we are but victims of circumstance beyond our control.

This delusion has given rise to the necessity for one who is opening to gain a more complete understanding of the workings of the principle of Inevitable Consequences: the law of karma. Until one at least recognises and acknowledges that one is in fact responsible for one's present state of affairs and accepts all that this implies, any attempt to avail oneself of the opportunity to change one's direction, to mature one's vehicles towards a time of transformation, and to be active in the personal assimilation of a change of consciousness – personally or collectively – will be in vain. Or at the least, it will be further reactive in nature.

In the lifetime of lifetimes during which the soul reincarnates and faces and experiences those consequences previously created by reaction and desire, the soul is ever maturing towards a time when it will no longer be necessary for it to undergo further birth and death. Eventually, there will no longer be any necessity for one to have a body to experience further consequences, because, due to a certain creative action which one can take, the consequences to be faced will begin to be diminished in number. The desire to experience will begin to diminish, and the cycle through which the soul has been travelling for countless numbers of lifetimes will approach a termination. As this termination of the cycle approaches, the embodied soul will eventually be relieved of the obligation to be reborn yet again and again.

The consideration of inevitable consequences, and at least a minimal grasp of the relative concepts, is important for many purposes in this Material:

- **Firstly**, and perhaps most importantly, for the assumption of responsibility;
- **Secondly,** for the consideration of that which one is to do with the consequences which one has stored and which still retain their characteristic of inevitability in light of the nature of the enquiry in which one opening will engage;
- **Thirdly**, in regard to the maturation and transformation of the life vehicles; and
- **Fourthly**, in relation to the assimilation of a change of consciousness which carries with it the increased flow of a different and Undefined Element.

The course of a lifetime is shaped largely, but not solely, by inevitable, though self-created, events and the activities in which one engages in relation to these events. However, this Undefined Element of Presence also helps to shape the course which one follows in one's lifetime. This is true even of a green or unevolved soul which labours through life almost, but not quite, completely at the mercy of the events which must be faced. This Undefined Element is the One which precludes all activity from being completely predetermined.

As one evolves and opens and becomes more aware, the course of one's lifetime is shaped decreasingly by these events and activities and increasingly by this Undefined Element, as one begins to take steps towards maturing the vehicles in preparation for a time of transformation. This discussion will be expanded in chapters of later volumes.

During the time of opening, one will be exposed to various avenues, attractions, and activities which may appear to be of help in the opening. One may find that one has an affinity or acute proficiency with some of these activities developed from past lives when one was involved in them. These avenues and attractions are described and discussed, to varying degrees, in the next few chapters. The attraction to such activities as one opens, or continues to open, is natural, but on opening one will be well advised to consider that an activity which may have been a helpful mode of expression in a day or lifetime past may now have become a hindrance and a distraction.

4   The Activities of Healing

As one gains an appreciation of the way in which consequences are created, one will wish to assess anew one's actions and reactions – physical, emotional, and mental – in light of their part in the creation of consequences.

One will also wish to reassess one's attitude towards the way in which one accepts or deals with the consequences which have been created, the ones which are now sprouting, and the ones which are presenting themselves to play out.

In this consideration, it is important at the outset to acknowledge and appreciate that a distinction must be made between the playing out of a consequence and the creation of a seed which gives rise to a consequence.

As one opens, one may be attracted to some aspect of the activities of healing. These activities may be of interest, as they may seem to be another expression of that Undefined Dimension to which one is opening. These activities of healing, in contrast with conventional medicine, may appear to draw on some undefined energy or force to accomplish certain results which are other than those results produced by the conventional learned approach to medicine.

Perhaps this is all that one will need to glean from exposure or involvement in alternative healing activities: that is, to see this Undefined Element at work.

For another, there may be a period of deeper involvement in order that one may acquire some familiarity with the activity.

For another who becomes involved, the activity may simply be a continuing fascination with a subject which one has pursued in other lifetimes and which now, again, presents an avenue of easy expression.

For another still, there may be presented an opportunity to display an ability or power brought forth from other lifetimes.

Each one must determine for oneself the degree of involvement required.

The various approaches to alternative treatments, corrective practices, and the elimination of pain, ill-being, and dis-ease are almost innumerable – perhaps incalculable – as well as indescribable. This subject covers such a wide area that it will be impossible to discuss many of the individual approaches in detail in this book. That, of course, is not the purpose of this book.

With the immense preoccupation with the physical body which now is emerging to grip the attention of a fresh culture which is awakening to dimensions other than those in which it has thus far related, there may occur a dynamic alteration of one's attitude when one witnesses an event of healing: that is, an event of otherwise inexplicable spontaneous physical correction. Such events may occur with or without the participation of another human being.

The avenues which such an event may follow are many and varied. They range from and include, but are not limited to, some of the following:

- the laying of the hands of one person onto the body of another, often accompanied by the recitation or formulation of a prayer for relief for the recipient;
- a gathering of persons to pool, by one method or another, their collective attention and energy and to send it forth by one method or another to a person, either present or distant, in order, once again, to offer some relief to the recipient;
- the asking for and the receipt of relief from physical pain and suffering either for oneself or on behalf of another, from or through another person whom one may revere and to whom one may be devoted;
- certain approaches to massage and manipulation; and
- the application of other therapies or practices which may precipitate a relief in an unconventional way, and so on.

'Healing', as it is commonly and popularly referred to, generally involves the attempt to relieve physical pain. Although there is, of course, pain which lies behind the physical and fleshly body, that is, the emotional suffering and the mental anguish which one incarnated in a human body will undergo, the outer manifestation of pain, that is, the pain in the physical, fleshly body, is the one most evident and most readily observed, and it is the one in which healing will be most commonly attempted and observed.

There are now emerging certain therapies and approaches to the relief of suffering which claim to operate behind the simple relief of physical pain, that is, in the areas of emotional suffering and mental anguish. Some of these claim to release or relieve – by manipulation or other means – a deeper cause of pain than just the physical symptom.

There is no question that relief of pain and correction of physical discomfort can take place as a result of some of these methods. Instances of it are mentioned through many writings of the ages, and such occurrences in this day and age are not uncommon. These events are quite often regarded as 'miracles'. A miracle might be described as something that happens which one believed could not happen. The secret, of course, is in the belief, and where the belief rests, how far it has developed, and whether one is open to believing things other than those which one now, or then, believes or believed.

There is also no question that many of the methods and practices that are being displayed and employed in the pursuit of healing actually do that which they purport to do: that is, induce some correction or relieve pain or suffering, generally of the physical, fleshly body.

One who is opening in awareness, one who has acknowledged the existence of a part of the self to which he or she has not previously related, may be drawn to such activities to correct a personal physical inconvenience.

Or it may occur out of curiosity, to see if it really works; or from a prompting from within, so that one may learn of some of the aspects of such work; or from a step in the direction of altruism. Such motives are also varied and involve only the person experiencing them.

To grasp or perceive some understanding of that which occurs in a process of true healing, it is necessary to have some understanding of the process beyond and behind the cause of the suffering. In short, it could be said that the cause of suffering is the appearance of a consequence which was personally inevitable for the one undergoing the suffering; and the healing or relief of that suffering is the diversion of that consequence. True 'healing' is the dissolution of the seed behind the consequence.

The process behind the creation and appearance of these consequences is discussed in the chapter on Inevitable Consequences, Chapter 3.

When an inevitable consequence arises, it either plays out or it does not play out. The laws governing the determination of which consequences arise to play out are complex, and discussion of them would involve the introduction of matters which are beyond the scope of the present discussion. That with which we are here concerned is that which happens when a consequence does arise to play out.

Although it may be difficult to perceive in the beginning, each such event which emerges to play out can be seen, if one views the matter with detachment, to either run its full course, or, in some instances, to play out an abbreviated existence, spontaneously decreasing its own lifespan.

When the event to be experienced is a pleasurable one, this abbreviation of the consequence is in itself unpleasant, for it appears that one is deprived of the pleasurable experience. However, when the event to be experienced is to be painful, the spontaneous remission itself becomes the pleasurable event. In either case, absent detachment, one will probably react, once again, to that event itself; that is, the event of the abbreviation of the consequence.

Healing, as it is commonly referred to, could then be said to be the abbreviation of an event or a consequence which has arisen and which one is now facing and undergoing, or overcoming, as the case may be. Spontaneous remission, or the unexplained disappearance of a physical illness, dis-ease or discomfort, is a fairly common event in itself, and there is a universe of consideration behind this one point alone; but this point also is outside the scope of this present discussion.

Further, there are instances where someone in possession of certain abilities and perception may intervene in such a way that the intervention itself becomes an event of spontaneity which relieves or diverts the consequence or symptom, or which dissolves the event which is transpiring or about to transpire, by dissolving the seeds from which the event or consequence has sprouted. This could be said to be True Healing, for True Healing is more than the mere relief of the pain of the consequence; it is more than the diversion of the consequence: it is the dissolution of the seed which has sprouted and given rise to the consequence.

The genuine occurrence of such intervention of this kind is relatively rare, and its sporadic appearance is generally inexplicable by reference to that which is stored in the circuits of present human knowledge. Such an occurrence is hence denoted to be something which cannot be denied, but which also cannot be explained: a miracle.

But what we are concerned with here at the moment in this chapter is the intentional abbreviation or elimination of a painful event or consequence by intentional intervention or interference on the part of another. Incidentally, someone with an overview may correctly observe that even the intentional interference by another is merely the working of a spontaneous intervention of the principle mentioned above, that is, spontaneous healing. In part, and in some instances, this is true.

The present widespread interest in healing – that is, the interest of many who are opening to engage in the relief of suffering of another – could be said to arise from a growing awareness on the part of everyone of the illness of the planet on which they are living out their seemingly endless existence. While opening, as one becomes aware of the suffering around one, the first suffering of which one will become aware is, of course, one's own. Then, one will become aware of the suffering of those who are close and whose suffering elicits vicarious suffering in the one who is opening and observing the discomfort of another. And finally, one will become aware of the suffering of those who are not close, and whose discomfort may, although at first apparently remote, become more of concern as one opens.

As this concern with suffering begins to arise and come forth to express itself, one may seek to learn how to relieve suffering: that is, to 'heal' others who are undergoing suffering and experiencing some unfavourable or painful consequence which they themselves had created. Much of the healing activity now taking place is the diversion of that consequence.

There are various ways, methods and directions of diverting a consequence, and, as mentioned above, there can be a dissolution of the seeds behind the consequences. Both of these matters deserve and will receive detailed discussion in chapters of the books which follow this one.

Our Opening of Awareness

Although the activity of healing, that is, the relief of physical discomfort, is fairly widespread now, it will be seen that for one to have the ability to relieve the symptoms of a consequence *by dissolving the seeds which another carries* and which have given rise to that consequence is fairly rare at the present time.

However, it will be seen in the not too distant future that for one to have the ability *for oneself* to relieve *one's own* symptoms, and to face and deal with *one's own* consequences, and *one's own* seeds which one has created and which one carries, will become a fairly common event as the Change of Consciousness begins to unfold.

It will also soon become commonplace for one who is opening to begin to be able to take positive steps to reduce *the creation* of the seeds of consequences. This process of Self-determination is an aspect of the Change of Consciousness, and it will be specifically discussed in chapters to come in the parts of this book which follow this one.

For these changes to take place, an immense expansion of one's own knowledge of one's own circumstance will be needed; an expansion of the understanding of the way in which the system or the process works; an expansion of the knowledge of the application of some aspects of the system; an expansion of the right kind of discipline to be able to act; and an expansion of one's own discrimination to know when to act, and when to refrain from action. In addition to this, it will be necessary for one to move towards a maturation and a transformation of one's behavioural patterns, for even the most scrupulous attempts to deal with one's own symptoms and consequences can be undermined by the retention and engagement, intentional or otherwise, of obsolescent behavioural patterns.

Until the Process of Self-determination begins to take root and bear fruit, the process of healing which moves from one to another will continue to gain attention, but on opening one should bear in mind that such an activity is merely a diversion of the consequence which was arising to play itself out. It is merely a diverting or a transferring of a consequence from one vehicle to another. It merely takes a different route to the same culmination. And the consequences of such diversion are often borne by the one diverting the consequence by some activity of healing: *the consequence is borne by the 'healer'*.

As the Change of Consciousness begins to descend, the first step towards self-determination, the first step towards the reduction of the creation of the seeds of consequence, and, of course, the first step towards any dissolution of these seeds, will be an assumption of responsibility for one's own trove of consequences. There will also be an expanded acceptance of Ultimate Responsibility by everyone opening for the relief of detrimental and deleterious inevitable consequences on a global and even universal scale.

And, of course, there will then be a relief from the suffering which afflicts one even from the remotest events or corners; there will be a reaping of the pleasurable consequences; and, as well, there will be a harvesting of the joys which will begin to benefit all.

5 Avenues and Attractions

We must now digress briefly to examine some of the other avenues and attractions which one opening may find of some interest. Some of these are discussed in varying detail in this chapter for the purpose of enabling one who is opening to become familiar with them and to gain some appreciation of that which has been available in the past. The reader's indulgence is requested, for the matters which are examined in this chapter may hold little interest except for one who follows or has followed the activities described.

Although in the beginning one may be unable to grasp the nature of the dimension to which one is opening, still one knows that it has a personal validity. One may, however, be unable to feel that this dimension can have an authenticity unless it is somehow phenomenalised, manifested, and seen to be believed and followed by others, and seen to have some kind of a past. On opening, one may thus attempt to find some interest in those activities which are already in existence, which have a past and a validity for larger numbers of persons and which may bear some resemblance or appear to have some connection to that which one is beginning to feel and experience within.

However, these avenues and attractions often work with a reflected image of that to which one is opening. If one attempts to correlate something which one is feeling with something which is phenomenalised, and, therefore, to some extent crystallised, the attempt at a precise correlation will be in vain.

With these preliminary points in mind, let us now look at some of the avenues and attractions which may present themselves to one who is opening.

Astrology

In the beginning, on opening one may wish to explore some of the hidden aspects of one's personality or to make some attempt to grasp the nature of one's fate. To follow this, one may feel the inclination to consult with an astrologer, a clairvoyant, a medium, mystic, or a reader of past lives. Or one may possibly visit some distant land to consult with the wise men and women who live there in hope of learning more of one's self.

Astrology is often of interest in the beginning. This is the practice of casting a horoscope chart to indicate the configuration of the stars and planets at the precise time of a certain event, usually the birth into the present incarnation of the person whose chart is drawn. The astrologer then attempts to interpret the configuration of the stars and planets in order to accomplish some divination of the events and tendencies during the lifetime of the person for whom the chart is cast.

This activity can give some interpretation to someone who has only newly come into contact with the concept of Inevitable Consequences and who may have some curiosity about past lifetimes, present tendencies, and future prospects. The astrological chart is really a summary of the inevitable consequences of past lifetimes, plus an indication of the consequences which one has chosen, or which have been chosen for one, to face, undergo, and to deal with in the present lifetime.

It can also give some indications of proclivities of character and give a hint of the course of the nature of the personality of the present incarnation. Astrology is a very old activity, and, in other cultures, those who became adept at its practices were well respected. This practice of astrology has reached proliferation and ramifications of almost unimaginable proportions. Some consider it an art; some consider it a science.

The casting of the chart in itself is not difficult. It is done according to a set of fairly rigid rules and procedures. The interpretation of the influence of the configuration shown in the chart is quite another matter. The interpretation and divination are usually done according to certain rules, but the ability of the individual astrologer will determine the blend of strict interpretation and intuitive perception that combine to give meaning to the chart.

For anyone who is opening to that which is described in this Material, astrology will probably hold little interest after the initial encounter and interpretation. One who is opening and assimilating a new awareness will probably correctly perceive early on that astrology speaks only of the way things are based on the way they have been. Astrology does not state how things must continue to be. Too often the person whose chart is drawn and interpreted accepts the characteristics, tendencies, and foretold events as die-cast, solid, and crystallised. Too often there is no room left in the mind for the possibility of change. If one accepts this view and accepts the interpretation of the astrologer, then one may well be tied to that interpretation.

The events and tendencies foretold in the interpretation can, however, be seen as characteristics and possibilities. That is, they can be seen positively as items of back-pressure against which one can test one's ability to change and develop creatively. They should be regarded as events and tendencies more to be overcome rather than to be undergone.

Spiritualism

Another way in which one may attempt to find out more of the nature of one's self or one's purpose is to make some attempt to consult with the 'spirit world'.

Our Opening of Awareness

For this purpose, one may consult with a medium or a clairvoyant. It is advisable here to define the distinction between the activities of a spiritual nature and the activities of 'spiritualism'.

Activities of a spiritual nature, as they will be spoken of in this Material, are those which are directed towards an identification, contemplation and unfoldment of another dimension of one's complete self, and a manifestation of one's own unique purpose through that identification. In terms of spiritual activity as discussed here, this also means the application of that study in one's own life towards maturing the physical vehicles in preparation for a transformation. These are matters which are founded in moving towards a realisation, that is a making-real, of the Spiritual Self. They are matters which are not grounded in secular, materialistic or competitive pursuits.

'Spiritualism', on the other hand, comprises those activities and matters which, while also portending towards asecular interests, occupy themselves with establishing contact with entities which are no longer incarnate – that is, no longer occupying physical bodies. These entities occupy various levels of existence which are slightly different in vibration from the physical earthly level of existence.

These other levels are, for the most part, not visible to the naked, untrained, and 'unopened' eye. This activity can also include the use of clairvoyance and clairaudience.

These entities are often called 'spirits' for the reason that they are no longer physical: that is, they no longer occupy physical, fleshly bodies. They are, nonetheless, still part of physical creation in the sense that the levels of existence which they occupy are of the physical or 'phenomenal' realm, as it is called in this Material.

Contact with these entities is often sought to be established through a person in a physical, fleshly body who is called a 'medium', for the purpose of securing some guidance or help in contacting another who has left the body.

Such a medium can operate in a number of ways. Sometimes, such a person will enter a trance or somnolent state and a faculty which has been developed by the medium is opened. Contact is then established with the other level of existence. The medium may then speak for one of the entities with which contact is made, or the medium may be used by the entity and the entity may speak through the body of the medium. Another method of operation of the medium is to establish contact with an entity while the medium remains in the waking state. The medium then speaks on matters which can be suggested by the entity with whom contact has been made.

Yet another method of operation between the medium and the entity is where the entity actually takes over the body and the consciousness of the medium and speaks through the physical body of the medium. In some cases, the medium may actually be completely taken over by the entity and the former personality of the medium is dis-integrated.

There is a religion – a spectrum of crystallised activity – that has grown around the practice of contact with entities which occupy levels of existence other than the earthly plane of existence. It is called Spiritualism or the Spiritualist Religion. It is a very old practice, and many find comfort in the receipt of advice given by entities through a medium who works in this metaphor.

The activities of these entities often bear little, if any, relationship to the activities and experiences referred to in this Material other than to illustrate that there are levels of activity other than the physical plane of earthly existence. On the levels at which these discarnate entities are active, there are those, as on all levels of existence, who are genuinely dedicated to the spiritual evolution of humankind.

Some of these entities who reside on planes other than the physical earthly plane have imparted some of their teachings through persons who were incarnated and who wrote down the lessons which they received from the 'spirit' entity. These written teachings have often gathered large followings of persons who study the writings and discuss them. They sometimes form groups, societies or orders for the purpose of collective study.

Many of such teachings have depth and substance for someone who is able to relate to them; however, such writings are often compilations of manifested teachings or knowledge or matters of an occult (meaning *'hidden'* or *'secret'*) nature.

Sometimes these teachings are so obscure that they are very difficult to understand or comprehend. They also often lack a teacher who would adequately interpret the deeper meanings of the writings.

Meditation

At various times, there have been some systems of contemplation introduced both by such writings or by the societies or orders which follow certain teachings, or by an individual who incarnates for the purpose of teaching the higher purposes of humanity's nature.

Those activities which are generically referred to collectively as *meditation* or *contemplation* include a host of approaches, techniques, and practices. In general, meditation, as it has been exported to the Western world, includes those activities which are entered into usually while one sits quietly, perhaps in a prescribed position, perhaps dressed in some prescribed fashion, perhaps holding the hands or the body in a prescribed way, perhaps breathing in some prescribed manner, and then concentrates one's attention at some prescribed point or on some prescribed object.

While thus dressed, placed and concentrated, one may then, according to instruction, proceed with any number of approaches including, but not limited to, watching the mind and the thoughts, reciting a word or series of words or sounds, holding the attention at some point or place on or in the physical body, imagining the face or countenance of a person, an object, a figure, or a diagram, or attending to some inner sound.

The purposes of these activities termed 'meditation' are as varied as the practices. Such purposes may include the quieting of the mind, the development of powers and abilities, the calming of the emotions, the inducement of a state of bliss, the cultivation of vibrations which induce a trance-like state in which one may oneself (rather than through a medium) contact entities which occupy planes of existence other than the earthly physical plane, and solicit or be receptive to their advice.

Many of the meditational disciplines now manifest and practised in the world, including some of those which have been imported to the Western world, do exactly what they claim to do. There are, in fact, for instance, certain words or syllables or sounds, which, when recited or repeated quietly in the mind, will cause a phenomenal event to occur or stop occurring. There are, further, places or points on or in the physical bodies upon which the concentration can be placed. When this is done, an event will occur or will be caused not to occur.

There are also methods of meditation which, when practised after the imparting of certain energy or energies from a teacher or guru, will induce a state of bliss, well-being, and, in some circumstances, these practices will open the recipient to various wells of energy or force.

One of the purposes of these practices has been to enhance one's ability to accept the possibility of incorporating into one's life a dimension which seems to serve or fulfil a need which was not previously served by either secular or materialistic pursuits, or the now existing religious activities. Some of these practices have enabled some persons to achieve a becalmed state, to face life with some feeling of balance and renewed personal purpose. To this end, the practices have served well.

One who is opening and entering a time of enquiry may be drawn to one or a number of these practices of meditation, and even to the lifestyles which often accompany the practice of meditation. Each person must decide whether and when to explore such an avenue. On opening, one will be advised to remain open to the possibility that one is to glean something from that practice and then to move on.

One who is opening in this time of transition is opening to avenues which are only just beginning to emerge for the expression of a fresh culture. One may thus find discontent with the existing metaphors of expression, even though one or more of them may serve for a time. When one approaches the time when the metaphor will no longer serve, there may be a feeling of incompleteness which eclipses the feeling of elation which one may have felt when one first gained exposure to the metaphor into which one has enquired and which one may have practised for a time.

It is that time, when the practice no longer serves and the feeling of incompleteness recurs, to which some of the comments in other chapters of this section and this Material will be addressed. In another section in this Material, there is a description of a newly emerging and unfolding method of meditation, or more properly, a method of going within which correlates more closely with that to which one is opening.

6   *The Attraction of Yoga*

One of the attractions which may present itself when one begins to open is yoga.

Yoga derives from a Sanskrit term meaning 'to join'. Through the ages, this term, yoga, has come to include many and sundry practices and disciplines which became available to one who was opening.

There are other names which have been placed on this activity. In some countries and in some languages, the activity is called other things. For the purposes of discussion here, we will refer to all of these as being within the purview of yoga, for it is 'yoga' which is often the avenue that is most attractive to one who opens in the West and who has found no other acceptable avenue now in existence through which to learn of that to which one is opening, or to express that which one may be feeling.

One attraction of yoga is that it has evolved through the ages to produce a metaphor through which certain truths could be and have been taught, truths which were to be taught to the existing cultures at the time, and which, until the time arrives for a Change of Consciousness, are complete in themselves and which extend to the limits of the abilities of those incarnating in a culture.

The activities of yoga take many forms, some of which include:

HATHA YOGA: the yoga of physical activity, including postures, breathing practices, cleansing techniques;

RAJA YOGA: the yoga of concentration of the mind. This is also known as 'the King of Yogas', as it is said that one who can control the mind can control other parts of the integrated life vehicles. This includes certain forms of meditation designed to help one calm and concentrate the mind;

LAYA YOGA: the yoga of the movement of energy by concentrated breathing practices and the inner will which moves the energy concentrated by that breathing. This also incorporates certain disciplines variously known as siddha yoga, kriya yoga, tantric practices, and *kundalini* yoga;

BHAKTI YOGA: the yoga of devotion which teaches that all can be accomplished without the need for the practices described above if one will follow a path of devotion to a guru. This is discussed in depth in a later chapter in this book; and

MANTRA YOGA: the yoga of the repetition of certain sounds, or chanting of certain sounds or verses or songs, most often coupled with certain aspects of bhakti yoga, and devotion to that or the one to whom the chants are sung.

The initial attraction to some kind of yoga seems harmless enough, perhaps a chance encounter with a suggestion floating in the air that some hatha yoga would help slim or improve the physical body. Many are attracted to the yoga of physical fitness, as it has come to be known and practised, as a way of personally correcting or decreasing a lifestyle which, in the Western world, has come to be filled with a bit more indulgence than is now acceptable to one who may be opening. One who is opening may wish to now correct some of the ill effects of such a lifestyle. Yoga appears to be a good way to do this!

Some will be attracted to the forms of yoga described here due to the many lifetimes which one may have spent incarnated in the cultures of the East. During these lifetimes, one may have achieved some adeptness in these practices and now finds them initially helpful and familiar.

With only few exceptions, the forms of yoga which have been exported to the West from the East work with an energy called 'Shakti' or '*kundalini*'. The activities of yoga, all yoga, were originally designed to be employed by someone who wished to devote all or most of their life to becoming enlightened, at least as that term was defined by the cultures in which these activities of yoga were developed over several thousand years.

Even for someone who only casually enters the practice of yoga, takes it up on a part-time basis, or for someone who turns to the disciplines which have emerged from these practices, this energy is awakened by these practices. *The practices do exactly that which they were intended to do.*

The word *kundalini* derives from the Sanskrit and is translated to mean 'fire in the pit'. It refers to the dormant force or energy which resides at the base of the spine.

Much attention has been paid to the *kundalini* in recent times, because the disciplines of other ages, times and places have been voluminously exported to the Western world as the advent of a Change of Consciousness approaches.

To appreciate the nature of the *kundalini* and its significance, it is essential to have at least a cursory understanding of not only the term but of the *kundalini* itself. It is intended here to offer that cursory examination, but to extend it only to the point to which one must go to glimpse the traditional view of its importance and presence, and then to examine its place in this different approach which is now emerging.

Traditionally it is and has been taught in many classic Eastern philosophies that the *kundalini* is the latent presence which lies dormant in humans at the base of the spine and which is 'awakened' at the proper time. In short, upon

Our Opening of Awareness

being awakened, the *kundalini*, also called the *kundalini* Shakti, is then guided or manoeuvred through a course of movement from its point of origin to a destination at the top of the head, or in the centre of the forehead, depending on which school one is attending at the moment. It is taught in most of these schools of thought that the *kundalini* must be awakened, moved and guided, and its journey completed for a man or woman to reach spiritual enlightenment. This is the essence of the traditional teachings concerning the *kundalini*.

There have been innumerable works written about how the *kundalini* is to be awakened and moved, what rules must be imposed for the proper working and movement of the Shakti, or 'power' which emanates from the activation of the *kundalini*, the practices attendant to the 'working with' the *kundalini* after it is awakened, and the 'siddhis', or abilities, or powers, which one can develop as a result of awakening the *kundalini*.

Although it is intended here to discuss only some aspects of this matter, it will be necessary to make certain allusion to particular aspects of the traditional teachings, both as a basis for certain activities which will arise in a New Approach, and as adjuncts to certain matters with which someone relating to this Material may come into contact.

It is helpful to have a view of some of the details of the traditional teachings in regard to the movement of the *kundalini*.

First, in working with the *kundalini*, it is absolutely essential to have the guidance and tutelage of an adept teacher, a master if you will, who knows what he or she is doing and can impart the details of the teachings to the student. For good reason, most of these details have remained secret, or occult, although some of the practices are beginning to surface in a broader diluted context in the present day.

Anyone who attempts to learn of the workings of the *kundalini*, or to awaken 'her' (the *kundalini* is most often described using the feminine gender as being the manifestation of the female creative aspect of the universe, the Divine Mother), or to attempt to guide and manoeuvre the Shakti after it is awakened, either from hearsay or from books, or without the guidance of an adept or accomplished teacher, is literally playing with 'fire'. The power or force behind the workings of this Shakti is almost unlimited, and the disastrous effects if it is misused or misdirected or misapplied can hardly be overstated.

Working with the *kundalini* is a highly specialised science which has taken thousands of years to develop and perfect. Most of what one can hear and read of this science and the effects it can produce is true: the effects of application of this power are limited only by the imagination of humankind. Various schools have adapted the art and knowledge of working with this latent force to the unique teachings of their particular philosophy. Tantric philosophy and teaching, for instance, incorporates various intricate breathing practices and exercises, called pranayamas and kriyas, as well as other activities which move the *kundalini* in a particular way to enable the practitioner to gain the benefits of its use.

Various other teachings use such practices as concentration, physical postures called asanas, the repetition of sounds or phrases called mantras, and the intentional and concentrated movement of energy called kriyas, to accomplish the purpose or goal which they seek.

As mentioned, these various practices are designed to awaken the *kundalini* and then to guide 'her' from the initial resting place upward through a series of conduits to the destination. Along the way, there are various dynamic nerve centres called chakras through which the *kundalini* moves and during the course of each movement, the *kundalini* awakens or 'opens' these chakras. These chakras, and the conduits through which the *kundalini* moves and which are called *nadis* (of which there are some 72,000) are located in the emotional or astral body of the person. This body is of phenomenal existence and is of finer material than the physical or corporeal body to which one generally relates in extreme external consciousness.

The *kundalini* can be initially awakened in a number of ways:

- it can awaken naturally in the course of one's personal evolution;
- it can be awakened by one being exposed to certain sounds or music (some would, and plausibly, maintain that this awakening and the others which will be described are merely forms of the first mode of awakening, the one in the natural course of one's personal evolution);
- it can be awakened by contact with an adept, that is, one who has the Shakti fully awake and is a 'master' of its use; and it can be awakened through various practices to which one may be exposed, e.g., hatha yoga, (which, far from being the harmless or simply helpful activity for physical fitness that it appears, can precipitate dynamic and subtle consequences for which the unaware practitioner is neither ready for nor equipped to handle).

Once awakened, it is intended that the *kundalini* should be guided through the chakras and that the Shakti which emanates from the *kundalini* should open these chakras and impart certain abilities to the practitioner.

There are basically seven of these chakras with which traditional practices are concerned: one at the base of the spine, one at the spleen, one at the stomach or abdomen, one at the heart, one at the throat, one at the forehead, and one at the top of the head.

The conduit through which the Shakti is guided to these centres is one of the *nadis*, a main conduit, called the *sushumnadi*, or *sushumna*, and it is located in the counter-juxtaposition of the physical spinal column.

There is, as mentioned a great deal of written material available to describe these matters, and to go into greater detail in this writing would be inappropriate, for it is intended here merely to impart a basic view of the subject.

The practices in which one is enjoined to engage can be rigorous and very concentrated and require a strict adherence to a particular austere physical lifestyle, and thought style, as it were, for the operation to be a success. The austerity required was for a reason; for example, if the *kundalini*, once awakened, was allowed to remain in the lower chakras without proper attention and correct practice, there might be precipitated a certain form of insanity. These matters are not to be taken lightly, nor engaged in casually!

Aside from the physical benefits, which are real enough in the beginning, there are other physical results that ensue as a consequence of engaging in the practices. One of these is that once the energy is activated, it cannot be stopped. Once the change is set into motion, it continues to move, even slowly, but it continues to move. There is also a change in blood chemistry which proceeds mainly from an alteration of the operation of the endocrine glands, those glands which secrete their emissions directly into the bloodstream and which are literally intended by nature to be 'mind-expanding substances'.

One of the main points to be seen at this writing is that the effort to be put forth to awaken, move, and 'raise' the *kundalini*, is an effort of force, push, or an expenditure of energy and effort which moves the *kundalini* much as one might, with force, literally spread a fire through a forest.

The guidance of the adept teacher keeps the path of the fire on course; in the absence of the guidance of a teacher who is totally and fully conversant with this energy, the fire burns out of control. This is especially so if the practitioner – ignorant of the pitfalls and dangers – fans the fire with practices without knowing their purposes or effect, and with the continuation of a lifestyle which is in basic disharmony with these new-found effects; the very effects which were intended to be produced by these practices and this force, but for a very different lifestyle.

7   *Beyond Yoga*

> Anyone who engages in hatha yoga, the practice of the asanas, or postures, can do so with relative safety if the practices are limited to the benefit of the physical body. Even some breathing exercises are safe when practiced with the asanas. Beyond that, the practitioner should be aware of the potential consequences of other branches of yoga, and beware of any teacher who claims to be able to teach those advanced practices who is less than fully adept.

The lifestyle which has emerged in the West over the past several decades does not lend itself well to the incorporation of the advanced practices of yoga and the effects which ensue from the involvement in such practices.

The practices of yoga cause the Shakti to move through the *nadis*, or conduits, and as the Shakti moves through these conduits, and into and through the chakras, or dynamic nerve centres, the effects which ensue are literally unimaginable to one who is opening. The movement precipitates experiences which are outside the realm of previous experience and hence are, to one still employing an obsolescent mentation process, indescribable and unrelatable.

The configuration of the bodies of a westerner attempting to employ the techniques involved inhibits the easier flow of the Shakti which would be experienced by brethren of another culture whose bodies are configured for and receptive to practices which have grown and developed in that culture over many thousands of years. In such a culture, the emotions and mental approach are attuned to such practices and the lifestyle required to work in harmony with such practices.

Briefly in this chapter, and to an expanded degree in a later chapter in this book, we shall examine the difference between the approach of an individual opening in other cultures, who can more easily adapt to such practices, and one who is opening in the West, as well as the difference between the approach and the energies employed in other times, and the approach emerging in accord with the imminent Change of Consciousness.

It is the object of the exercise of the traditional disciplines which deal and work with the Shakti to produce exactly the experiences and effects which ensue from the practices, and it is the intention of the student working at the behest of the adept teacher to cause these experiences to happen.

One who enters the practice of such activities and attempts to casually combine it with the lifestyle which prevails in the Western world will begin to have some different experiences at some time. The experiences may be very subtle; they may simply involve a subtle awareness of matters which previously escaped one's attention. Or they may be more dynamic, including violent physical reactions, emotional upheaval, or mental instability.

Generally and conventionally, in the metaphor in which these disciplines have been found and in which they originated, the student had so arranged the details of life so as to be able to adapt to the experiences and the consequences which ensued, for that had been the object of the activity. Often, the student had been required to renounce the world and all other activities solely to be able to handle the ensuing experiences.

With the advent of a Change of Consciousness on this planet, there being no other presently existing or developed discipline or framework in the West into or through which one could open to that which could be loosely described as 'spiritual enlightenment', these specialised disciplines, with their intricate and unique practices, found wide acceptance in the spiritually virginal Western world.

Unfortunately, most often the instruction presently given in these disciplines, even that given by teachers from abroad, is given by someone who is less than fully adept; not only at imparting the practices, but also in the personal ability to implement them, as well as being deficient in the ability to provide the correct guidance to one whose Shakti becomes active. The species of fully adept teacher, or master, of these practices is now so rare as to be said to be endangered.

Certainly the imparting of instruction by anyone who is less than fully conversant with all of the implications and complications would be said to be at the least dangerous, not only for the recipient student, who, having unleashed the energy, must now cope with the physical, emotional and mental consequential experiences which ensue, but also for the teacher, often also a neophyte, who must bear the inevitable consequences which result from the imparting of lessons incompletely learned and only partially active, even within that teacher.

The physical bodies which are occupied by the human evolutionary wave now sweeping the planet, especially the Western world, are ill-equipped to devote the time and concentrated attention to the proper implementation of the practices which they are importing. They are ill-suited to accept and assimilate the consequences of engaging in such practices in the casual manner in which such activities are generally approached by those who have become exposed to them.

Even if the Shakti does move correctly, in a controlled and restrained way, the consequences of its movement are to arouse and awaken latent abilities – nay, powers – which will enable the practitioner to see things which one may not be ready to see, or to do things which one may not be ready to do. The awakening of such powers and abilities must be accepted with a humble attitude. The acquisition of powers often leads to the further inflation of an ego already oversized in a society and way of life which places a high value on accomplishment and encourages the display of accumulated acquisitions and the retention of that which one has won or gained.

It should be remembered that in the beginning, the purpose of working with the Shakti was for the ultimate enlightenment of the neophyte student, and that the acquisition of powers was considered, by an era of seekers humble enough to handle that which they had awakened, merely to be another step on the way to the sought after enlightenment.

Many an enlightened and adept spiritual teacher has advised his or her sincere follower to avoid like the plague the 108 siddhis, or powers, for distraction can entrap the attention of someone who is even momentarily tempted by the flare of an active imagination when viewing or experiencing one of these powers for the first time.

Generations upon generations of practice by those admitted to the secret chambers of these activities, which had taken so long to develop, have refined the vibrations and circumstances wherein the ego confronted the pitfalls of the occult practices.

The maturity with which they were able to approach the fruits of the practices enabled them to accept the fruits without attachment, display or pride. The adept teacher who imparted the practices would also then impart these refined vibrations to the student, along with the practices.

The luxury of such adept guidance is largely unavailable to those now opening in the West. It is also unnecessary. The previous disciplines and ways are unsuited to the needs of those now opening in the West in a new time and in a fresh enquiring culture with needs of its own.

These Western physical bodies are of a different configuration from the bodies of those who have lived in the established cultures for lifetimes upon lifetimes, and who grew in each incarnation with the evolution of a method which had been manifested specifically for that culture and which was uniquely suited to the needs of that culture in which it evolved.

The bodies of a westerner – being configured to a different time, a different circumstance, a different cosmic need, a different evolutionary purpose, a different heritage – are, accordingly, ready for a different discipline, a different approach.

It is time for a fresh culture to set aside the old ways, rendering them the respect they deserve, to open, and to manifest a new and different way. While it is true that the awakening of the *kundalini* Shakti is, in fact, a part of the spiritual evolutionary development so that one who is opening can experience a full realisation of that to which he or she is opening, there is, fortunately, no need for these practices and disciplines, which have served well in another time and place, to be brought forth to be incorporated into a different approach which is now emerging and will fulfil a need arising from a basic Change of Consciousness in a fresh new culture.

There is a new approach emerging, and the need which it is to fulfil is also different: the practices of old are ill suited to meet that need.

This can be seen by the consideration of one simple fact: the point of destination of the practices of old is the point of beginning of the practices of the new which will emerge from a Change of Consciousness. *The new starts where the old finished.*

One who is opening in this time of transition and seeking to identify with their spiritual nature, even if realisation of that identification is less than instantaneously complete, opens to a *Positive Presence* which was scarcely available even to someone who had received the most complete guidance and had succeeded in reaching that far destination which was the goal of their efforts.

Anyone who attempts to follow imported disciplines from other times and cultures may face the daunting realisation that that for which they have fought and struggled is now obsolete.

Creation is sustained and manifested by two aspects of Divine Energy: a Positive Aspect and a Negative Aspect. The Negative Aspect is the energy of phenomenal creation; it is the energy of procreation; it is the Shakti or power of the manifested universe. The Positive Aspect is the Presence which descends from the aphenomenal into Negative Aspect. In many teachings and cultures, these energies have been anthropomorphically denominated the Father and the Mother.

The Positive Presence descends into the Negative Realm and sustains whatever is created by the Negative Aspect. This sustenance is provided by an infinitesimal flow of the Positive Presence. Reflected change, that is, the change which occurs in the Negative Realm, is a manipulation and rearrangement of the energy of that Realm, that is, the Negative Energy.

True change occurs when there is a larger inflow of the Positive Presence. This occurs at various stages of evolution in order to transform the state of the Negative Realm. For this transformation to occur and for True Change to be implemented, there is a transitional time in which the awareness of the Negative Realm opens to the increased Positive Presence and preparations are made for a Change of Consciousness.

Each individual soul incarnated into a set of integrated life vehicles is like unto a mini-universe, in that its personal universe is sustained by a small flow of Positive Presence. Its actions and reactions, and the vehicles through which these actions and reactions are expressed, are manifested with the Negative Energy – the energy of creation.

With only few exceptions, the passing disciplines worked almost exclusively with the Negative Creative energies, developing them and refining them, and with the conduits and centres in the physical bodies through which these energies flowed. The practices developed were for the purpose of moving those energies and working with them, as described elsewhere in this book.

The way which is now emerging for a fresh culture in the West is not merely for the purpose of giving the West another way to work with these energies; it is not merely to provide another way simply so that the present state of creation can be rearranged in yet another configuration.

The movement of evolution and the state of matters on this planet at this time preclude yet another rearrangement in any attempt to maintain or retain the status quo.

The way which is now emerging will enable one to accept an additional inflow of that Undefined Element to which one is opening and to assimilate and synthesise it with the existing creation to effect a True Change.

This True Change comprises an opening of awareness, a transition and transformation, and the ultimate assimilation of a Change of Consciousness – *of the culture as a whole* and of each individual incarnating in that culture – to the degree that each is able to assimilate that change according to his or her own unique state of evolutionary development.

The challenge for a fresh young culture is to traverse this time of transition with as much equanimity as possible, *gently* accepting the new, and maintaining a balance along the way.

The opening to the Positive Presence enables one to commence an intertwining of Positive and Negative aspects of the Divine purpose, and instead of the need for the perpetrator to blindly force the Shakti into areas which are dark until she enters them, one is able to *allow* the Shakti to move freely into the Light.

She gently opens the chakras as she goes, flowing harmoniously without force, ever moving in a divine intercourse, orchestrating the manifestation of needed abilities at the proper time and to the proper degree; and as she moves, healing, enlightening, opening – joyfully changing and strengthening the phenomenal vehicles to accept not only that which came from the antiquated practices which surfaced from working with only one side of the Divine Energy, but also bringing forth in a balanced manner that which is needed and called forth at any given moment – enabling the opening soul to take part in the play, in oneness, not only to be an observer, but a participant as well; ultimately enabling one not only *to* experience, but *to become* the experience... not only to see the event, but to *become* the event: *to be the event*.

8 The Avenue of Devotion

In this age, in this time of transition, with the dawn of a change of consciousness only just visible at the horizon of humankind's awareness, there is a key which has survived many ages and which, if brought forth from the disciplines of ages past, and allowed to mature, will enable the one opening to traverse the time of transition with relative ease.

This key may be found in some aspects of the Avenue of Devotion. In the past, the application of devotion was on the part of a devotee, or a disciple, and, in the first instance, it meant devotion to the guru: 'the one who waits'. This principle of devotion, or *bhakti* as it has been called for many ages, is very much present in the world today in many forms. Traditionally in the passing system of the search for truth and enlightenment, the one who practiced bhakti, called the bhakta, was required to devote one's entire being and energy to the guru: the teacher who waits.

For one to find one's way to a guru was a true blessing. This might occur after the potential devotee had begun to open and had followed a path of opening or enquiry for quite some time. Often an adept teacher would be aware that this potential devotee had indeed entered the path and was wending the way to the teacher, even though the potential devotee might be some physical distance away. Such a guru, if truly adept, could help and guide the potential bhakta even before the latter had physically arrived at the 'feet of the guru'.

Once at the 'feet of the guru' the potential devotee would prostrate the body to the feet in a gesture of humility and respect and devotion. If the guru found that the aspirant was sufficiently humble, the guru would accept the aspirant as a devotee and perhaps eventually as a disciple, meaning one who disciplines him/herself after the example set by the guru or the master, as one is sometimes called.

If the guru or the master was a true guru or true master, the aspirant was truly blessed, for such ones were, and still often are, well hidden and hard to find. They are also, for a new system, emerging for a fresh culture, something of an anachronism. The aspirant would present one's self for acceptance, and if accepted would then enter a time of cleansing and instruction.

Depending on the nature of the energy of the guru or the level of evolution of the guru, the cleansing would be done mostly by the aspirant being exposed to the vibrations or the presence of the guru. This more highly refined presence and vibration of the guru would permeate the aspirant and would catalyse certain changes in the aspirant, usually beginning with an initial mental rearrangement, an emotional upheaval, and physical cleansing.

The aspirant would be expected to accept completely and without question anything that happened. One would do this to effect a gradual, complete, unconditional surrender to the will of the guru. In fact, this surrender and devotion was often initiated by the belief and acceptance on the part of the aspirant that the one to whom one had found one's way was in fact a true incarnation of God.

This belief was that God had manifested before the aspirant in this body called the guru for the purpose of bringing enlightenment to the aspirant and, probably only incidentally (in the eyes of the aspirant), to the other devotees who surrounded the guru and had been accepted as devotees or disciples by the guru.

In such a time and on such a path, it was the guru who had the veto: it was the guru who decided who would be accepted as a devotee and disciple, not the other way around. This relationship which was entered was complete, comprehensive, and forever.

If the guru was genuine, then the guru would guide the aspirant, sometimes gently, sometimes other than gently, through the quagmire of the aspirant's personality and through the aisles and alleys of tests and questions where there is no right answer. The dilemmas forced upon and faced by the aspirant were momentous and in most cases seemed irresolvable. What the aspirant often did not know was that the important element was not the answer, but the question. And even the nature of the question was not of the utmost importance. What was paramount was the asking of the question – the facing of the dilemma – and going through the experience of it. It was, of course always resolved… eventually… *by the grace of the Guru.*

In these paths or disciplines of other times and other cultures, the aspirant would often experience an ambivalent feeling towards the guru, for the true guru was a very dangerous person. In time, the feeling of devotion would prevail if the aspirant remained to become a devotee or disciple. By this time, the disciple knew that acceptance by the guru would mean the ultimate destruction of the personality and the ego, as one had previously believed these to be. This destruction was accepted not only willingly but also enthusiastically.

There was of course an added dimension to the experience which would begin to emerge as the aspirant proved worthy of the attention and acceptance of the guru. This involved the dawning of the emergence of a flow of a new force within the aspirant. Such a force, called the Shakti (see previous chapters), would then enable the sincere and devoted aspirant to begin to approach the time when one would begin to be permeated with the same force which energised the guru, and one too would then begin to know certain things that the guru knew.

But to discuss such matters at this point is premature, for there is an important step which the aspirant had to take before this happened, and that must be seen first. Before this step is discussed, it is important to examine further the relationship and exchange which occurred between the guru and the aspirant-cum-devotee-cum-disciple-cum-adept.

For this discussion, it is assumed that the guru in question is genuine and sincere. This point may seem elementary, but there have existed and do exist those who profess to be able to lead and to cleanse and to teach, but who do so for the most part to gain a following for the sake of having the following.

In the melding of the cultures of the East and the West in recent times, where a dawning spirituality has blended with materialism, the prospect of accumulation, gain and power has been too tantalising for some who might have otherwise been able to maintain sincerity and genuineness (again, assuming it was present in the first place), and a would-be guru or teacher may have succumbed to the temptation to convert the devotion of another to their own purpose.

It is not intended to be within the purview of this discussion to examine the conduct and consequences of someone who attempts to develop a following for the extension of their own purposes and designs and to further their influence. The consequences are too dire to consider here, and it is intended that this Material should find its way to those who would have already recognised the need to ignore such entreaties if they were confronted with them. It is not assumed, however, that the naivety of an aspirant in transition has been dispelled, and that which is offered here is given for the information of such a one who knows within the self the feeling of that which one seeks and towards which one aspires, but who wishes to gain some understanding of the old so that the best of the old may be blended with the new as the new emerges.

If it be assumed, then, as it is for this discussion, that the guru is or was genuine, and sincerely had the welfare of the aspirant at heart, and had the abilities necessary to accomplish the task and the wisdom to know how to apply the abilities, it will do well to examine the nature of the relationship between the guru and the disciple, to see what it was that was to be accomplished; for there are aspects of this relationship which may have some significance for someone now opening and which may apply in this time of transition.

For the good of the aspirant, the guru would probably exact some promises of conduct, or vows, from the aspirant. The first of these and the most important on the path of devotion was the promise, vow, or commitment of devotion: absolute, complete, and utter devotion to the guru, and attendance to every word, as if that word came from God Him/Herself. Very little was left to the discrimination of the aspirant. It was the complete belief of the aspirant that everything which happened actually transpired at the behest of and by the grace of the guru. Everything that the aspirant did, was able to do, acquired, learned, thought, ate, felt or experienced was by the grace of the guru. The genuine guru accepted this responsibility for the aspirant. And it was done.

One of the first and primary effects of the outlaying of this devotion on the part of the aspirant or seeker was the complete subjugation of one's own will. There could be no conflict of wills between the guru and the devotee: the will of the guru must always prevail, regardless of the strength of any feeling of disagreement on the part of the aspirant. There was no room for a difference of opinions.

The guru knew this, of course, and was placed in a position of tremendous cosmic responsibility, for even the slightest instruction on the part of the guru, even the tiniest morsel given by the guru brought the guru to a position of complete responsibility, not only for the welfare and well-being of the aspirant, but also for the karma – the Inevitable Consequences – of the aspirant. How such a responsibility on the part of the guru was discharged is the concern of another discussion.

What effect, then, did the subjugation of the will have upon the aspirant? First it began to empty the will within the aspirant to any purpose save that of serving the guru and attending to every word and every wish. This devotion proceeded from a *love*, the nature of which is largely unknown and enigmatic to those currently occupying bodies which dwell in the Western world. It is a love which comes from a personally desired and intended surrender, a love which requires constant and, at the least, mental prostration; it is not a love which is experienced with the arms folded, the head cocked, or the eyebrow raised. Prostration of any variety is for the most part foreign to anyone occupying a body in the contemporary Western world.

Even if one is able to bring one's bodies (physical, emotional, and mental) to any position of subjugation or prostration, the effectiveness of the experience may be diminished by the internal scramble to justify it, examine it, understand it or even shorten it.

It was a love which transcended and survived any trace of suspicion or hesitation on the part of the aspirant. While it was true that the experiences which were designed and manufactured for the benefit of the aspirant were often calculated to introduce doubt, the purpose of the experience was to dispel that doubt, to build a faith which was unshakeable and unmistakable.

In building the faith in the guru, of course, the aspirant began to build faith in one's self, at least a faith in one's ability to obey. This was one of the first characteristics which the genuine guru watched for in the devotee.

The ability to follow the every word and wish of the guru was the nature of another vow which the aspirant accepted, that of *obedience*.

In the beginning the obedience was to the literal wish of the guru, and most commands were explicit, direct and clear. Often, these first commands or wishes on the part of the guru involved further vows including one of *poverty*, in which all of the possessions of the budding aspirant were given to the guru (often a stumbling block for many an aspirant, and generally an obstacle which most westerners will not even consider, let alone transcend).

Another of these vows was *celibacy*, the purpose of which was at least initially twofold: to minimise distraction and to conserve and marshal one's energy. (It could be said that in many cases the latter undermined the former.) The nature of these vows, their evolution, their maturing, and their efficacy is discussed in detail in later books which will follow this one.

The extent of the structural proliferation of the rules and practices imposed on the devotee-cum-disciple, and the ramifications and implications of this proliferation of rules, often progressed to a state and degree which would stagger the imagination of even the most expanded intellect.

The rituals which were designed, designated and imposed by the successors of the guru (who were most often formerly chief disciples) gradually obscured the original nature and purpose of the devotion and the loving subjugation of the will of the aspirant.

Even the surrounding community would often look to the guru – and to the chief devotees or disciples – for their religious, and sometimes spiritual, guidance. As the practices and disciplines promulgated by the guru began to filter down and outwards to the secular community, there then developed various social stigmatic reprisals, which were directed towards those who even slightly questioned the purpose of such rituals or directives. Thus was born religion.

Although the essence of its structure was long ago imported by a confused young culture which needed strength, the true nature and essence of this path of devotion did not survive for the Western world. And although it found the strength of *form* in the imported essence of bhakti, it has yet to find its strength in a viable *substance*.

The form of devotion has survived and been transformed from its original shape and depth to become worship. The need for substance will lead the West to bring forth the desirable aspects of this once effective path and to incorporate them into an integrated path of form and substance, freshening the essence of devotion and blending it with the 'knowingness' which will replace the blind faith of an outdated way.

9 Transcending the Past

One who is opening and preparing for the assimilation of the first aspects of a Change of Consciousness will find in the time of transition that there are basically three areas of adjustment which one will encounter and which will require attention.

- **Firstly**, there is the adaptation to the changes which are necessary for one to effect a mental rearrangement. This is a change in the way in which one thinks, the way one goes about thinking, remembering, making decisions, and so on. The introductory discussion on this matter is found in the final two chapters of this section. A detailed discussion is found in other books of this Material.
- **Secondly**, there is the consideration of the energies which are involved. These energies are present and viable and active in one who is opening; one must give consideration as to how one works with these energies. As the Change of Consciousness descends, there will be a shift, a change, a difference in the way one who is opening works with these energies. The introductory discussion on this subject is in the chapter which follows this one.
- **Thirdly**, there is the consideration of the development of a proper personal approach which one will have towards the matters discussed in these final chapters of this section, and in the publications of this Material which follow this book.

The development of this approach is the subject of this chapter.

The development of this approach comprises the creation and the shaping of an inner environment, an *attitude*, by which one can approach these matters and through which one can more easily adapt to the changes which will come. In the beginning, there is very little in the way of action which one must take to be receptive to that which happens when one opens. It just begins to happen.

There is, however, an action which one can take that enables one to adapt to what happens. The first action which one can take is the beginning of the cultivation of a proper attitude *towards* what is happening. This begins with the acceptance of a key which is buried in an avenue of the passing disciplines and which is foreign to the mode of Western thought. There may be other ways in which one can approach and relate to that to which one is opening, and it is not claimed that the approach described here is the only way. But the approach described here can help: it is one which can enable one to maintain some semblance of a balance.

The key to the approach which is suggested here cannot, in the beginning, coexist with the present approach of the Western mind when a new concept is broached. In the present condition of the human mind at this stage of evolution in the Western world, the two approaches are mutually exclusive. If one approaches the matter correctly, however, there is a convergence which occurs later on – a blending of the two – in which each complements the other and makes the other more meaningful.

The first step in the application of this key is the acknowledgement that something is happening within which is presently inexplicable; this acknowledgement must be made *aloud*.

The second step is a determination, a decision, made within the self that what is happening within is *next* – that it is personally inevitable. If there is any possibility that one can determine that one has a choice as to whether or not to follow what is happening within, then, in all probability, one would have to admit that what is happening within is *not* happening.

However, if one determines that one must move with what is happening within, and if one acknowledges that what is happening is inexplicable, and if one then acknowledges this determination, then one has thus effectively gained access to that key which is available.

There is one further matter of which one should be aware: that there will be, at least in the beginning, a recurring and sometimes continuous conflict, and that this conflict will resurface as one opens.

This conflict will have two aspects:

- **Firstly**, it may ask for an explanation of that which is inexplicable; and
- **Secondly**, it can suggest that one has a choice as to whether to proceed further.

If one determines in the midst of the conflict to allow either aspect of this conflict to express itself, then one may temporarily lose the precious balance which one seeks to maintain. If one determines to dissolve the conflict, then one need only apply the key to which one has already gained access and which is available simply by its application.

If one follows these steps towards the creation of this inner environment, then the environment will, so to speak, begin to create itself. It is there, waiting, ready to be accepted, but it must be accepted to be effective: it will not force itself upon one opening. If it is accepted, it will begin to expand and to bring with it certain changes. These changes, like the inner environment itself, need only be accepted to become effective. The opening to the acceptance of these changes allows them to become self-expressive and self-determining.

Our Opening of Awareness

The first of these self-implemented and self-expressive changes is really more of an experience rather than a change. It may come suddenly, or it may dawn slowly over a period of time. It is not really something which one must do. It requires little action on one's part other than the openness and acceptance. It involves the transcending of certain bonds which have held one in ignorance and have distorted one's ability to see. It involves the transcending of something which is built into most of the existing approaches which are now being employed and taught in the world, and, ironically, it is the very thing which most of them purport to transcend. *It is the experience of transcending the delusion of duality and the luxury of blind obedience and attribution.*

The duality and the blind obedience, and the attendant attribution (that is, attributing events in one's existence to an external force or being), which are present in the avenue of devotion that have come forth from other times, and which are still subscribed to and followed by many, provide a touchstone of hope in a sea of chaos, confusion, and uncertainty. For one immersed in this approach, there is a certain undefined assurance that, even if one did not oneself know, at least there was someone or something – 'out there' – which *does* know. An attitude of devotion towards that someone or something instilled a reverence and humility, or at least a fear.

Most of the viable teachings over the past several thousand years have been introduced by an enlightened and evolved soul or being who was at least a little bit ahead in time and who incarnated into a culture for the benefit of that culture. Almost without exception, these evolved and incarnated souls or beings would state that they were one with the Source. This Source might be called by different names at different times. When it came time for the teacher to depart the culture, and perhaps leave the realm, those who succeeded the teacher and who continued, or attempted to continue to promulgate the teachings of the one who had departed, could rarely, if at all, sustain the upliftment which was present when the teacher was still among the culture, unless they too had gained the enlightenment which the teacher carried.

As the years passed, the attention and adoration was thus turned away from the Source, with which the original teacher was one, and which was certainly apparently present so long as the original teacher was present. The attention and adoration was redirected, not to the Source, but to the form, or the memory of the form, of the now departed teacher.

Duality once again descended. This duality re-established the gulf between one and the Source, of which the teacher had spoken and taught. This duality provided both a delusion and a protection. And the former – the delusion – was sustained for the latter – the protection of the culture – at least until the time came for another teacher to incarnate to help enlighten a culture, a tribe or a nation.

The energy which went into feeding and sustaining this duality was immense: the worship, the rituals, the sacrifices, the prayers, and the collective desire of the culture or tribe to elevate someone or something to a position of worship and adoration. This duality is present in almost every remaining discipline now existing in the cultures and tribes which inhabit this planet. Their approach, almost without exception, is characterised by a relating to something or someone, now alive or once alive, and now removed, who or which, it is believed, holds the key, the power, and the authority from which one, and the culture as a whole, can benefit, if properly approached.

The really great teachers instructed the cultures in their charge to approach the Source, with which they are one, with reverence, humility and enthusiastic surrender. The evolutionary state of humankind in these tribes and cultures had not yet been developed to such a degree that they were able to do this and to know the Source and to become one with the Source. This was, of course, convenient to the culture, and to an individual, which did not wish to accept all of the consequences and implications which would come with the assumption of Oneness. Such is still the case.

When the time comes for one, or a culture, to transcend this duality, the duality becomes an obstruction to the identification necessary for one opening. In this time of transition, the immediate, initial identification with the Spiritual Self is a necessary step to be taken, even if the realisation of that identification is less than instantaneous.

In the past, it was the nature of things that when a teacher would appear to help enlighten a tribe or culture or to help it move on to what was next for it, the members of the tribe who were in the spiritual forefront, so to speak, would wish to know what the teacher knew. They would wish to be what the teacher claimed to be and what they believed the teacher to be: One with the Source.

To the sincere members who approached the matter with humility, the teacher would impart certain teachings, which, if followed, it was said, would aid those who followed the teachings to know and to be what they wished to know and to be. The more highly evolved the tribe and the culture, the more esoteric were the teachings. Conversely, the less evolved the tribe and the culture, the more explicit were the teachings.

For a tribe or culture which was evolutionarily elevated only slightly above its lower nature, there were explicit rules and commandments instead of guidelines. These rules were to be strictly observed, and they were strictly enforced by a hierarchy of authority structured either in the religious or the secular segment of the culture.

Blind obedience to the teacher and the teachings had some benefits. The most obvious benefits accruing to the members of the tribe which strictly followed the rules were the rewards of living a peaceful life, unharassed by authority. Conformity bequeathed comfort. For the members of the inner circle who had access to the teacher and who received the teachings which were proffered for their benefit, their adherence to the rules provided periodic insights into their own being and enabled them to move towards an accomplishment of their goal – oneness with the Source – which the teacher enjoyed.

Blind obedience bequeathed other fruits as well. Some of these will be explained in the publications which will follow this one, but a word at this point will help to plant the seeds which may sprout later.

When properly applied, obedience with awareness (as distinguished from obedience with blind faith), can form the foundation for one of the characteristics which will necessarily be developed in one opening in this time of transition: that of an *Inner Discipline*. Obedience to an authority – *without* – can mature to become a discipline within. It can enhance the ability to move with that which one knows within the Self: the ability to move with that which one sees as one begins to Discriminate.

Obedience to that *without* – an authority, a leader or a teacher – is merely a less refined version of the ability to be obedient to that which is known *within*; for, although blind obedience is an obstacle to be transcended, obedience with awareness is an avenue to inner Self-discipline. Not everyone who opens needs to experience blind obedience to develop this foundation of discipline, but if on opening one has been fortunate enough to have the benefit of some kind of training – even secular training – which required obedience in some form prior to the time of opening, one will find that the circuits of the integrated life vehicles are much more able to place into action the promptings or nudges which come as one opens.

Any person who has avoided the development of obedience by escaping the imposition of authority – and the obedience thereto – either by rebellion or by guile, has deprived himself or herself of a cornerstone from which he or she could move more easily towards that to which he or she is opening. Anyone who has actively avoided the imposition of outside authority, the obedience to that authority, and the benefits which he or she could have gained as a result of learning obedience by adhering to the rules of some authority, must now face the inevitable consequence that the opening may be more difficult because of that avoidance: there may be a lack of *Inner Discipline*.

One's acceptance of this link or connection can be most helpful in creating the essential inner environment and Inner Discipline.

In a later book, we will explore how obedience can be a foundation of that Inner Discipline which needs to be developed and how that obedience and discipline can ripen into a characteristic trait which is absolutely essential to one now opening in this fresh culture.

The disadvantages of blind obedience, however, overshadowed the benefits. Blind obedience is an obstruction to one's ability to Discriminate. It encourages the abnegation of, rather than the assumption of, Responsibility. This is because the other side of blind obedience is attribution: that is, the attributing to one to whom obedience is given the responsibility for one's own actions proceeding from the obedience, and the responsibility for the consequences of those actions and the present state of one's affairs. In this climate of abnegation and attribution, there grows a dependency which inhibits one's unfoldment. Being devoted to and blindly obedient to another can obscure one's own truth by finding purpose in the object of devotion. Devotion to another's purpose prevents one from bringing forth that which waits within one's self to come forth and be manifested.

If on opening one opens to, accepts, and follows the proper approach which will unfold from within, then the gradual experience of the Oneness will enable one to begin to see a hint of one's purpose as it begins to unfold. When obedience is ripened into integrity, and one develops the Inner Discipline to be able to act, the duality of attributive devotion can be transcended. This will then enable one to glimpse and begin to know one's own purpose.

10   A Reorientation

It is an evolutionary fact that if one is incarnated at this time on this planet in the condition that the planet is in, one is now facing not only one's own trove of personal evolutionary inevitable consequences but also facing, in some part, the consequences which the planet must inevitably face as a whole, as individual tribes, and as a collection of tribes and nations. Thus, by one's presence on this planet at this time, one is, by definition, involved in this present state of affairs and in the changes which are now taking place.

This has implications both for one as an individual opening to a new direction of enlightenment, and for one's purpose or the part one plays in the alleviation of the condition of one's tribe, nation, or the planet as a whole. The degree to which one is personally affected by the state of things and by the changes occurring at this time is a reflection of the extent to which one has been involved in some way in determining – by actions or involvement in past lifetimes – this present state of affairs. It is an indication of the degree of one's involvement or participation in the implementation of change.

Now, with consideration of many of the disciplines, practices and techniques behind us, it is time to turn to the new, to consider the differences between what has gone before, and what is now to be incorporated into the spiritual practices as one is opening. It is time to consider how this will change one's lifestyle, thought style, emotional mode, and so on.

After the discussion of these matters in this chapter, we will then, in the final chapters of this section, look at steps one can take to begin to change the operations of the mind so as to release some of the obsolete patterns one is retaining, and to begin to educate the mind to that which is coming next. This is in preparation for those matters which will be discussed in later publications on this Material.

There is a very basic difference between the old approach and the new approach. There are differences in the experiences which one will have, in the way that one relates to those experiences, and in the way one goes about the very everyday activities of thinking, relating and living. These everyday activities are shaped by what one experiences as one opens.

The difference in approaches is so basic as to be foundational. It involves the difference between concentration and non-concentration: the difference between placing energy into a place, spot or point where it is **concentrated** *and the placing of awareness so that it is present and* **concentred***, but not* **concentrated***.*

- **In the first instance**, there is the consideration of the different energies involved.
- **In the second**, there is the consideration of the different approach to these energies, for each energy or Presence, as one of them could be called, requires a different way of relating to them.
- **In the third instance**, there is a consideration of the different methods of assimilation and implementation of the energies.

Concentration involves and requires the presence of a particular kind of energy to be accomplished. This energy is employed by one every day in many ways. Most often it is used for the accomplishment of the various little tasks which are required of one to get through the day: reaching for an object, grasping it, lifting it, releasing it; or attempting to recall a name, fact, concept; or presenting an argument to make a point, or controlling a flood of emotion such as anger or embarrassment.

All of these activities require one to concentrate, that is, to amass one of the energies of the body into a place or into a flow into a certain direction. One is taught from early childhood to concentrate in even the simplest ways to be able to learn how to perform the simplest tasks of life. Let us draw a comparison between a concentration which is familiar and one which one often uses but which is less familiar.

It is a familiar activity to clench the hand around an object. In much the same way, one with a developed concentration can employ that concentration in the mind. It is as if there were a muscle of the mind, or muscles in the mind which, until developed, energised and made fit, are flabby, uncontrolled, and slothful. They roll and flow this way and that way with any thought which enters the mind. The muscle of the mind can be developed to enable it to hold its concentration around an object (a thought or concept) and to concentrate energy in a certain direction in the mind to pursue a line of thought or rationalisation. To some degree, this muscle of the mind can be developed to project thoughts to the exclusion of other undesirable thoughts.

It is well known in the disciplines of old that there is an energy which is employed to accomplish such a task. First, there is the development of the will, that is, the will to do something; and then there is the energy which is employed actually to do the task desired. It is important, for this discussion, only to recognise the existence of the first: that is, the will.

It is the second – the energy which is employed by the will – with which we are concerned here. It is this energy which has long been the subject of work in the disciplines of old so as to enable one to gain a mastery of life, of the elements of the created universe — the phenomenal realm — that is, the realm in which phenomena occur. This energy has been called by various names.

The practices which work with it seek to control it, and it is controlled by concentrating it and then directing it, and then by controlling the movement of it in the direction in which it is sent. To develop this control requires practice, dedication and hard work. Even someone who lives only a quiet but active secular life must work hard to develop the control of certain aspects of this energy just to be able to function in normal everyday life. Of course, one who is opening in awareness must retain one's ability to concentrate certain energies in the everyday activities of life.

In this time of transition, one will also need to be able to work with and develop the new approach: the ability to become concentred without employing concentration. For a time in transition, concentrated activities must continue to be used. They complement that which is seen and experienced in the opening. They complement the experiences which result from the development of the ability to become concentred without employing concentration.

In other times and cultures, those who began to open into matters which went beyond the normal activities of everyday life were developed and taught by someone who had developed these techniques and control to lengths and abilities which can truly stretch credibility. They could use this energy for many various purposes. The use of these techniques and the development of the ability to use them involved a determination which became ironclad. It required a concentration and direction of will and energy which had the force and tenacity of a steel trap. It required a repressive control of emotion. All of this gave rise to a delusion that one was growing spiritually.

Now, let us look forward, quite a way forward, for just a moment and see just how that to which humankind is now beginning to open will differ from that which is described above. It is difficult for one to do this, for even the attempt to understand or grasp that which is now described employs the very energies and techniques of concentration of which mention has been made here. So, it is advisable at the outset to begin to view matters in a different way. Please note: the advice here is to *view* matters in a different way, not to *try* to view matters in a different way. To *try* is to begin to gather and concentrate energies. To *do* that which is now described is to abstain from trying. It is not refusing to try, for that too would require concentration. Rather, one is advised to remain concentred in neutral, to become gently receptive by relaxing the concentrated energies with which one normally works, and to relax the will which gathers and directs those energies.

To be most effective, real change must come from within outward. Hence, it is helpful to discard any notion that the first part which must be relaxed is the physical body,

That with which one will begin to work should begin in the mind. Actually, it begins beyond the mind, but it will first enter the waking awareness in one of the levels of the mind. Once begun, it can then be moved into the emotions, and then into the relaxation of the physical body. To attempt to relax the physical body first invites frustration in the emotions and the mind. Purely physical relaxation often leaves the mind more active and uncontrollable than before. At the least, it causes one to become more aware of its uncontrollability.

Attempts to take control of the mind in the beginning will be futile. With the state of consciousness of humankind in general at the present time, there is no way the mind can be fully controlled. There are techniques to suppress or eliminate thoughts and ways in which the mind can be emptied of certain activities, but control of the mind implies control of those regions of the mind of which one is generally unaware.

Control of these regions is not possible at this present state of evolution, before the implementation of the coming Change of Consciousness. There are, in those regions of which one is unaware, certain seeds which sprout into consequences which one must inevitably encounter. If one were fully aware of those seeds or of those coming consequences, one would attempt to predetermine, by use of obsolescent mental processes, just how one would meet those consequences. This would deprive one of some of the items of back-pressure which one needs to shape one's own evolution and spiritual development in a milieu of Self-determination.

Attempts to control the mind employ the very energies which stifle and foreclose the possibility of real change, for these energies are developed to be dominant and repressive. As each level of one's being takes its direction from the level above it, the emotions become restrained and frustrated by an attempt to control the mind. There is a diminishing of the breadth of expression and development and evolution of the emotions and the physical body. They are constrained and forced to conform to dictates which proceed only within a narrowed pattern of thoughts in the mind, rather than being able to expand and develop and flow towards new realities.

At the present time, the mental process employed in the human mind is negative. This means that it receives stimulus from outside or from within its own regions, or from levels of one's integrated vehicles below the mind. This process then prompts us to react to the stimuli which it receives. It also receives stimuli from what it attempts to anticipate, and it reacts to what it sees in anticipation.

Control of the mind, or, rather, control of the direction of the mind, will eventually become possible, but instead of being a repressive control or a negative process, it will be done by a positive mentation process. This is a process whereby the thinking process itself becomes emanative, positive and creative, rather than negative and reactive. It will become evident that there is a distinction between positive thinking and thinking positive thoughts.

The beginning steps into the acceptance of a new approach require one to gently set aside, at least for the moment, the need to understand what one is about to consider. It is helpful if one will make another acknowledgement in the manner in which one has been advised earlier to do. This acknowledgement is that what one is about to consider cannot be understood; and this acknowledgement also should be made aloud. When an acknowledgement is made aloud, there is no doubt that it will have been heard by all levels of one's integrated vehicles.

That to which one is opening in the way of a flow of a Positive Presence requires not only a relaxing into but also a welcoming of, instead of a searching for and a grasping at. Thus, there is first a gradual reduction of concentration of the mind. This reduction of concentration, and the relaxation which follows, will then filter downwards to the other bodies. There is a diffusion and release of the energy which had previously been concentrated. There is then an opening to and a welcoming of a very gentle and non-controlled, non-controlling, and non-concentrated Presence. This Presence will enter only into an atmosphere of receptivity, and it will become elusive if any attempt is made to chase, grasp, understand, control or direct it.

This activity invites one to do almost the very opposite, in almost every way, of that which one has spent most of one's waking moments in the whole of this lifetime – and many before it – developing. And sometimes we have developed this to a degree which is most elegantly refined. In many instances, it contributes to a delusion of self-satisfaction and a fiction of self-sufficiency.

If one has been involved in activities of a so-called 'spiritual' or personal development nature, including the activities of yoga, meditation, tantric practices, spiritual study, breath control or pranayamas, then one is called upon to open to a new approach.

This new approach will go about things in a way which is almost certain to be almost completely in opposition or contravention to that which one has been developing and employing in one's practices, techniques and thoughts.

This variance in approach will affect one in the full range and spectrum of one's activities, from the normal little everyday actions to the very most refined considerations of one's spiritual evolutionary development.

There are some initial steps which one can take in order to implement a new approach.

The first of these includes a consideration of the memory or recall process presently employed in the human mind, and how one can begin to change it. This step also employs a consideration of the decision-making process presently employed in the human mind, and how one can begin to take steps towards developing a new way of reaching decisions.

An introductory discussion of both of these considerations follows in the final two chapters in this section of the book.

11   Being and Seeing

Memories just aren't what they used to be.

Once upon a time, one could employ the circuit memory or recall process for just about any purpose, from the fond recollection of times and experiences gone by to the practical recall of events and their lessons, to enable one to make a decision in regard to a matter of present concern.

One who is opening now in this time of transition may find that the recall process, or the circuit memory, of even a short time past is becoming less effectual. One may also perceive that the items recalled, the memories themselves, carry less and less significance. If the memory itself does serve, the lessons recalled seem to have lost their impact and substance, and cannot be used as they once would have been as a source of criteria, standards and procedures to be employed for the purpose of making a decision or resolving a question or dealing with a crisis.

In these final two chapters of the first section of this book, we are going to examine two aspects of the mental process as they are now employed by much of humankind on this planet: the recall process, and the decision-making process. We will look at how they interrelate, how they are becoming less functional and reliable in their present form, and what steps one can take towards dismantling those parts which are now of dubious value with an eye towards building that which is to come next and which is in harmony with a Change of Consciousness.

The discussion of these matters here is only introductory and the treatment is necessarily cursory, for these matters are not discussed for their own importance but rather as steps towards matters of further importance; that is, to facilitate an easier maturing and transformation of one's vehicles and the maintenance of a balance in the assimilation of a Change of Consciousness. The processes themselves and that which will replace them will be discussed in later sections, for, although an introductory understanding of them can help one to move into the new, there must be some action taken before the full implication of the change can be seen and appreciated.

To a large degree, the memory process in the human brain at this stage of evolution is and has been, with occasional exceptions, limited to a recall of matters held in the circuits of the physical brain. These matters are for the most part the formulation of a framework or method whereby an event can be structured and stored for the purpose of recall. For this process to be effective, the first requirement, obviously, is for a physical body and a brain, both of which must function well anatomically and physiologically.

The little sparks of energy which dance around the ends of the nerve cells in the brain must have a well-oiled and organised playground or workshop, as the case may be, to be able to jump the proper gap and connect with the proper item of storage to bring it to the fore on command. This requires at least some concentration of energy, that is, concentration of energy as described briefly in the chapter called 'A Reorientation'; at least some development and toning of the muscle of the mind is indeed so that it may seek out, wrap around, and clench and bring forth the item to be recalled.

The present recall process is limited, firstly, to the recall of matters on a certain level of activity, of which more will be said presently; and secondly, to a particular kind of item which can be recalled on that level. It is further limited by an influence below the mind, that of the emotions. When the emotions are exerted, they can cause a supposedly reliable mental recall process to break down. More correctly, it will distort that which is recalled and refuse to function to an otherwise acceptable level of performance.

The human memory at its present stage of evolution is, for the most part, limited to functioning on a linear plane of time and space, and its function of recall can extend in depth and height only to certain extremes. The limitation of depth might be said to be the inability to recall those matters buried in that which is often called the 'subconscious'. The limitation of height applies to matters which have transpired at moments in time or places in space which are presently inaccessible. The matters at these levels may become accessible as one opens. Likewise, the limitation of height applies also to those matters – or inevitable consequences – which are still in seed form, yet to be sprouted, and which must remain, for a time, beyond the limitations of one's personal recall ability.

While there are events which one's personality has experienced in this lifetime or in other lifetimes which it might wish to recall, still some items of memory are shielded from availability either by the emotional barriers erected, as mentioned, or by the Discrimination of the Spiritual Self. The Spiritual Self selectively determines which matters would be better left unavailable for the serving of the Optimum Purpose of the experiences of the present lifetime.

If on opening one is emotionally vulnerable, either from the present state of one's own emotional predisposition or from a fragile condition due to a change, as if in a 'time compression' where events present themselves with shattering velocity and ferocity, then the Spiritual Self will shield the personality from seeing – or recalling – matters which might otherwise exacerbate the already precarious position; that is, it will shield one from such matters until it is time for one to see them.

Our Opening of Awareness

This protective barrier can be broken by the use of certain hallucinogenic drugs and substances, by emotional crises, and by the improper use of or indulgence in certain so-called yogic practices, some of which were discussed in the chapter called *'The Attraction of Yoga'*. If the protective barrier is broken in one of these ways, the results can be devastating, for one may see or experience something for which one is not ready.

There is also a change in the memory simply by the appearance of natural evolutionary phenomena.

With the advent of a Change of Consciousness on this planet, there is now such a natural evolutionary change occurring. Those opening are experiencing certain phenomena, both within and, perhaps, in the physical circumstances of their lives and relationships. For the acquisition of these phenomena, they have seemingly put forth no effort. These phenomena seem to appear for no reason and without explanation. These experiences by those opening are natural, even if sometimes disconcerting.

The opening and the expanding of awareness have brought along certain ancillary processes including an overhaul of the present memory or recall process. One of the first things one may notice as one opens is that the recall of little everyday matters, which theretofore seemed to be routine in the way of remembering where something was stored or when something occurred, or what is the name of an object or person, may be becoming a chore of almost impossible proportions. As one's awareness expands, one will find that one is drawn more and more to live in the infinite present, if not in the eternal, and that being in the present precludes living in the past or projecting into the future, at least in the way that one may have been accustomed to surmising what the shape of future events would have been according to the procedures which are now obsolete or non-existent.

One may feel that one has lost one's memory. This is in fact only a move as one opens to be more in the present moment, from which one will rise to a point of transcendent vantage to view the past with objectivity, to view the future with more clarity, and to view the present in a way which requires only the experiencing. From this vantage point, one will not need to process the experience for storage or accumulation, and one will not need to draw on that which is already stored and accumulated in order to give authenticity to the present experience.

The mental recall process, as it has been employed in the past, has always been basically only just reliable at best. It is generally characteristic of those employing it to embellish and even distort the original experience, and that which is recalled of it, in order to render that which is recalled compatible with the way which they would prefer to remember events to have been. As we will see in a later discussion, one's emotions also alter the 'purity' of an experience when viewed in retrospect.

The process by which *accumulata* of the past could previously be recalled is becoming obsolete. It is the disintegration of this process which one may view as the 'loss of memory'. One who is opening who is of advanced physical age may take comfort from what is being described here, for it is not necessary that memory should decline with ageing. For one who is opening towards a new consciousness, 'memory' will be converted, transformed, and changed to a new system, a new process, which will be of much more reliability, more keenness and more clarity.

If one is able to 'see', then that which one sees replaces that which has grown and developed as a substitute for the ability to see. This substitute for the ability to see is a complex and intricate process of surmising, deducing and plotting, and it is now supported by energies and motives which are no longer of use to humankind. This 'substitute process' can be dismantled and unlearned as one opens. In fact, the unlearning of this interloping and distracting process is one of the things which does happen naturally as one opens. The time of the personal transition is largely occupied with moving from the old process to the new one.

The inability to see derives largely from humankind's desire to be able to think; that is, to be able to think in the way in which humankind has come to view thinking or the thinking process. To 'see', one must 'be', in the present; and there is no way that one can 'think' about the present. In the present process known as 'thinking', all thoughts which present themselves in the thinking process are either of the future or of the past.

If one attempts to 'think' of the present, one will naturally transcend, even if only slightly and if only for a short time, the plane of time and space; one will thence gain at least a momentary experience of *being* in the present. This experience will necessarily bring the focus to the self.

To 'see' requires that one must 'be' in that experience of the Self which is not of the plane of time and space. As there is no way in which one can think about the present, so there is no way that one can 'be' here, now. If one can be, one can and does transcend the planes of here and now: that is, the planes of space and time. Thinking likewise ties the attention and the focus to the here (that is space) and the now (that is time). 'Thinking', as it is spoken of by humankind at the present time, is simply the full linear spectrum of that which is called memory, even though memory commonly denotes thinking about the past or recalling the past.

Although the present thinking, and memory or recall, process precludes one from thinking of or recalling the future, there is, built into this obsolescent process, a way in which a substitute procedure is employed in an attempt to anticipate the future. This is done through this intricate and complex weaving of conclusions, surmises, theories and probabilities by which the human mind is deluded into believing that the process works effectively, and that it can make some determination of the events of the present and the future based on events and conclusions which are recalled from the past.

This process can be unlearned, and the tenacious grip which it has on the human mind can be released and relaxed. It is not necessary, fortunately, to begin at the outside and unravel from the outside in. It is not necessary to regress through the physical events which have transpired and affected one in this incarnation, for they have done their bit. They were inevitable consequences which arose when their time was right; they were encountered and they played out.

Unfortunately, one so encountering such consequences probably related to the event and the consequences thereof rather than the true lesson which was inherent in the experience. These events of the past have little or no relevance for the present, and they have relevance for the future only insofar as the true lesson, the essence, of the experience can be distilled from the experience to shape the personality of the present incarnation, and to enable one to take the residual vibrations of such experience and lesson to be retained by the seed atom which will shape the nature of the vehicles and personality of future incarnations.

For one to see the true lessons of the experiences which one undergoes, and for a tribe or a nation to see the true lessons of its history, there is a need to transcend the past. This is done by acknowledging that the experiences of the past were inevitable consequences which have already occurred and which cannot occur again. At least, they will not recur in the precise form which they assumed in the previous encounter.

The decisions which one makes about 'what to do' should then come from the present, from the present moment, and from what one sees in the present moment. This in itself is not difficult, but there is, or there can be, a difficulty in retaining the purity of what is seen in a present moment. The force behind the invasion of thoughts, that is, items of the thinking process, deductions from the past, or from anticipation of the future, is very strong.

This force has behind it the strength of generations upon generations of events, incarnations, and refinements of the concentration of energy of the phenomenal realm. It is in this realm wherein humankind has fed fear and superstition, and devised the decision-making process which now does all that it can to prevent one from being in the present moment, and to prevent one from being able to see and to determine what one should do in a way which is pure and clear and devoid of self-interest.

There is no need to dismantle the outdated recall system to be able to see. There is a need simply to *be in the present*, to see, and then to be able to dismantle the consequences which arose from the inability to see. To accomplish this, one must be dedicated to maturing and transforming the bodies and to accepting change which is *truly new*.

Now, what steps can be taken in this direction? To determine the steps to be taken requires first a discussion of the background of the decision-making process as it now interrelates with this faulty recall process.

12   First Steps: New Decisions

In this final chapter, we will first examine the nature of the decision-making process employed by the human mind and illustrate how it binds and limits the ability of that to which one is opening, the Spiritual Self, to gain full expression. We will then look at some of the practical steps which can be taken to begin to rearrange the mind and its working so that it may be receptive to that which is later to be presented.

As one begins to dismantle the past, take a new approach to an old recall process, examine reactive behavioural patterns, and approach the possibility of moving towards a transformation, there is a vital and essential procedural change which must take place in the workings of the human mind.

The mind in its present form uses a very strict and staid system for reaching decisions. It is this decision-making process which we are going to examine now. The mind, as well as other parts of the integrated vehicles, will begin to open to an Undefined Element. This will enable the integrated vehicles to move towards the assimilation of a Change of Consciousness, but the present decision-making process inhibits the acceptance of the *new*.

In the beginning, it is well-nigh impossible for the mind to accept new concepts, for the force and amount of energy which has been placed into building its decision-making process and energising the circuits in and through which the process works are literally almost infinite.

This development of this energy and the quickening of the circuits in this direction have been done by choice by generations upon generations of development of the human mind on this planet. As with other evolutionary matters, when it was brought forth and manifested, it was a revolutionary as well as an evolutionary development. It was a great step forward for humankind to be able to 'reason' in any way at all. This was true, even though it was a process which made reference only to that which had gone before in order to make a decision having to do with the present or with the future.

The process by which the human mind reaches decisions at this time and up until now, that is, since the last major breakthrough in the development of the process with which the mind works, enabled humankind, at that time, to bring some order into the chaos of the way we did things.

If we can remember that when this reasoning process emerged, humankind was in a state where its main concern was merely to be sure that there was enough food available, that one could keep the body warm at night, and that one could satisfy those basic urges over which one had virtually no control and which had to be met when they arose, then this reasoning process was a dynamic change. It offered some hope that the needs which man considered vital and over which one had no control would be met. This was to be done by referring, as best one could, to the way the need was met the last time it arose.

This of course gave birth to *memory* as it is known today. It enabled one to remember how a need was met in the past and then to move towards fulfilling the resurgent need by moving to the point, place or procedure by which the need was met before. This process and its limitations were discussed in the previous chapter.

Then, there arose the problems, of course, of what happened when events did not go as they should have: that is, that they did not go as they should have, *had matters been as they were remembered to be when last left*, or as they should have been, given the probabilities that the resources should have been available this time, since they were available last time they were needed!

Up until the development of the reasoning process as it is known today, and which is presently employed by most of the tribes of humankind as a whole, these needs which arose were met in a haphazard sort of way. One had to rely basically on chance. Reference to the manner and place in which a need was met the last time it arose enabled one to begin to move with some certainty. This of course gave rise to the fact that one did not have to spend so much time fulfilling these needs and was able to give attention to other matters. It gave one time to devise more interesting ways of meeting needs. It even gave time for one to begin to wonder a bit.

Then, variations in the fulfilment of need gave rise to pleasurable fulfilment of desire. And, thence, to the variations in the pleasurable fulfilment of desire; and thence to the divisive and intentional pursuit of the fulfilment of intentions which were designed to produce neither the fulfilment of need nor the fulfilment of desire, nor even the pleasurable end of either. These became ends in themselves: that is, done merely to see if they could be done; and then to see if they could be done in a more clever way.

The fruits of the venture no longer were important, and the action was undertaken merely for the purpose of doing the action and satisfying the urging to accomplish an end to test or exhibit one's guile, cunning, and wit.

Not the least of the ultimate products of this process was the emergence of boredom due to the absence of further needs and desires to be fulfilled and the distraction which resulted. One was then called upon to create new needs to fulfil and new desires to pleasurably satisfy. It would be abhorrent or even unendurable to envisage a situation in which one had no further desires left to fulfil!

Massive distraction then ensued; that is, the distraction of the attention from that which one *is* to that which one had *created* – even to the point of identifying with that which had been created.

Thus, the ability of Humankind, especially of the Western world, to fulfil a need far outstretched the need itself. Our ability to imagine and visualise, not to mention our ability to desire, far outreached our ability to devise ways to satisfy or accomplish what one imagined or visualised.

Now, Humankind in the Western world is reaching the point where even the most outlandish desires are within easy reach.

All of this was further complicated by the retention of and attachment to a reasoning or mentation process which was originally designed to meet a need which arose aeons ago and which was for the purpose of merely remembering where one got one's last meal. There was a probability that there might be something there to eat the next time the need arose.

Now where does this leave Humankind? With a new hunger! It leaves us with new needs – really new needs – from projects which we have manifested into thought-form and further into the form of desire-plan. But it also leaves us with a mentation process which is ill-equipped to deal with even a fraction of the intricacies, details and creation of the articles of fulfilment of these new plans and intentions.

Even given the possibility that Humankind can redirect the ability to produce from the purpose of seeing if it can be done to a purpose of meeting a new need, imagined or otherwise, Humankind is left with the massive problem of devising and accepting a new mentation process to meet even the form, let alone the substance, of a new purpose.

We are left with the massive problem of how to meet the consequences of desires and actions, let alone the incomprehensible consequences of the gargantuan proportions to which the individual as well as the collective ego will expand as a result of the accomplishments and the pride taken therein.

Now let us look at the complications which arise as a result of the continued use and retention of this antiquated decision-making process, which served well in the times when it was needed but which now has been far surpassed by humankind's present needs and abilities.

If we remember that this mental process was designed for the purpose of fulfilling simple needs as they occurred or recurred in a manner in which the similar need had been formerly fulfilled, then it can be seen that the principal purpose therein was the assurance of comfort and security.

If one growingly wishes to begin to move with the promptings which are emanating from within, it is understandable that one's interpretation of such promptings will be coloured by or subject to the need to be assured that one's needs will be fulfilled.

Self-preservation is the first and foremost instinctive need which we wish to fulfil. It is a long way from the need for self-preservation to the prompting to exhibit behaviour which is magnanimous, altruistic and generous. Even such action when it first begins to emerge is coloured and shaped and limited by a generosity which remains only after the fulfilment of one's own needs and wants is assured.

Even one who is beginning to have promptings from within as to the action to be taken will almost inevitably retreat to consultation with the mind, or the circuitry of the intellect as it is now employed, to determine if one should accept the prompting, or if a reason therein exists which will justify one ignoring the prompting.

So long as one falls prey to the temptation to engage in such a consultation for such a purpose, one is limiting the possibility of *creative action*. Creative action requires the introduction of something new – truly new – and not just a rearrangement of the old.

And certainly not for the preservation of the security of the fulfilment of the basic needs of life which was long ago assured many times over for most people – at least in much of the Western world.

Initial promptings from within or from one who can help, even those promptings with an unmistakable Ring Of Genuineness, will carry no reason or substance which can appeal to the reasoning process as it is now known. These initial promptings, as well as those which will follow, if the present decision-making process is not evolutionarily overhauled, will be subject to this basic test of self-preservation in the form of a question, proposed to the intellect. This question may take the form of, 'Is there any reason why I should not follow this prompting and undertake this action?'

If there is any possibility that any part of the integrated being will be threatened in any way, the answer which will be thrust forth by the intellect on behalf of the rest of the being will be a resounding, 'Yes, there is a reason: don't do it.'

This answer will, defensively and mistakenly, be taken, in the beginning, as something which one believes that one feels within. It will not be overcome by that which carries the Ring of Truth, for the energy which sustains the process which assures self-comfort is stronger, at least on the level on which it operates, than the Presence which manifests and moves the Change of Consciousness and the true positive changes inherent in it.

One who is opening to that which is known within will recognise what is being described here. The issue which arises may not be the correctness of this discussion, but what is to be done about it. On opening, one will find within, even within the lower bodies, the desire to move out of the confines of a continuous programme of self-preservation. It is difficult to overcome a process which is energised by generations and generations of ramification, variety, refinement and indulgence.

How then is one to dismantle this self-limiting syndrome? There are two basic simple steps which one can take.

The first involves the approach to that which arises from within the Self in the nature of a prompting – a 'knowingness' – that one is about to be called upon to do something or take some action, the nature of which, at least at first blush, is *unsupported by any 'logical' purpose*.

This approach involves the asking of the question, *'Is there any reason why I **should** do this which I am prompted to do?'*

The answer to this question will be a sounding and resounding, 'Yes!' *But this answer will not come from the mind.* It will come from the depths of That to which one is opening within. And then there will be silence! The mind will wait in vain for a further answer. The question has been answered!

'*Yes*, there is a reason why I should do this.' There is a reason; that is enough.

The second step involves the development of the ability to move to the action to be taken after perceiving only the initial action to be taken. This comes without knowing or being able to perceive the actions which will then follow, or even the reason for the first part of the action to be taken, let alone the entire operation.

This will take practice; it will take time; and it will take hard work, especially to be able to relax into it.

Until one is able to move with these two steps, one is still operating at the mercy of events, still being manipulated by inevitable consequences as they arise, and there is very little that one can do in the way of moving to Positive Action or Positive Creation and manifestation.

One who can begin to work with that which is described herein will be ready for the Material which will follow in the next section.

Our New Human Consciousness

Our Path of Self-discovery

An Overview

As we move towards a New Human Consciousness that comes with this new century and a new era, **The Path of Self-discovery** may be the only path available to us. But this is not a path for the faint-hearted. Although there are no rules, there are some **Guidelines On The Path of Self-discovery**. You start in the here and now; you don't have to clean up your mess, get forgiveness, or even pack a bag before you start this journey. You are the only one who can approve or disapprove of your actions, and you will develop the tools to do this and to gauge your own process as you go along.

So, if you start this path here and now, it is best to recognise **The Way Things Are**. You need to become acquainted with The Three Realities: that is, the way things are, the way we think they are, and the way we would like for them to be. The need for Discrimination begins to arise when our neat, clean and tidy scenario begins to disintegrate, to come apart – that is, when one begins to suspect that things are not the way one views them. There is also a benignly smiling paradox which peeks around the corner of one's awareness inside and says that one cannot really change the way things are, but that one could begin to sort out **the way things aren't**.

This is the time for **Beginning Discrimination**. Discrimination is a process. It is a continual and continuous process of sorting out that which is real from that which is unreal, that which is important from that which is unimportant, and that which needs and deserves attention from that which does not need or deserve one's attention and effort. Many of us live either in the past or in the future: it is a rare person who lives in the present. It is not difficult to live in the present, but there is a condition that most are unwilling to accept: that is, those items that belong to the past or the future must be left there. This takes guts! It takes guts, determination and a strong will to accept that which one sees. The trickiest task at this time is **Keeping a Balance**. The process of Discrimination can lead to a balance in one's life, a balance that is difficult to maintain with first, the present system of thinking that most of us employ; and second, with the emotional structure that most of us have as a result of our heritage and education from the culture into which we have been born.

So this process begins by **Making the Shift**. As one commences to use Discrimination and prepares to enter the Path of Self-discovery, one is standing at the doorway to a new dimension, and the shift in personal consciousness that one faces can alter one's evolutionary position. One of the things that one will experience is a feeling of coolness, a feeling of objectivity, a feeling of detachment. This feeling is basically foreign to the nature of the personality that we of the Western world have developed over the past many centuries. It is not part of our inherent way of life. When one has a glimpse of the way things are, or at least a glimpse of the way things aren't, there will be **A Consequence of Seeing**. This is the start of a journey – a journey that has no ending, that has no goal, that has, as its sole purpose, the travelling on the journey itself.

It is the most exciting voyage one will ever make, and it culminates in the knowledge of and the being of that for which the soul has been searching since it first began its involution into matter and its wanderings through creation. The major consequence, then, of seeing or sensing at least a little bit of the way things are is that one knows that this is what one wants. One also knows that there is such wisdom and clarity and truth in that which one sees and senses within that one in fact would like for things to be the way one has seen them within.

It is then that one begins to see the difference between **Aspiration and Inspiration**. The accomplishments to be attained and towards which we are motivated are most often the definition of aspirations that we hold deep inside. These aspirations appear from time to time and are often called 'ideas', but, in fact, most of them are inevitable consequences that come to the surface and that themselves were the result of some desire or some reaction. When a true artist moves to work in his or her medium of expression, the inspiration comes first and then the aspiration follows; that is, the vision of that which one wants to do comes first, and then the motivation to do it can be summoned to provide the energy and resources to move to action. The motivation that then produces the action can thus come from a desire to express that which was seen in the moment of inspiration. Many an artist has lost the inspiration to create by reversing the priority and placing the aspiration first. That which happens in this process is called Discrimination, and the process itself is called the Enquiry.

Genuine inspiration comes **From the Inside Out**. It is not found by peering outward. Nor, for that matter, is it found by looking inward, at least with the present condition and state our minds are in. There is an optimum attitude to be adopted that enables one to adjust to the way things are, to accept that the way things are may not be exactly as one has believed them to be, and to harmonise the way one wishes things to be with the way things are. The technique of seeing how things are is not difficult to practise. It is simply to focus the awareness at this Point of Becoming. To implement that which is being described here, one will experience **The Dawning of an Inner Discipline**. There is a special discipline, an Inner Discipline, that one must develop for one to work with the inspiration that comes From the Inside Out, and the purpose of which is to bring with it that which is new and to manifest the way things are and the way things are changing. This is the training of the mind, the emotions, the body and the personality to act on that which is seen to be needed to be done. Discrimination is the essential ingredient in seeing what needs to be done; Inner Discipline is the essential ingredient in doing it.

There may be a desire to 'get on with it' accompanied by a feeling of impatience. Impatience can be unnerving at the least and at the outside dangerous and even devastating, for it is at such a time that one can become most vulnerable to an attack by the ego. Now one may begin to undergo a **Self-transformation of the Ego**. Attendant to impatience – the desire to 'get on with it' – one will also find the erroneous notion that constant action on one's own part and by one's own efforts must physically and actively be put forth. There is a tendency to do everything within one's power to exhaust all efforts at one's disposal to aid and further the impetus which is in fact self-perpetuating, but which, deceptively, induces one to action, precipitated by the notion that the more energy is expended through action, the greater will be the progress.

One who is firmly pursuing the enquiry will soon find that there is a connection between **Self-reflection and Self-discovery**. Self-reflection is a very practical process by which one can begin to harmonise one's life with one's own unique set of inevitable consequences and the purpose of one's life. Self-reflection is a medium- to long-term project, but it will have short-term effects and consequences as well. No matter what other practices one has worked with or what paths one may have explored or followed, when one first begins to practise Self-reflection, one will open one's self to a Positive Presence. The discovery of the Positive Presence is part of the process of Self-discovery.

13 The Path of Self-discovery

> As we move towards the major change of consciousness that comes with this new century and a new era, the Path of Self-discovery may be the only path available to us.

What's wrong with the way things are now?

We seem to be eliminating or rejecting most of the existing paths to spiritual enlightenment. Indeed, the Path of Self-discovery is probably the only path that we will accept. It is the path that will answer the question, 'Who am I, and why am I here?'

But this is not a path for the faint-hearted.

The Path of Self-discovery can lead to realisation of the Spiritual Self. Traditionally, this has involved a search towards a goal, but this is not a goal to be searched for or selected, but rather a state of being to be accepted.

The main barrier that now stands between one who is opening in awareness and this state of being is adherence to a crystallised set of beliefs rooted in the past.

The traditional paths of the search for truth and enlightenment have often been revealed to or through an incarnation, who then passed on the truth of the moment to his or her followers. Inevitably those teachings became crystallised into dogmas. In an attempt to keep the teachings alive, religions were formulated to perpetuate the dogmas.

This worked for a while, but then the times moved on, and the teachings of the religions, fastened as they were to a moment in time, began to move into the past and become increasingly irrelevant. The ring of truth might remain in the moment, but the experience too often became vicarious. This can mean that those opening to enlightenment may have had nothing to rely on but the teachings of others and of the past, the relevance of which, to one's own search, is questionable because most of the important matters are decided by someone else.

What are the demands of a new generation of opening souls?

These traditional paths offering vicarious experience are not generally acceptable to those who are now opening in awareness and who are not willing to wade through or accept ancient teachings and outmoded disciplines.

They want enlightenment, *and they want it now!* In essence, they are saying, 'I want the truth, and I will find it for myself.' When one makes this statement, the onus shifts: the seeker says, in effect, 'I will decide what is relevant for me, and I will find my own way.' In essence, this statement initiates the first step on this new path: this is the step of discrimination, the process of sorting out what is relevant and what is irrelevant. The first declaration of spiritual independence may be made with some bravado, but the process itself must be carried through with genuine bravery and courage. It is not for the faint of heart or the weak of resolve. Why not?

How does this affect 'me'?

Let's bring this experience close to home.

Immediately upon making this first statement of spiritual intent, the onus shifts onto one's own shoulders. There is a major change of assumptions, and it can be scary stuff. As one reaffirms that resolution daily, the results can be frightening to say the least. Even if one says it only once, there is no going back, because it means that one accepts the responsibility for one's own path.

If one knows within that this is what one must do, one can make the statement almost effortlessly. The process of putting it into action, however, takes every ounce of effort that one can muster every minute of every day. The effect of making this declaration to pursue the Path of Self-discovery is much the same on every one of us: we are on the path together, but we travel it alone.

What happens when one makes this declaration?

In effect, this declaration is a statement of the self to seek the Self. This is not a play on words; it is the initiation of a personal path to move from who we *think* we are to who we *really* are.

This is a natural evolutionary move, given that we are developing a paradox in our growth as a culture. We know from trusted teachings that with beings less evolved, the soul of each is bound to a group soul. As we move from this lower consciousness, we begin to create our own destiny as individuals. We create a manifestation of the higher self that projects into a lower self, and that lower self begins a return journey to find the higher self. This much we all know or have been taught.

So, what is the paradox of the Path of Self-discovery?

The paradox is that the divergent path we begin when we start on the path of self-discovery will, once again, converge with the original path when we begin to discover the higher self. So, the path is really a journey by the self to discover the Self. This may sound like a cliché that restates all of the truisms that we have heard from teachings of the past, but the experience of making the journey is anything but a cliché; it is a rugged trip and a ruthless experience.

This is not some namby-pamby peace-light-and-joy singalong.

Why are things happening and changing faster and faster?

As a culture, we have no choice but to make a shift in our consciousness. As the exponential curve of change grows steeper, our evolutionary growth is far outstripping the growth of our behaviour patterns. We still retain attitudes and behaviour that we should have rejected long ago. In spite of the fact that there is an infinity of levels, even on our planet (from the most rudimentary forms of life upwards through the most rudimentary forms of human life and on upwards to very highly evolved souls incarnated into human bodies) the entire spectrum of life on the planet is due for an upward shift: a Change of Consciousness.

Those of less awareness will be swept along and have little choice in the matter of changing their consciousness. Those whose awareness is open will have the option open to *choose* to shift their consciousness and to participate in the overall shifting of consciousness of the culture. It is these latter persons who can accept the Path of Self-discovery and who will initiate themselves onto this journey.

Why is this so difficult?

This will be a difficult change for everyone, no matter where they were when the change started in them. For those with little awareness, it will be hard because they will not know what is happening to them. The changes will be decided at a higher level of consciousness, and they will need only, so to speak, to 'go along with the programme and follow the path'. For those of more awareness – that is, those who choose the path of self-discovery – it will be more difficult, but in a different way; for by choosing to initiate themselves onto this path, they will also *choose* to help design **the programme** and to help find the path.

This is doubly difficult because we are cutting a new path through uncharted territory; we are making it up as we go along. We are cutting the path through a wild jungle. In essence, the choice is a choice only so long as one chooses it. There is a story from an old Indian holy man who said, 'You can walk down to the water and jump in, or you can stick your toe in and then walk in, or you can stand there and wait to get pushed in from behind.' Most of us who choose this path made the decision to choose it long ago.

So, where is the 'onus'?

Now what does this mean to you if you choose to enter the journey of self discovery?

It means that you become the initiator, the perpetuator, and the regulator: you start yourself on the path, you keep yourself on the path, and you monitor your own development.

So the onus shifts onto your own shoulders. This is a major change from the way of seeking truth and enlightenment, both from the past and from other cultures. Those who have embarked on this path are forging their own development; they are charting their course.

Where this course goes is determined by several factors:

- The influence of the unique set of inevitable consequences (karma) that we each have created ourselves;
- The speed by which we are able to discriminate and discard matters of irrelevance;
- The degree to which we commit ourselves to be trustees of sacred knowledge in forging the path for others;
- Our ability to keep a balance between growth and distraction; and
- Our acceptance of grace.

It is the last of these that we will look at first, for there is a major hurdle to overcome as soon as one declares the intention to follow this path.

Whom can I follow? Who will tell me what to do?

This Material is written mainly for those in the Western world who have chosen to incarnate at this time of the emergence of a new culture with a new consciousness. Those who have incarnated in this new generation comprise people of all ages from early childhood to elderly adulthood. They begin this journey with a major handicap inherited from the culture as they have joined it: they carry a burden of guilt that comes from our cultural heritage. According to this heritage, we *start* this journey as one who is laden with sin and who must be cleansed. This is perhaps the first antiquated and irrelevant relic from the past upon which we must exercise our discrimination and gently but firmly reject and relegate to our psychological dustbin.

This is a 'bootstrap' exercise, and it goes to the very root and heart of the ability to embark on the path of self-discovery. As a bootstrap exercise, it is something that we each must do for ourselves. No one else can do it for us, no one can tell us when we are ready to do it, and there will be very few if any who stand on the sidelines to cheer you on when you do it.

This assumption of guilt is one that we have lived with for so long that we have accepted it as part of our being. It is a cultural paradigm, a pillar of our belief system so deeply ingrained that it cannot be expunged by the means we have been told to use by our religious teachings. To attempt to use a little water to cleanse us of our deeds is like throwing a towel into a pond so the fish can dry itself.

One of the first things that one rejects upon entering the path of self-discovery is the notion that someone else has the answers to our problems. *My problems are my problems, and I must find the answers.* This is not always comfortable; we like to be told what to do and how to do it.

You may say, 'I am independent, and I think for myself. I reject outside authority.' This is the bravado to which reference was made above, and such a statement may carry one well in the marketplace where the modes of behaviour and the codes of practice are well established; where one knows where the boundaries are and when one crosses them. But the support of one's bravado will dwindle when one enters the wilderness of one's own mind and the labyrinth of circuits, conclusions, beliefs, prejudices and base desires that each of us carries deep within.

Even though each of us has these gremlins deep within us, each of us has a *different* set of gremlins unique to us. The path of self-discovery is about you dealing with your own gremlins and me dealing with mine. This is not *learning how to deal* with them; this is *dealing* with them. To say one is totally alone on this path is not completely correct. *Help is available.* There are some techniques that help. But there are no rules, and even if there were, they would not work across the board for all of us because of our uniqueness, and further because there are no two gremlins alike, not even two of yours or two of mine. No matter how fast the fish rubs, it won't get dry with a wet towel.

So we have to back up and take a look at the broader picture. Many of us were taught from very early childhood that we are sinners and that we would need God's forgiveness before we could be whole.

The problem was that forgiveness supposedly came from God through so many channels that by the time it reached us it had a great many strings attached. This meant we got caught in the net, unable to find our way out. There is some suspicion that this was the purpose of the system in the first place.

This is all built on a myth, a fiction, but it is a fiction that came from teachings formed by a 'truth-giver' very early on. If you read history, you can find out why a truth-giver had to make such harsh statements to a tribe that needed to be dug out of the mire of their own collective consequences. They needed a shake-up. And they got it. The problem was that those teachings found their way into the scare tactics of those who said they could forgive those sins, and they have passed that tactic down through the ages. Somehow, it survived right up into our present day.

But now there are those walking and talking in our culture who are rejecting this teaching out of hand: they will not even listen to the authority that tries to ram it down their throats. They may not know exactly how to go about finding the truth yet, but they know that what is on offer is definitely not the way for them.

First we question the basic assumption upon which a lot of this is based: that we are bad to begin with, and we must somehow become good. If you wish to believe this and continue to accept the practices that are supposed to correct the situation, then you must do as you believe. It is possible that this Path of Self-discovery is not for you.

But if down deep somewhere in there you suspect that you are *not* bad to begin with, that you are *not* a sinner to be cleansed with someone else's towel when they decide to use it, that you are *not* one who needs to rely on the judgment of someone else who claims authority from a source so remote from you that you cannot relate to it, then consider this:

What if you are not that which you have been taught to be?

Consider for a moment a hypothetical proposition. Consider that you are not as you believe yourself to be; that is, you are not a person who is a sinner and who needs to be forgiven by someone else, but rather that you are the occupant of a set of life vehicles, and that these life vehicles are your articles of expression in a life on a plane on which you are dealing with consequences that you have created in the past, and that you will occupy those life vehicles until you have completed dealing with an allotted quota of those consequences at which time you will remove yourself from those life vehicles. Let's leave it there for the moment; we will deal later with what you did before you entered this set of vehicles and what will happen after you leave them.

While you are here in these vehicles, you must do what is fair: clean up your own little set of consequences of things you have done in the past. In these vehicles, you have a *mind* to think through what you are going to do and to try to figure out what life is all about; you have an *emotion* so that you can feel good about what's fun, so that you can feel as you must about your part of the mess, and so you can scare yourself to death as you think what life is all about; and you have a *body* to jump, dance, and shake, to feel pain and pleasure, and to help the emotion create some more desires that go on up to the mind. Your mind will then try to figure out how you can get more of what made you feel good and less of what made you feel bad.

Then one day, you twig. 'Hey,' you say, 'maybe if I had some more information about all of this, I could stop causing myself so many problems. Maybe I could begin to unravel my own mystery.'

That's where it starts. But where does it finish?

14   Guidelines on The Path of Self-discovery

Although there are no rules on this path, there are some guidelines that might help one along the way.

What are the basic guidelines for this Path of Self-discovery?

Here are a few basic guidelines about how this path works:

- You start in the here and now. You don't have to clean up your mess, get forgiveness, or even pack a bag before you start this journey;
- You can have instant enlightenment right here right now if you can handle it;
- You are the only one who can approve or disapprove of your actions, and you will develop the tools to do this and to gauge your own progress as you go along; and lastly
- You can set your own pace and work your own system as you see fit, except that, if you pledge yourself to assist in the implementation of the Change of Consciousness, you may be subject to a superior itinerary or agenda (more about this later).

When you apply these guidelines, they add up to a fluid paradigm that answers to no one except your Self: no blame, no attribution.

This may sound selfish and arrogant, and *it is*. Once you begin to get a handle on your own inner growth, you will then begin to develop a new *personal* consciousness.

So, where do we start?

The first step is *Re-identification*.
　　When most of us say 'I', as in 'I think' or 'I will', the statement carries an implication of *inappropriate identification*. If you say 'my higher self', it implies that you, the speaker, are focused at somewhere other than in that higher self.
　　Identification is a very important beginning point of reference for one who wishes to pursue self-discovery. If you are identified with some part of you that refers to the Spiritual Self as *'my'*, then there is, additionally, a factor of possession. *It is that part of you where you are focused and which refers to other parts of*

you as 'my' that will control the source and nature of your energy and your identification.

Thus, there is a very important question that you can ask to help reorient your focus to that part of you from which your Light proceeds:

Who is the **I** that says *'my'*?

Who is the I that says 'my higher self'?

Who is the I that says 'I am not in harmony with my higher self'?

Even if one wishes to take a 'logical' approach to this question, it is not the 'Higher Self', for the Higher Self does not refer to ItSelf as being something possessed by or outside of itself. The 'lower self', on the other hand, has indicated that, in its separateness and in its separation, it has become aware of a 'higher self', and in doing so has made a great leap forward – *if there is a forward to go.*

Where does this path take me?

This brings us to a consideration of dimensions. In the realm of the Higher Self, is it possible to go forward? Is it possible to progress? This question might be answered – or at least examined – by asking the same question regarding the 'lower self'. Is it possible to have 'progress *forward*' in the realm of the 'lower self'? Yes, it would seem so, for the lower self is firmly anchored in the negative realm, the *phenomenal realm*, the dimension of time and space, and that is where *movement forward*, or *progress*, can be envisaged. In the Higher Self, can there be progress to anywhere else besides where it Is?

Of course these questions sound philosophical and very basic (especially to one who has already enquired into such matters), but they do have some value in the 'reorientation' process, or the act of identification: an essential action to establish the right foundation for realisation.

The point of focus in most of us was, or sometimes still is, anchored firmly in the realm of the 'lower self'. It may be the 'lower self' that is seeking some point in the darkness where one could attempt to place a hand on the doorknob of a door in a dark room.

We have some clues to help us remember where the doorknob is located if we get distracted by something over there in a dark corner that calls plaintively to us to remember and long for something from the past.

It is the 'Higher Self' on the other side of the door that we long to find when we have mistakenly believed we were *that* which inhabits the dark. But when we find that Self on the other side of the door – even for just a moment – then we can remember that it was that Self that projected into the dark room, closed the door, and threw away the key of enlightenment, orientation and identification.

So, who is the I that says 'my'? Who is it that says 'my door', 'my doorknob', 'my light', 'my Higher Self'? Even if the answer is not realised, it can be hypothesised. By that I mean that it can be postulated and considered as a guide to reorienting the Identification. Just consider, how would it be if you said, 'I wish to bring my lower self into harmony with Me?' The answer might then come more easily to the question:

Who is the I that says 'my'?

15 *The Way Things Are*

The best place to start on this Path of Self-discovery is where you are now, with things as they are now.

How can I find out how things really are?

Things are the way they are.
In the beginning, the way things are comprises:

- The way things are;
- The way one *thinks* things are; and
- The way one *wishes* things were.

Psychology differentiates between a psychotic person, a neurotic person, and a distressed person.

The psychotic person says, *'I know two and two are five.'*

The neurotic person says, *'I know two and two are four, but I have a lot of trouble with it.'*

The distressed person says, *'I really wish two and two were six.'*

Although all three of these views of reality are amalgamated and synthesised, (that is, admixed and interfused), and although each is affected and influenced by the other, still each of these retains a certain 'quantitative integrity' – that is, a kind of separateness from the other.

This is not as difficult to see as it sounds. For instance, even when the three of these are amalgamated, there is still a separate reality: *The Way Things Are*. This reality goes beyond the way things are when amalgamated with the way one thinks things to be, believes them to be, and the way one would like for things to be. Whether one knows of this *'reality beyond'* or not, it is there.

This third element, that is, the way one would like for things to be, is still shaped almost completely in the beginning by this amalgamated or synthesised way that things are. The change that one can make, that is, the extent to which one can wish things to be other than the way they are, is limited in scope of both conception and imagination.

How do things change when the awareness opens?

When the awareness begins to open, all of this begins to change.

When one begins to open in awareness, one begins to wonder firstly how things are and then one begins to enquire into *the way things really are*. One begins to suspect that things may not really be the way that one views them; one begins to enquire as to whether things are really the way one believes them to be.

One begins to wonder if it is possible to change things from the way they are to the way one would like them to be. One may begin to wonder if it is possible to begin to take a hand in *shaping the direction* that things take in one's personal life, and in the part that one plays in the life of one's community and one's world.

Before one begins to open in awareness, these various factors cannot be distinguished one from the other. In fact, it will not even occur to one not yet opening in awareness that there may be a distinction of these factors one from the other, for when this thought does occur, one has begun to open in awareness.

When we say that these factors are amalgamated, that is all mixed together, we mean that each influences the other. The way one views things and believes them to be is determinative in shaping the way things are. One's ability to wish for things to be other than they are is shaped by the way things are, which in turn is shaped by the way one views things. And the way one views things and the way one wishes things to be are clearly active in shaping each other.

How is 'the way things are' different from 'The Way Things *Are*'?

Here we are speaking of the way things are and we are not yet speaking of the way things *are*. When we speak of the way things are, we are speaking of the way things are in the phenomenal realm – the created universe, the world of humankind.

When we speak of the way things *are*, we are speaking of that into which one begins to enquire when one begins to open. But first, one must and will make an enquiry into the way things are. The way things are is a reflection of the way things *are*.

One may ask, 'How did things come to be the way they are? Are they the same for me as they are for others? Do I have a clear perception of things? What, if anything, can I do about things?'

These are very explosive and exciting questions, for part of the way things are determines whether one is able and ready to find the answers to these questions, and this is determined by whether one is able and willing to ask the questions.

When one begins to ask these questions, one is already on the way towards finding the answers. And when one begins to see the answers that come in response to asking these questions, the way things are will change. And it will then be determined by what one does with the answers one sees whether one can then begin to enquire into the way things *are*. And that which one is able to do with things when one begins to see some answers will be determined largely by one's ability to use Discrimination.

What is 'Discrimination', and where does it fit in?

The way things are has been determined largely by the decisions which one has made at other times, and in other places. The way things are is also affected by the decisions other people have made at other times insofar as those decisions have been related to the decisions we have made. The way things are is also affected by the desires we have and the desires of others when mixed with the desires we have. This is something like a cosmic collective bargaining process. It works as a flow or a wave.

It is not necessary to have a complete understanding of these matters in order to be able to see the way things are. It is enough, in the beginning, if one will just slightly shift one's approach to things. We might say that it is enough if one shifts one's attitude or one's posture towards things. It will probably be enough in the beginning if one changes – or at least becomes willing to change – the nature of one's beliefs.

For instance, when one begins to open, one has certain beliefs, a certain view of the way things are. This has largely been determined by that which one has been told and that which one has been taught. There are certain assumptions on which one will base one's actions. These are not necessarily assumptions that we make consciously. In fact, most of these assumptions are so basic as to be foundational and in that part of us which rarely makes an appearance in our external awareness.

So, what is one supposed to believe?

When one begins to open in awareness and to wonder how things are, it would be helpful if one might say to oneself that one will now believe that things probably are not the way that one believes them to be: that is, that one will now believe that things are probably other than as one views them or thinks things are. For the moment, this is a good place to start.

It is a safe place to start, for already there may be a dawning somewhere inside that there is a possibility that this is the case. It is safest to acknowledge this fact as soon as possible, for there may be a part hidden down deep inside that does not want to see this for fear of the consequences. But those very consequences themselves are compounded if one hides this fact or hides *from* this fact.

Before this began to happen, *the way things are* mixed with *the way one views things* mixed with *the way one would like for things to be*, and they were all nicely integrated: life went on, if not smoothly, at least, well, acceptably. Things were rather on automatic, and there was little concern about the way things are. Decisions were made in accord with the rules inherent in the way things are, and most events were attributed to either luck, chance, or some other inexplicable fortuitous circumstance.

The need for Discrimination begins to arise when this neat, clean, and tidy scenario begins to disintegrate, to come apart – that is, when one begins to suspect that things are not the way one views them. There is also a benignly smiling paradox which peeks around the corner of one's awareness inside and says that one cannot really change the way things are, but that one could begin to sort out ***the way things aren't.***

Discrimination could be said to be this sorting out of the way things are from the way things aren't. It is a tricky business in the beginning. Indeed, it is tricky at any time, and if one believes that there is no need for the sorting, that is, that there is no need for Discrimination, then one is not ready to sort it out. In such case, one will probably retreat into the safety of some re-patched, re-glued, and hastily reassembled, temporarily effective, but unsatisfactory, integrated set of beliefs.

What happens if I start to believe this?

If one can acknowledge near the beginning that the way things are is not quite the way one believes them to be, discrimination can begin to develop from within. It is not necessary to find something else to believe – or to believe in. It is not necessary to find something else to replace that which one formerly believed or believed in, but rather it is enough to open the matter up, to hold the slate clean, as it were, and to just wait for a while.

This is a bit tricky too, for the mind wishes to have things in a neat little package and to believe that it knows how things are; more importantly, it wants to know *that* things are.

When one opens to this possibility that things are *other* than as one believes them to be, then one has opened to the possibility that things *are not* as one believed them to be, and the mind may not take kindly to this.

So it is best to be as gentle as possible to start with. It is best to gently begin to sort out the way things are from the way things aren't. And this is where discrimination comes in. Discrimination makes the difference. It is the one thing that keeps one together when things begin to come apart, and it has a mode of operation all its own. It is available only to someone who is ready and willing to use it. It is the catalyst in the enquiry, and it is only for someone who wants to know *the way things are.*

Each of us has an apparatus that is capable of knowing the way things are, and each of us has the capacity to use discrimination to begin to see the way things are. When the possibility of employing discrimination arises, there are many other possibilities that will arise as well.

How does one deal with the changes?

There are some steps one can take to start dealing with changes.

> **The first step** is to welcome change. The first of these is probably the ability to welcome change rather than to resist it. Some go even further than resistance; some deny the existence of change. Discrimination enables one to open to the possibility that change does exist, must exist, and it enables us to redefine the status quo from something which *tries to stay the same* to something which *can stay the same by becoming different.*
>
> This wonderful faculty of discrimination enables us to start right here in the middle to sort things out, rather than trying to find the beginning and to understand how the whole thing works and how things got to be the way they are. Again, it is enough if one simply says that one now believes that things are other than the way one has believed things to be. One does not have to know the way things are – at least *not yet*. One will find that out by not trying to find the beginning but by starting here in the middle, right in the middle of the way things are – right now.
>
> So, accept things the way they are.
>
> **The second step** is to accept the way things are, even if one does not yet know the way things are. This means that one is able to accept the way things are without knowing how that is.
>
> What an exciting time this is! Here one has the opportunity to exercise one's first step in real discrimination. Here one has the opportunity to make a major change in approach, and it is different. For here, one can say, 'I accept the way things are even before I know what the choices are.' This is a major departure, for most often the way we work is to say, *'Show me the choices, and then I will tell you which one I want.'*
>
> To accept the way things are before one knows the way things are will probably exacerbate the disintegration of an unreal reality which is already underway, but by now it is already too late to turn back anyway. Once one

accepts this new possibility, then discrimination begins to become very prominent and very energetic in one's own new mode of thought.

What a relief! Now one can begin to see that the way things are, is the way things are and that it makes very little difference how one *views* the way things are. And in fact, the way that one views the way things are becomes, at least for a time, almost irrelevant. But that's OK, because by now, one begins to see that the way that one *views* the way things are is not the way things are at all, but only the way that one *believed them to be*.

Discrimination is the one key in the midst of all this disintegration that enables one to keep things together.

Where does faith come in, or go out?

There is another way to keep it together: faith. But if one is ready to begin to use discrimination, faith becomes ineffectual except insofar as it matures into trust. But that is another matter to be discussed later.

Faith will have a hard time coexisting for very long with the discrimination, which begins to grow and to emerge in one who is brave enough to acknowledge that things are not as one believed them to be without knowing the way things are. But once one begins to feel the freedom from the fetters of belief in things *that one has been told*, the freedom from the fetters of blind faith will soon emerge as well.

Once one begins to discriminate to any degree, blind faith begins to lose both its ability to help one in one's ignorance and its ability to *hold* one in one's ignorance.

When one lets go of faith, one can then move towards finding out the way things *are*. And to find the way things *are*, one must begin to refine discrimination.

16   *Beginning Discrimination*

Now that we know where discrimination starts, let us have a look at how it works and where it works. For one who is opening and who will soon be enquiring into the deeper nature of one's own being and purpose, discrimination offers a possible way for one to begin to work with things the way they are, even before one knows the details of the way things are.

What is 'Discrimination'?

Discrimination is a process. It is a continual and continuous process of sorting out what is real from what is unreal, what is important from what is unimportant, and what needs and deserves attention from what does not need or deserve one's attention and effort.

The true purpose of this process is really seen only when one begins to work with the higher reaches of the emotions and the mind and begins to perceive certain spiritual or inner truths. But it is important to begin the application of this process early on, before one begins to deal with such higher and loftier matters, for by then one will see that a good and solid foundation must be built in the lower parts of one's being and activities before attempting to work with the higher matters inside.

So, the place to begin is here and now, and it begins with a recognition that there are certain things that one knows within oneself, or suspects within oneself, and has within oneself that are unique to oneself. After one accepts that recognition, the process of discrimination begins to help one make decisions or to assess matters in a different way and with a different set of criteria.

For instance, the process of discrimination enables one to stop and to reassess the importance of pursuits in one's life that one had previously considered to be important or essential. It enables one to reassess certain 'truths' that one may have accepted and taken for granted. In applying this process, one will begin to have an appreciation of relative truths; that is, that there are aspects of truth that have various shades of truth in them, and these truths can vary from day to day or from moment-to-moment. When something that is true or important one moment becomes less true in some later moment, it is for some persons impossible to acknowledge this fact, for the possibility may not have occurred to them that something could be true and relevant one moment and so irrelevant the next moment as to have virtually lost its truth as that matter applies to their own awareness and state of consciousness.

Although at this time we are speaking of discrimination as a process, and, indeed that is what it is in the beginning, later on it will become more than a process. It will become more and more a part of one's being, so much so that it too becomes foundational, applicable at all levels of one's being, enabling one to eventually perceive the highest truth that is relative to one's own peculiar and unique state of consciousness, and the degree to which one is able to open one's awareness at this time in this body in this lifetime.

How does one start to apply Discrimination?

The practical application of discrimination begins here and now, as soon as one who is opening, or open, can acknowledge the fact that one is opening, or open, and as soon as one determines that one wants to *know*.

The first step in this practical application is to accept things as they are, to accept oneself as one is, now. This is both easy and difficult; it is easy to say and difficult to do. But it is difficult only in that it relieves, or deprives, one of certain beliefs that one has been nurturing and nursing and to which one may have become very attached.

These beliefs, as they are called here, are not limited to the beliefs as such, but rather they include certain goals that one may have set for oneself at some time earlier on in life. They can include certain illusions that one may harbour deep within as to the way that things are in one's life. They can include the nature of relationships that one may have developed over a period of time and to which one still clings, in spite of the fact that certain events or developments make it absolutely clear, when viewed with discrimination, that those relationships have long outgrown not only their usefulness but also even their form.

The form of such relationships, goals, beliefs and illusions remains fixed in a memory system that is a process that humankind has developed as a result of a faulty reasoning process, and the memory process itself has now become faulty. It has failed to develop with humankind's ability to think in a new way. It fixes images in a part of the mind and those images remain crystallised, safely deposited and hidden in the deeper recesses of one's mind until one retrieves them, dusts them off, and then attempts to apply them to a present event, decision or situation. By then, these old fossilised antiques and relics of some past thought are totally inapplicable, useless, and even unworthy of being considered important for the present moment.

What use is the old memory process in Discrimination?

This process of retrieving these old relics did have some merit at one time, in at least two ways, and to some extent it is still useful. In fact, it must still be used at least for a time as one traverses a transition process when one opens.

The first of these merits related to the time when the process developed more than in its application. In past centuries, life moved more slowly, change happened at a snail's pace, and, when it came to depositing something for future use, whether that deposition was of a utensil in a drawer of the cabinet or of a thought into a drawer in the mind, there was, as a result of the fact that change went slowly, the good possibility that the item so deposited would still be there when one went looking for it the next time it was needed. The second of these merits was that there was a good possibility that the item, be it thought or utensil, would still be useful.

The process still applies fairly well to physical items, as we will see; but the fact that change is now not only increasing in its pace, but also increasing at an increasing rate, renders the probability of usefulness of many items previously deposited less and less likely. We are now riding an exponential curve of change.

This is a phenomenon to which humankind has not yet awakened to any large degree, and it is the one phenomenon that must be acknowledged by humankind as a whole and by the individuals of the human community to enable humanity to go through the Change of Consciousness without losing its collective mind.

To start with, this new process must be applied by each of us as individuals. When we return to look for an item, especially a thought previously deposited, the initial application of discrimination should touch a little trigger inside that says, *'First, let's have a look and see if this thought, concept, goal, or whatever, is still viable. Is it still applicable now, where I am standing here today, as it was some time ago when I formulated it and deposited it safely away in my trove of perceptions?'*

This may appear to be a cumbersome process, and, in the beginning, it is cumbersome and time-consuming. But like all phenomena that are new, and that are new to the mind, it will become more easily applied and employed as it is practised.

Where did the concept of Discrimination come from?

The idea and the process of discrimination itself are not new. It has been known and practised as a part of ancient spiritual disciplines for centuries upon centuries. But it is new to the Western world, the Western mind and way of thought, and especially to the Western ego. And it will take some getting used to. It is not mandatory that one practises it, but it does offer a way for one to adapt to the increasing pace of change.

Our Path of Self-discovery

This applies to one who is opening and whose pace of change is increasing as a result of an expanding awareness. It also applies to one who is not necessarily opening in awareness but who is stranded by a twist of one's own inevitable consequences in a world and a society that are about to undergo one of the biggest changes in the last 2,000 years. One who is both living in this world and opening in awareness is well advised to begin the practice of this 'new' process of discrimination, or to find something that will accomplish the same thing in some other way.

Discrimination is, or can be considered to be, a basis of a new way of thought and a new way of living, for it enables one to live in and relate to the way things are rather than the way one thinks they are or wishes them to be. This is a fairly simple and seemingly innocuous statement, but when considered in its most subtle form with its subliminal consequences, one can see that there are vast implications for one who opens it for consideration.

How does Discrimination help us live in the present?

Many of us live either in the past or in the future. It is a rare person who lives in the present. It is not difficult to live in the present, but there is a condition that most are unwilling to accept. This condition says that if one lives in the present, then those items that belong to the past or the future must be left there. The past shapes what we consider to be the present mainly by attempting to foist on the present these memories or crystallised fossils of concepts that were formulated in another era and are now applied in their old form. There is nothing wrong with applying these antiques, but to become useful in the present they must be updated.

Likewise, for a hope or an anticipation of the future to be usefully employed in the present, it must be 'downdated', as it were, or 'backstepped', to coincide with the conditions of the moment into which one may be attempting to utilise it.

Discrimination enables one to do this, but discrimination cannot be applied to these items of future or past in the way that the items themselves were formulated. Those items, either memories of the past or hopes of the future, were formulated by drawing a conclusion from something that one may have seen in the mind, an experience that one may have had that was either pleasant or unpleasant, or an anticipated experience that one either hopes or fears will happen or will not happen. To be truly effective when applied in the present, each of these items must be examined, if only momentarily, to determine if it is still applicable and relevant, if it is still viable in this moment for this purpose to which it is about to be put.

This cannot be done by looking at the original moment when the item, be it memory, hope, or fear, was formulated; for the moment of its birth is gone.

The item must be seen as having the form and attributes of the moment in which it was formed rather than including the very attribute that is most essential of consideration now: that is, that of the *condition* of the present moment in which it is to be applied.

Discrimination offers the consideration of that condition, but it does so with a pure and simple litmus test that can quickly determine the viability of the matter at hand; devoid of the pitfalls of the faulty reasoning process that drew certain conclusions with regard to the item in another time; and free from the emotional distortion that occurs when someone of Western heritage has the opportunity to perceive something in its pure and presently relevant truth, but *refuses to accept that which he or she sees!*

This takes guts! It takes guts, determination, and a strong will to accept what one sees and to accept the message of the test applied, without distorting or colouring it with the various and sundry shades of influence that are vying for attention and crying to be heard. This is the beginning of being able to see and to accept that which is known within the Self.

What happens when one begins to use Discrimination?

The first thing that will happen when one really properly applies the process of discrimination will be a flash of a realisation that something, probably something that one has kept safely hidden away, is no longer necessary. There will be something that says, *'If that is true, this other thing is not true, and I believed it to be so true!'*

The ability to accept what one sees when one begins to apply discrimination will come first from at least a cursory understanding of 'the way things are' as described earlier. There must be a resolution of the 'stand-off' between the mind and the system (the way things are), for the mind refuses to accept until it knows what is available, and the system refuses to show what is available until the mind says it will accept it, virtually sight unseen!

Until one overcomes and transforms the arrogant attitude of the mind that claims a right to prior inspection, the truth of the way things are will remain hidden until the mind and the ego either agree to accept the possibility that things are other than as they believe them to be, or to shakily agree to acknowledge the imposition of a new and changed reality – and consciousness – which refuses to be ignored and hidden behind some ill-conceived misconception concocted in the past and energised by a deluded belief in some relative truth that may have at one time carried some validity, but which now has been rendered inoperative and obsolete by one's own evolutionary growth.

In short, then, discrimination is the process that sorts out the things that make up one's own unique and personal existence. And this applies to the individual person and to the whole of humankind, for each of these has certain matters that need sorting out. In the process, one discards items of the past that one carries and that are no longer useful, and one revises those items that one carries that relate to the future but which are no longer effectual or feasible.

It is essential for one to be able to begin to apply this process as one begins to open, for soon one will begin to enquire into 'the way things are', and 'the way things are' must and will take precedence over the way that one believes things to be.

If one develops discrimination, then one can minimise the conflict when the time comes to determine which is which – even at those moments when one has quickly become the other.

17   Keeping a Balance

Keeping one's balance on this Path of Self-discovery is very tricky.

If one can begin to grasp the concept of discrimination and begin to apply it to the little everyday decisions with which one is confronted, eventually the process will find its way into the other parts of one's personality that are crying for attention, if not for transformation.

How does one keep a balance?

The process of discrimination can lead to a balance in one's life, a balance that is difficult to maintain with the present system of thinking that most of us employ and with the emotional structure that most of us have as a result of our heritage and education from the culture into which we have been born. Even so-called modern psychological theories tell us that one of the secrets to a good life is being able to let go of obstructions and relax. Oh, that they could tell us how!

The theories that speak of such 'letting go' often miss the point of the matter, for there is most often the suggestion or the implication that once something is let go, there is something or there *must be* something to replace it. Real discrimination – Evolutionary Discrimination – does not deny this suggestion, but there is another and better way to replace that which is released.

At present, the replacement is provided by a process of the mind and the emotions that is terribly archaic, both in its operation and in the items that it has available to replace whatever is released. Too often, that which replaces what is released is merely a rearrangement of the same thing that has been released. Sometimes, something – a thought or an emotion – is suppressed, and then it seeps out under the door in another direction, causing just as much trauma as the first avenue of activity.

The mind often gets stuck in a rut. It goes around in circles searching for an answer that just, as yet, does not exist; or the mind attempts to devise an answer that is in consonance with what it knows or with the way it believes things to be. It claims to be looking for something 'new' or a 'new way', but in fact it leaves no room for anything really New. It is willing only to accept a rearrangement, and often the acceptability of this rearrangement is governed or determined by how much and what one will have to give up if this rearrangement is accepted.

What is the 'internal bargaining process'?

All of this gives rise to an extremely complex and intricate bargaining process that transpires in and among the various parts of the personality, the mind, the emotions and so on. Not the least of the matters considered in this bargaining process inside is the matter of how one will appear to others when one comes out of the bargaining session and a joint communication is issued to the outside world. This, however, is a matter for another discussion, for just now we are concerned with the internal negotiation that goes on.

Discrimination provides a way out of this circular trap. One who can begin to discriminate may see that when it is time to release something that is obsolete, firstly, there may be no need for it to be replaced; and secondly, if it is to be replaced that it will be replaced with something that is perhaps not yet in existence, or at least not yet in one's own personal existence.

The introduction of such a possibility enables one to open, even if only slightly, to the possibility that things are not as one has believed them to be. One can perhaps glimpse that the way things are extends beyond the limits of one's own personal perception and perhaps beyond one's own personal ability to perceive the way things are.

How does the ego get involved in this?

The acceptance of this existence of this limitation on one's personal perception is repugnant to the ego, which has grown far out of proportion as a result of the Western way of thought. The Western mind, mainly from the erroneous thinking process that it calls 'scientific', has deluded itself into believing that it can understand its own workings, and it arrogantly refuses to accept any suggestion that this is impossible. And it does this even in the face of the occurrence of something that it cannot understand or explain in terms of that which it has already 'discovered'. Generally, it will simply dismiss such an occurrence as a 'miracle' or an aberration and refuse to acknowledge it.

We are now witnessing the disintegration of this so-called 'scientific method of thinking'. It does not work! Individual persons and humankind as a community are coming face to face with the undeniable fact that there are certain things that are happening within each of us and within us as a communal body that either cannot be explained or are simply unacceptable.

What about miracles and 'acts of God'?

Some phenomena have long been dismissed as 'miracles', 'acts of God' or the 'result of faith'. They can actually be quite threatening, for the matters that are unacceptable are causing the breakdown of the social order and are actually threatening the ability of the individual human being on this planet to maintain a sane balance in his or her own life.

Primarily, this is due to the inability of the individual human mind to fit that which is happening, *that which is blatantly and undeniably happening*, into the way it believes things to be and the way it wishes things to be. This proposal can be applied both to the everyday life matters that we all face, and it can be applied on a larger, national or even global scale.

At this point in time, many still deny that there is any change needed, let alone that change itself is inevitable. Even when one does accept and acknowledge that change is inevitable, one may still deny that it is needed. And if one accepts that change is needed, one may still deny the possibility of any change that is at odds with the way one believes things to be or the way one wishes things to be.

When change itself begins to happen, it really takes very little notice of such arrogant attitudes, especially when the evolutionary requirements of one's own growth demand that one move into a new and different space.

Socially, we wait until the change is declared by some outside authority and then imposed by that authority, and any acknowledgement or acceptance of the change is done grudgingly or at least with reservation.

Does one have to 'make' a change?

Discrimination allows one to move with change and to maintain a balance, but the balance to be maintained has a 'mind' of its own. Discrimination opens this airtight conundrum and can enable one to dismiss the erroneous notion that one can maintain one's balance by 'making' a change.

In fact, there is no change to be 'made' by someone who becomes unbalanced.

It is the balance itself that moves and engenders change, and it moves and changes according to the way things are. It moves and changes unhindered and unaffected by the way one believes things are or the way one wishes things to be.

What happens when one 'loses the balance'?

One may egotistically declare that one has 'lost one's balance'. In fact, it is the balance that has lost you! It is the balance that has moved, and unless the person who wishes to keep a balance scurries along and moves with the point of balance, then the 'unbalance' gets bigger and bigger.

What is happening could be described as *Trap-Gap-Snap-Zap*.

When one is attracted by something desirable in the present moment, and that to which one is attracted crystallises in the mind and the concept is stored away, one has succumbed once again to the trap of the mind that remains in a passing moment and drifts into the past. The mind loses its focus in the present and begins to think about the past or the future, depending on the nature of the concept, thought or experience that has transpired.

Trap!

The way things are is always in the present. On the spectrum of time and space, anything other than the present is either the way things were or the way they will be. The way they were can and does influence the way we see things and believe them to be; at least, in the present mode of thinking this is what it does. Soon, there will be another way of 'thinking' in which one can accept or deny that influence on the way one thinks and believes things to be. It is discrimination that enables one to do this.

Gap!

But let's stay here with the discussion of the moment for the moment. If the attention has been trapped in the passing moment and slips out of the present there is a gap created between the present and where one is focused – that is, in the moment that has already passed. So long as one continues to hold that memory, or the crystallised concept of the way one believes things to be that is no longer in the present, the gap becomes wider and wider. It grows and stretches that little thread which connects the way things are with the way one believes them to be.

Snap!

Then we have a snap of one kind or another. If the thread between the way things are and the way we believe them to be snaps in two, and one leaves the body because of the shock, that which one has experienced is called death. If the thread snaps and one does not leave the body, that which one experiences is called insanity.

But the other kind of the snap that occurs is more common. It is the snap when the attention is snapped back from the concept of the moment that has passed to the moment of the present, and one is literally forced to acknowledge once again the way things are, and, at least for a moment, one is once again in the present. As a result, the way things are and the way one believes things to be are at lease very close if not the same. And then, time once again begins its courtship of the mind and emotions with fantasy and desire, until one once again succumbs to the guile of the lovely and wonderful energies of creation and the seduction is again complete when the gap begins to widen.

This is something that we all experience every day. It is common for one to experience something that one refuses to acknowledge as having happened. Contemporary psychology has recognised, if not explained, this phenomenon. It is said in psychology that we blot out an experience or suppress its memory out of the trove of the external or available awareness.

Zap!

Many persons in relationships with other people in their family, or in relationships with their work, or in relationship with habit patterns in their lives, will retain a crystallised concept of this relationship when the true nature and the form of the relationship alters with time.

In the mind, however, the relationship clings to a concept of a form of another time. It not only refuses to acknowledge that the nature of the relationship does change or has changed, but the possibility of the existence of change does not even enter the realm of thought. Then some event transpires that renders it absolutely impossible for one to retain the faulty concept of the change in the relationship.

For instance, someone dies or departs from the physical presence of the person living in the illusion, or the nature of one's employment changes or terminates, or some physical disability or condition renders the continuation of a certain habit pattern impossible.

This suddenly brings the attention back into closer focus with the way things are, and one has the zap: one gets 'zapped' into the present. Often the zap into the present is traumatic; but, again, it is recognised even by the incomplete and inadequate theories of present psychology that if one acknowledges how things are and undergoes the trauma of the adjustment, even though it be emotionally devastating, once the emotions have been played out and the mind accepts the new concept, one can resume a 'normal' life.

Where does 'attitude' fit into this?

It is not only conceivable but it is entirely possible for one to alter this pattern merely by assuming a different attitude towards that what happens in one's life.

This change of attitude may occur as a cause; that is, it may be something that one deliberately and intentionally decides to do. Alternatively, it may occur as an effect; that is, as the culmination of events or matters moves one into a position where the change of attitude simply appears and dawns within one. In either case, it is a natural consequence of the opening of awareness that is taking place and it is the natural beginning of the process of discrimination.

With the change of attitude, there also occurs a shift of position, as it were, inside. There is in this change of attitude the beginning of the shift of identification from one part of one's integral being to another. It occurs as the focus of one's identity moves from that with which it *has been* identified to that with which it *will* identify as a result of the opening of awareness that is now occurring.

In essence, it is a shift across the gap that appears and widens when the balance moves on and leaves one standing behind, attached to a moment that was born in the present but which has flowed on into the past, carrying one's attention with it. It is an awakening to that which some have called another dimension within one's self, but, in fact, it is the awakening to the Self, itself.

18   *Making the Shift*

As one commences to use discrimination and prepares to enter the Path of Self-discovery, one is standing at the doorway to a new dimension, and the shift in personal consciousness that one faces can alter one's evolutionary position.

How does one make the 'shift'?

When the time comes for one to make the shift across the gap from one side of the delicate inner balance to the other side, the experience may occur in any of a number of different ways. One of the things that one will experience as a characteristic of this shift is a feeling of coolness, a feeling of objectivity, a feeling of detachment.

This feeling is basically foreign to the nature of the personality that we of the Western world have developed over the past many centuries; it is not part of our inherent way of life. We feel a very warm, endearing closeness to most of the things in life with which we identify, especially life itself as we understand it. Those objects that make up our 'life', including friends and loved ones, possessions, relationships to other persons, relationship to 'myself', bear to us a position of importance.

Sometimes, when we are immersed in an experience of life which has come upon us as a result of the appearance of an inevitable consequence, we may be in the midst of deep grief or extreme elation. At the extreme peak of emotional expression, this seemingly strange feeling of detachment or objectivity may suddenly and fleetingly appear to disengage us from the emotionalism of the experience. It may seem almost as if one is watching oneself from inside as one cries or laughs or in some other way emotes.

Sometimes when this happens, we may feel uncomfortable, for it may feel that we have not only been deprived of the experience of deep emotion that was transpiring, but there may also be a feeling of a separation from the experience, a 'dis-integration', as it were.

'Dis-integration' is essentially what has happened, and there has been a separation from the experience, and one may have momentarily, in the separation, viewed the experience with detachment, without involvement. For a moment, even if only for an instant, one has viewed the experience as the experience *'is'*. One has viewed the emotionalism of the experience with objectivity. Sometimes this is not very comfortable, for the experience has at least momentarily separated us from a part of that which we have considered to be ourselves: that is, a deeply entrenched emotional pattern or circuit.

At some time, one opening will experience that which was described above: that is, a twinkling of a separation from the experience. One will have a momentarily objective view of the experience, a feeling or a glimpse that that what one is or has been seeing is not what one thought it was.

How does one use this experience to make the shift?

It is at this time when one can make this shift across that gap between a consciousness that was melded and amalgamated with the experience and a consciousness that one feels within oneself is a separate and distinct identifiable 'touchstone' with which or through which one's perspective can view that which is happening.

This phenomenon can be approached intellectually as well, but, in essence, this is merely another approach to the same experience in a little less abrupt and perhaps a little slower method. One may, over a period of time, have an intellectual inkling that something is other than as one has viewed it, and there are numerous writers who have waxed forth in large quantity and varying quality on this subject. There are even certain spiritual teachings and disciplines that can guide one through the maze of thought processes to arrive at an intellectual conclusion (an anachronism that is still considered essential to the contemporary conception of advanced thought) that one is other than that which one has believed one to be and that things are other than as one has believed them to be.

Regardless of how one has reached this point of experience, regardless of which avenue one took to arrive at this point, the experience is basically the same: a momentary separation from that in which one was immersed in the way one believed things to be, and a momentary identification with that which is an inseparable part of the way things are.

This is a crucial and momentous experience. It is the moment when one first has the opportunity of glimpsing something that will take one out of the realm of illusion and enable and allow one to see and experience at least a little bit of the way things are.

How much 'free will' does one have in this matter?

It won't last long the first time. Our nature is kind enough to allow us to believe that we have a choice whether or not to pursue this new-found experience, and, for a while, we do have this choice. Up until this point, there has been little in the individual repertoire of reaction that could be considered to be 'free will'. Most of the experiences that we have confronted and faced or avoided were brought to the fore by the inevitable consequences that each of us creates for ourselves. These are stored in our trove of forthcoming events.

For a great deal of the journey of the soul in this created phenomenal realm, we will react to these consequences. Then, as the soul evolves and we have an increase in wisdom and knowledge of the way things are, we can begin to take some active hand in shaping the nature of our being. In the end, we actually become creative, not only in the further shaping of our own nature but also in the evolutionary shaping of our environment.

Before this can happen, there is a lot of sorting out to do. If the dawning of the separation of awareness from the event was slow and gentle, then one will probably approach the task at hand with an open mind, depending on how closely and firmly attached one is to one's concept of the way one believes things to be. If the confrontation with this separation from an event was sudden, as in the midst of an experience of grief or heightened ecstasy or elation, one may be so charged with enthusiasm that one pursues this new-found reality with vigour and energy.

Or, if one is closely attached to the objects of the senses, one may be very frightened by the experience and retreat into the recesses of phenomenal creation and avoid any further contact with the experience or the opportunity at hand. There will be some temporary comfort in this latter approach, but still there will always be a next time after the first time. And there is a first time for everyone; it is inevitable.

What happens when one glimpses the way things 'aren't'?

Here we are assuming that one who is opening has had, in one form or another, a glimpse of the way things are, or at least a glimpse of the way things aren't, or a glimpse that things are other than as one has believed them to be. For the moment, we are unconcerned with the matter of how one wishes things to be.

If one has had this glimpse and wishes to pursue the matter, either with vigour or with caution, one can make this shift or move slowly – or rapidly – over to a position where one can commence this sorting out process. This process begins to sort out the way things are from the way things aren't or the way one believes them to be. This can take a long time, but there can be moments of intuitive insight that result from a combination of detachment, inevitable consequence, and Evolutionary Grace, a matter on which more discussion will appear later.

What does one need to see in the 'glimpse'?

Discrimination is the process of sorting out that which is seen and experienced in these moments of insight so that one can retain that which is important and essential and which can be gleaned from the moment of insight, and reject what is of no further use.

There are two important things to see at this point:

- **Firstly**, that which applies to one person in this process may not and probably will not apply to another person – even another who is following the same process; and
- **Secondly**, that the criteria that one has in one's storehouse to sort things out in the old way are almost certain to be inoperable and useless.

Both of these matters can cause deep and endless concern, if not disruption, to the one who is opening and beginning to discriminate the real from the unreal, so it is important to be aware of these two points.

In the opening of awareness that occurs in the lower levels of creation, even in the lower levels of one's own consciousness, the physical and emotional experiences that we have, there can be certain generalisations made. There can be some sweeping statements made that apply to all, for the further out towards the periphery one moves, that is, the further out towards the periphery of physical creation and experience one goes, the more applicable and enduring will be the statement of relative fact. This is a fact inherent in the evolute or outwardly occurring creative process.

What is a 'cosmic life-print'?

But when one turns one's direction and begins to seek the Source, there is, literally, a turnaround, and an evolutionary process begins that is as unique to an individual as are one's fingerprints. It could be said that there is a 'cosmic life-print' that is unique to the individual. If one identifies with the physical body and the physical realm that it occupies, then there are certain generalisations that can be made and which apply. And it is likewise with the emotional body and the emotional experiences.

However, one can observe that the statements that can be made about emotional experience begin to lose their universal application as generalisations, and we begin to see even more that that which applies to one may not apply to another. The further inward one goes, the truer this becomes. When we approach the upper mental realms of one's being and then the matters of spiritual opening and evolution of the individual soul, there is a uniqueness that begins to emerge and for which there can be very few generalisations made.

How is this experience unique to each of us?

It will be helpful if one acknowledges at the outset that that which one is experiencing, or has experienced in the opening and at the beginning of the discriminating or sorting out process, and that which one is to experience in the opening, is *unique*. In fact, it is the heart of the Evolutionary Discriminative process that enables one to sort out not only how certain truths operate, but also which of these truths operate for oneself.

This other matter of how these truths operate involves the second matter that is bound to cause some concern at various points along the way: that the criteria by which one in the past has measured and has assessed what one is experiencing do not apply. In fact, criteria that were, like certain relative truths, operable and viable only moments before may quickly fade into obsolescence and deteriorate before one's eyes.

Now all of this may sound or appear very daunting, and it is. But after a certain point, it is the only game in town; it is the only thing that will become important, and it is the one thing that will occupy all of one's thought and all of one's time and all of one's effort.

And, once one acknowledges that this *is* what is happening, it is the most exciting thing ever to happen to a person: a soul whose consciousness has projected into the matter of physical bodies, has been immersed therein, and who now has the very real opportunity of sorting out the delusion with which one has heretofore been melded and amalgamated.

One can now make that shift *from* being continually and continuously rocked to and fro by merciless consequence, and *from* being a victim of the way one believed things to be, *to* that part of one's being which can see the experience with objectivity and begin to identify with at least a part of the way things are.

19 A Consequence of Seeing

> When one has a glimpse of the way things are, or at least a glimpse of the way things aren't, there will be consequences – neither good nor bad consequences; just consequences.

What happens when one begins to 'see'?

This is the start of a journey – a journey that has no ending, that has no goal, that has, as its sole purpose, the travelling on the journey itself. It is the most exciting voyage one will ever make, and it culminates in the knowledge of and the being of that for which the soul has been searching since it first began its involution into matter and its wanderings through creation.

The journey on which one now embarks is literally a quest to find out how things are – to be able to see the way things are; to be able to feel the way things are; to be able to *be*. It is a quest for True Knowledge, not for mere learning. It is a labour that one undertakes for the love of the Self.

It begins with that first glimpse, that first experience that lasts perhaps only for an instant. What one sees in that instant completely changes the way one is, the way one sees, what one knows, and how one goes about things.

There are many ways to go about moving into that which one has seen, glimpsed, experienced or felt, and each new era brings a way that is well suited to those who are alive and embarking on this journey at this time. One who is alive and experiencing that glimpse now is one who is more experienced in the ways of physical evolution than some who have gone before and who found other ways in which to gain their knowledge.

How does this differ with the way things were in the past?

There is presently, in this fresh culture, not only a wish to know the way things are, but also the ability to see the way things are and to move into harmony with that which one sees: that is, to assimilate, to practise, to incorporate that which one sees and that which one is coming to know. This ability to personally know and see the way things are without the need to accept something that is taught and learned on faith is a major departure from the way things have been in the past. But first-hand knowledge carries with it certain responsibilities as well as abilities.

If one has a glimpse and wishes to know more, one must be willing to take some important steps, and these steps are mainly taken on one's own – *one must go through this alone.* There are certain matters that need to be decided, and certain determinations that need to be made.

What criteria can one use to determine what to do?

If one chooses to enquire further into what one has seen, it is essential to be willing to make these decisions and determinations for oneself, for one of the characteristics of the way that is opening up for many who are having the first glimpse is that there are precious few, if any, external criteria that one may have learned which will help one in the decisions and determinations one must make.

These matters are to be decided in a new and different way, and it is a way that is not to be learned from any existing structures of education, teaching or learning.

This new way is one that is ever new, ever changing and ever dynamic. It constantly changes its direction as well as its colour, its shape and its expression. It moves from the inside out, and it emanates from that place within one that is part of the way things are. It is ever present, ever energised, always reliable and always right.

Now, the trick is to be able to see it, to know what it says, to do what it says, and to adjust to the changes; this is no small challenge.

> *It is the ultimate game, the ultimate test, the ultimate victory over an illusory foe whose purpose in being created was solely to provide a worthy, loyal and able adversary against which one could wage a battle whose outcome was already decided before it began, and in whose result all, including the foe, will rejoice.*

What are the guidelines one can use to see?

Throughout the journey, there are certain things that it will do well to keep in mind, so to speak; certain guidelines that may be helpful. One of these is that it is the journey itself that is important rather than what one may conceive to be the destination.

It is the process of discovery that is essential rather than what is discovered. It is the 'ever-newing' that is the essence and manifestation of the way things are, rather than that which is produced by the manifestation. Even if one believes that one knows the nature and shape of the destination, it will change before one arrives. Even if one believes that one knows what is to be discovered, that too will change when it is discovered. And even that which is produced and is new and exciting immediately becomes old as soon as it is manifested.

It is thus the process that is important, and it is the process that will enable one to sort out the way things are from the way things aren't. When one sees for the first time that point of balance, when one first peers through the mist across that gulf from one side to the other, there is inevitably some concept formed of what one believes one has seen. There is something that forms in the mind, something that begins to relate all of the other concepts that are held in the mind to all of the variants and gradations of emotional responses that are held in one's reactive repertoire and to the various little physical habits and practices that one has developed and honed over many years and lifetimes as a result of the accumulation of experiences and conclusions drawn from experiences.

How does one control the mind in this experience?

When the mind observes an experience that occurs in the world in which we live, certain impressions are recorded, certain conclusions drawn, certain assumptions made as a result of those conclusions, and certain behaviour patterns are then formed as a result of all of these processes. It is common for one, after an experience, to make the determinative statement that one will *know how to handle* such-and-such a situation the next time it arises. That works fairly well for some of the more physical experiences of life, in that physical reactions can be fairly well observed and generally predicted given certain sets of circumstances.

This procedure will however prove unreliable if one attempts to apply it to that which one has glimpsed within the Self, and it will not work when one attempts to place something into practice from that which one has seen or felt within the Self.

There is a different process available, and essential, to placing these new matters into operation.

- **Firstly**, they are not lessons to be learned and applied; they are items of knowledge that are sensed, assimilated, and that become part of the very make-up of one's nature.
- **Secondly**, each item seen, sensed or felt, produces an absolutely distinct and unique result in each one of us.

Again, it is helpful to recognise that matters on the periphery of existence are fairly predictable and can reliably be set into motion, but these matters of which we speak here, these matters that come from the inside out, these matters that are ever-new are not only unique in themselves, but they are also unique in their application to each individual person. They operate, if you will, not at the periphery of one's body, but from the core of one's being.

When the mind perceives the occurrence of such matters within its circuits, it draws certain conclusions about what it has seen. The attention that one has previously placed in the glimpse of something new is thus diverted back into the mind to assess and analyse what has been recorded. The attention then is no longer on that which is part of the way things are, but now the attention is back in the mind. It is back where one thinks about the way one believes things to be. It has recorded an impression of what it has seen, or what it believes it has seen, and that impression is then, to some extent, crystallised in the mind. It becomes an image in the mind – a paradigm. It becomes – at best – a reflection of that which the mind believes it has seen in the glimpse.

This is normal. This is the way the mind works now. This is the way the mind records the impressions that it gains from the senses that in turn have gained their impressions from the world around one: that is, the world that houses all of the little – and the big – impressions, reflections, images and creations that have long ago crystallised and that now exist for their own purpose of being enjoyed, to one degree or another.

How will this change?

This is all about to change as a result of the *glimpse*.

This new experience of seeing, feeling or suspecting within that things are other than as one has believed them to be will, at first, be only fleeting; it is there only for an instant. To draw the curtain aside too far in the beginning causes, or enables, one to see too much.

In antiquated cultures or disciplines, where one respected the person who could teach and in whom one who is opening could repose an unquestioning trust, the strings of the curtain or the veil remained in the hands of teacher, for they knew just how far they should open new matters to be seen. Such a one could judge just how much another could handle.

Part of the new way is that one who is opening to enquire into the way things are generally demands to judge for oneself what one will see and how much one can handle.

This is fair enough, but there must still be some inbuilt safety precautions, and there are. These 'safety switches', such as they are, are part of the new process itself. They in themselves are something that one will see or feel in the glimpse; they are something that one must sense within and that one must apply for oneself, for that is what one has demanded to have the right to do. And that is the way things are now.

How fast can one 'progress'?

So, when one first glimpses, and when one first sees, that which one sees is limited to that which one can handle, and so it is throughout. A little bit taken from time to time can be digested and assimilated into the fabric of one's manifested nature – that is, into one's personality, one's concept of the way things are, and eventually, even into the way one would like for things to be.

It is the reflection of the glimpse that gives rise to the delusion. The reflection of that which one sees in the glimpse descends into the mind and is then assessed and analysed in the only way the mind presently knows – that is, by comparison, analogy, assumption, conclusion and reaction.

The problem arises when what one has seen within, what one has sensed within, does not fit into or coalesce with what the mind knows, or believes, as a result of being confronted with something New. Truly New.

Collectively, the cultures of history record such events and the reflection of their occurrence. If such occurrence can find a niche in the learned and recorded knowledge of human history, the occurrence is called fact; if not, it is called a 'miracle', or act of God. In truth, it is neither fact, miracle, nor Act of God: it is merely New.

It is the assimilation of that which is New which is of major concern here, and it is the process of the recognition of that which is New that comes first. This process forsakes the old processes of assessment and adjustment, for these two processes have a different source, a different purpose, and each has a different way of application. Most of the characteristics of each that differentiate one from the other will become clear to one who is beginning to see, and this will occur as one recognises the difference and begins to at least recognise that the old way does not apply to the New.

Does one need to know how this works in order to use it?

It is not important or necessary to know how the new way works, except to recognise the little hints that have been given here and to recognise that there are differences. It is not necessary to know how things are before one can begin to work with things the way they are. To believe that one must understand how things are first is the old way. It begs for a reflection which it insists must fit into a slot that it has already designed. The New is not concerned with the size or shape of the slot, and it is not disturbed, in fact, if there is no slot available. It is content to wait.

It is the mind that then becomes impatient, for its concept of orderliness and its delusion of self-understanding have been disturbed by the introduction of something which it could not and did not conceive of existing and which it now is forced to admit does not cohere with the finite intricacies that it has designed to explain to itself its own workings.

Once one has seen and sensed within, even if for a moment, or even if that seeing and sensing are only a glimpse, the consequences begin to flow. One of those consequences is that one will wish to see and sense even more. It is now, at this time, that one will probably be opening the serious enquiry into the way things are; but there are adjustments that must be made in the personality so that one may accept and assimilate that which one sees within.

The major consequence, then, of seeing or sensing at least a little bit of the way things are is that one knows that this is what one wants. One also knows that there is such wisdom and clarity and truth in what one sees and senses within that one in fact would like for things to be the way one has seen them within. One would like to believe that things are that way, and one will know that one would like to bring the way one has believed things to be into harmony with the way one has seen them within.

This feeling will be with one so long as one continues to tap into that place where one has seen the way things are. It is the gradual assimilation of and placing into practice of what one has seen that enables one to wish for more and to accept more.

It is the assimilation process, the deciding what to accept and what not to accept, what to use and what not to use, that is now important. There are many adjustments to make.

And one starts here.

20 Aspiration and Inspiration

> **When one begins to see, things begin to change. This does not mean that the way things are begins to change. It means that one begins to see the changes in the way things are; that is, that the way things are is change.**

How does one begin to see inside?

If one begins to feel the cumulative effects of what has been described in the previous chapters, one may begin to see also that there is a positioning of the awareness inside that can help one to keep one's balance, to go about one's daily work, and to keep one eye open to see what comes from that place where the glimpse took place. This is a bit tricky in the beginning, for it involves the bifurcating or dividing of the awareness, and most of us are not accustomed to doing this – intentionally.

An example of this little activity could be described in the physical world as looking at one object and being aware of another out of the corner of the eye, or looking at one thing and thinking about another out of the corner of the mind's eye. This is not difficult to do; it is simply an exercise to which we are not accustomed and which, until it is experienced, generally would not occur to one who had not experienced it – consciously.

When one can begin to do this, all kinds of nice things can begin to happen. One of these is that one can begin to have access to that place where the glimpse was first experienced, for, in the beginning at least, the ability to see the way things are cannot be experienced by looking to see how things are, and that spot where one had a glimpse cannot be seen by looking directly at it.

The experience is something akin to looking at something in the night-time. It is easier to see an object in the dark if the vision is placed slightly to one side of the object rather than focusing the vision and concentration directly on the object.

It is in that place where the glimpse takes place that one can see the way things are, and this first glimpse may last only for a split second or two. Anyone who attempts to regain that experience will most likely be seduced by the reflection that, once manifested in the circuits of the mind, takes its place on the plane of time and space and begins to move to the back of the temporal spectrum floating into the past.

Anyone who focuses on this reflection that, in its original form, was a glimpse of the way things are, will also drift into the past and out of the moment that is midpoint in the temporal spectrum and from which, when one is focused therein, one can disengage the attention from the temporal spectrum and rise above the plane of the way things will be and enter into the flow of the way things are. But this is a bit advanced for one who is just beginning to glimpse.

Where does one find the motivation for all of this?

To be able to do this at all requires some movement in one's motivation and some alteration to one's attitude, and the opening of the 'mind' (for the lack, presently, of a better term) to considering the possibility that there may just be a difference between the way things are, the way one believes things to be, and the way one wishes things to be.

The movement in motivation is extremely important, but as with so many other concepts and things that one will encounter in this journey, it is important to remember that it is virtually impossible to define the movement to be made ahead of time; that is, *it is enough at this point if one will merely accept that there is a movement to be made.*

This acceptance, as with other matters which one will encounter along the way, can be made voluntarily and easily early in the piece, or it can be made at a later time under some duress, and, if made very late, will be made in desperation.

How does conventional motivation differ from the motivation needed here?

Normally, motivation in the conventional sense comes from a desire for a gain of some kind; that is, monetary, intellectual, or for some tactical or strategic advantage in the game of life. To follow through with this motivation, to pursue it, requires energy – or, more properly, the concentration of energies.

Each of us has access to a certain amount of the energies that can be so concentrated as to manifest an accomplishment towards which we are motivated. In all but very few cases, the motivation is to accomplish a rearrangement of things so as to bring them into some configuration that is consonant with the way we believe things to be or the way we wish for them to be.

What is the difference between aspiration and inspiration?

The accomplishments to be attained and towards which we are motivated are most often the definition of aspirations that we hold deep inside. These aspirations appear from time to time and are often called 'ideas', but in fact most of them are inevitable consequences that come to the surface and were themselves the result of some desire or some reaction. When we see or feel something towards which we aspire, the motivation follows, and, depending on the strength of the aspiration, we may feel great motivation to accomplish the goal; that is, we may feel *inspired* to work tirelessly and endlessly towards the end that we see as 'desirable'.

Most of our aspirations are stimulated by the perception of things in the physical world as we believe them to be or wish them to be; that is, most of our intended accomplishments are defined by desire. Often, the inspiration follows the appearance of aspiration.

When a true artist moves to work in his or her medium of expression, the inspiration can come first and then the aspiration follows; that is, the vision of that which one wants to do comes first, and then the motivation to do it can be summoned to provide the energy and resources to move to action. The motivation which then produces the action can thus come from a desire to express that which was seen in the moment of inspiration.

There is a little bit of the artist in each one of us – a small quiet place that wishes to create, to bring forth, and to express. But so often there is little inspiration from which to work, or it is so buried as to be almost non-existent. The artist, if truly working from that space, works to create rather than to complete. Artists work from inspiration, and from that inspiration comes the aspiration. Many an artist has lost the inspiration to create by reversing the priority and placing the aspiration first.

How does one use this in the 'real world'?

For someone who is accustomed to living in a competitive world and working towards goals for the purposes of accomplishment and accumulation, it is difficult to work without the definition of something towards which one aspires. Aspirations and desires are the things of which life is created; but the truly beautiful, creative and worthwhile materialisations of life come forth from inspiration first and *then* the aspiration to see that the inspiration is made material. The product of the true artist who has worked from inspiration to aspiration and then to creation is unique: it cannot be duplicated. Any attempt to duplicate moves from a position that places aspiration ahead of inspiration.

It is hence difficult to conceive of a new state of inner consciousness that could continuously move from aspiration, and, in the present state of human consciousness, this is largely the case; it is virtually impossible. But for one who has had the glimpse of the way things are, a new state of inner consciousness can become a possibility and then a reality.

In the moment when one glimpses the way things are, and even in the contemplation of the memory or reflection of the way things were when one saw things the way they are, or at least the way things were when one saw the way they are, there is something in one that says, 'You can know more about this if you wish.'

If one, in response says, 'Yes, I want more,' one sets into motion the Basic Change – that is, a major shift – and enters a period of transition in which one will effectively reverse the priority of one's motivation and begin to move towards that time when one will work from *inspiration* first and then from an aspiration to fulfil or manifest that inspiration.

This will take some time.

Everything in the material or phenomenal world takes time.

It is best not to be in a hurry.

It is best to slow down and to have a look at just what one has said that one wants.

What is the 'aspiration-inspiration' hierarchy?

There are other things that have been reversed besides the order of the aspiration-inspiration hierarchy of values. When one has had the glimpse of the way things are and expresses the desire to know more of the way things are, one at least implicitly expresses also the desire to further *manifest* the way things are.

The ease or difficulty with which this takes place is directly proportional to the divergence or differentiation between the way things are and the way one believes things to be times the way one wishes things to be.

How does one harmonise the various realities?

In other words, the process that one sets into motion at this point is the process of bringing the way one believes things to be into complete harmony with the way things are – *and not the other way around*. Since this is the case, the process that moves one's beliefs towards the way things are also necessarily reverses the procedure by which one wishes, because now, instead of wishing to bring the way things are towards the way one believes them to be, one implicitly has expressed the wish to bring the way one believes things to be into harmony with the way things are.

> **That which happens in this process is called *discrimination*, and the process itself is called the *enquiry*.**

If one begins to move from inspiration, the inspiration that is seen in the momentary glimpse of the way things are will never present itself in exactly the same way twice; that is, *it is unique every time it is seen or felt*.

How long is a glimpse valid?

If one whose mind is still used in the conventional way does not act on that which is seen in any momentary glimpse, that glimpse and that which is seen in the moment crystallises into reflection and then moves onto the conveyor belt of time and space and can then exist only as a reflected memory. It has a useful timespan in which action can be taken, but if action is not taken, that which was seen moves too far out of present usefulness and becomes obsolescent and then obsolete. The moment is then lost for that concept. If the inspiration comes again, even for the something that appears to be the same concept, there will be just an ever so slight difference, perhaps almost imperceptible, between the concept as first presented in the inspiration and the concept that seems to have reappeared.

It takes a great deal of discrimination just simply to know whether there is now a new concept appearing from inspiration or whether it is merely the recollection of a reflection of an inspiration that has previously come forth and crystallised. It is hard to tell the difference, for the mind is very clever and it can duplicate almost anything.

Almost.

But it cannot duplicate the Ring of Genuineness. It cannot duplicate the Light of the Source from which inspiration comes.

But it can reflect it. There are ways to test it and to tell. One way to test it is to look and to see the nature of the motivation; that is,

if the prime motivation is aspiration, one has probably been seduced by the reflection; if there is also ambition, one has not only been seduced by the reflection, one has also been victimised by its energies.

How does one differentiate between the 'real' and the 'unreal'?

There are two things that cannot be imparted from one to another:

- **Firstly**, the ability to distinguish between the genuine and the reflection; and

- **Secondly**, the discipline to place into action that which is seen in the genuine inspiration.

Only one who wishes to *know* and who has expressed the wish to know can begin to develop this within oneself. In the ultimate test, there can be no comparison of experiences from one person to another, for each experience of discrimination from one person to another is unique to each person. And, in the optimum moment, there can be no discipline drawn from another's trove to manifest that which is uniquely one's own.

If one has glimpsed the way things are and wishes to move with what one has seen, it is essential that one have one's priorities in proper order and acknowledge that one wishes to move from inspiration first and aspiration second. To approach what one is moving into with these out of order invites chaos on top of confusion.

There is only one way to practise discrimination and that is to practise discrimination. In the development of this unique practice, there are many tests and trials that one encounters, and one will make many mistakes.

There will be countless times when one is seduced by the aspiration and forsakes the inspiration. There will be innumerable occasions when one mistakes the reflection for the Genuine Article.

But not to worry.

Is it not better to at least see the Genuine Article once, even for only the first time, and perhaps for the only time in a long time, than to continue, as one has been for countless lifetimes, to be seduced by the mere reflection of that which humanity has memorised and retained from past creation?

21 From the Inside Out

> Genuine Inspiration comes from the inside out. It is not found by peering outward. Nor, for that matter, is it found by looking inward, at least with the present condition and state our minds are in.

What adjustments does one have to make to move from the inside out?

There is a way to see it, to feel it, and to express it as it comes, but there are adjustments to be made so that it can be seen. These adjustments have much to do with motivation, as we have seen. They also, as we will see, have to do with a technique: the skill of 'going within'. But before this technique can be studied, there must be a willingness to adjust the attitude.

The concept of *attitude* is a wonderful thing. It says so much, and, if it is grasped and put into action, it can change much of what happens to us by changing our approach to that which happens. The *attitude* of which we speak here is different from the common definition of the term.

Here, it is more akin to the concept of attitude when that term is used in aeronautics, as in the angle of approach that an aeroplane has to the wind into which it is flying. When the 'attitude' in this sense is correctly defined, the aeroplane can obtain a maximum of lift and benefit from the wind it meets, and at the same time it can minimise the resistance. With the right attitude, it can flow with the changes of current and still maintain a steady course in spite of the ups and downs that occur as it moves from one air pocket, flow or crosswind to the next.

What is the 'optimum' attitude one must adopt?

There is an optimum attitude to be adopted that enables one to adjust to the way things are, to accept that the way things are may not be exactly as one has believed them to be, and to harmonise the way things are with the way one wishes them to be. As with the change of motivation, this change of attitude cannot be readily defined ahead of time, but it can be set into motion voluntarily. This adjustment also is one of 'ever-newness' – that is, it is ever redefining itself – and it needs the energy of its own presence to be able to continuously redefine and express itself.

Although it is somewhat difficult in the beginning to know what the new attitude is, it is not difficult to see what it is not. We might say that the old attitude came from aspiration and the new one comes from inspiration. Aspiration, in turn, comes largely from desire, and desires are sparked or stimulated from without, from the world around us that one observes and lives in. Inspiration, on the other hand, comes from something other than desire as we know it now.

Inspiration comes from the inside out. If there is a desire involved at all, it is a desire that comes from once experiencing this genuine inspiration, and wishing or desiring to experience it again, and then further to take action on it. The nature of this inspiration is so pure and so exciting that other desires pale beside it, but it cannot be expressed solely from its purity; it needs the element of desire to bring it forth, to express it, to manifest it. Even the form that comes from it is open to creative definition. But we are getting ahead of ourselves just now. These matters are covered in depth in later chapters of this book.

Where does the change of attitude come from?

The change of attitude that begins to make this possible and to enable one to begin to move and flow with genuine inspiration is one that should be acknowledged, recognised and then set into motion. The first change that takes place within this process is the alteration of the attitude itself from being stimulated by that which has already been created to being inspired to create that which one has seen in the moment of inspiration.

This is not so difficult to see as it may sound. In the present approach to what we often call 'creativity', which is really mostly a rearrangement of that which already exists, there is a whole host of influences that cause, shape and define the desire or aspiration from which one moves. The study of these influencing factors has given birth to the modern science of psychology. But this science carries a delusion from an erroneous basic assumption that it has never questioned. More about that later.

How does it work?

The way it works is fairly observable. Great store is placed on the senses that observe, interpret and record that which already exists in the world. This includes not only the physical world of wood, stone and dirt, but also the world of emotions and thought patterns that are much less observable but which are still quite capable of being seen in their effect. The end result of creation stimulates various desires to see more, feel more, know more, experience more, own more, write more, etc.

Unless aspiration has bowed to inspiration, there is also the desire to do

Our Path of Self-discovery

these things for some purpose, some gain, some increase in tactical or strategic advantage in the intricate game of life. The stimulus from which we move thus meets us from the outside, and is processed to determine if it can increase that advantage or fulfil some desire that surfaces in response to the force of the stimulus. The action then taken is devised, engineered, and then turned back into the created world from which the stimulus came.

This is a circular, or at least a half-circular, activity; and, once it is sent forth, we then wait to reap the benefits of the action, or reaction, that we have thus re-sent into the created world. This stimulus-response works well on animals, and it works well on the part of the human being that is still immersed in the world of the animal. The lower the point of impact of the stimulus, the more shallow is the place where the response or reaction is shaped. In the lower points of impact, there is little depth, and the reaction is largely instinctive. As the point of impact is raised, that is, as the point of focus of awareness is raised out of the physical, through the emotional, through the mental, and upwards, there appear dimensions of more depth, and the response can be of higher quality, so to speak: more subtle, of deeper beauty.

How does one adopt the 'optimum' attitude?

At the point of optimum – not highest – impact, there can be a meeting and a harmonising of the maximum depth of calling from the stimulus that comes from without with a maximum height of creation from the innermost parts of one's self that has uniquely manifested into the personality one carries in a particular lifetime.

There can, at this optimum point of stimulus impact, also be a change set in motion that alters the attitude, the angle of approach, which one must have to express the ultimate form of that which one is stimulated to do.

This is still not the highest form of expression. That proceeds from genuine inspiration from within. But if one can see how the process described alone works, one can gain at least some appreciation that it is merely a reflection of the way things are: that is, the way true and genuine inspiration expresses itself.

How does the proper stimulus come from the inside out?

We could roughly say that stimulus in the lower strata of creation is a reflection of the inspiration that comes from the higher areas of being, and true and genuine inspiration comes from places higher still. These higher places, one will eventually see, are not outside, but within oneself. This genuine inspiration, then, one will also see comes from the inside out.

Such things have been known to occultists throughout the ages, and it is a commonly observable truth that when the time comes for the world to have a certain thing, it moves from being hidden to a place of open knowledge.

So it is with things that come to a time when they are to be known. When it is time for a certain thing to be known by the world, it moves from something that is known in the occult (that is, in hidden form) to a form that can be known by all. There are innumerable examples of these phenomena now occurring, and one of these examples is the perception of the difference between reactive rearrangement and creative expression: the latter proceeds from within, from genuine inspiration.

The point at which genuine inspiration enters the realm of possible creation is the same point at which one can find and maintain perfect balance and peace, and it is at this point where one sees the way things are. Once one has seen this point, once one has been there, one wishes to go there again; one wishes to know more of the way things are.

How does one access this 'Point of Becoming'?

The technique of seeing how things are is not difficult to practice. It is simply to focus the awareness at this Point of Becoming. It is important to know how to do this, and we will discuss this in depth later in this Material. What is more important at this time is to know how to handle what happens when one first focuses at this Point of Becoming and first sees, even if only in a momentary glimpse, the way things are. What is important now is to begin to develop the proper attitude.

The development of this attitude takes time. The time wherein the attitude is changed is a time of transition wherein the awareness opens. The practice of applying this developing attitude during this time of transition is the practice of discrimination – sorting out the way things aren't – that is, the way one once believed things to be, from the way things are. And the way things are is the way one is now coming to know things to be.

When one begins to see the way things are, one wishes to know more of the way things are, and before one asks to know more of the way things are, there is something very important that must happen. It is absolutely essential that one must make a change of attitude before the enquiry is opened.

How does one 'see' at the Point of Becoming?

Here one begins to see some things out of the corner of one's eye of perception. But these things will quickly disappear or fade into the shadows of the mind if one places one's gaze directly upon them. These things that one can now begin to perceive evade concentrated scrutiny and examination, but they are quite willing to become more and more clearly seen and known if they are viewed firstly with the right motivation and secondly with the right attitude.

This essential attitude and the attitude that one must develop so that one can see more of the way things are is an attitude of humble receptivity that agrees, ahead of time, to accept that which one sees, even before one looks. It is an attitude that is devoid of desire and devoid of aspiration. It is an attitude of open enquiry that says, *'No matter what I am going to see, it is exactly what I must know, what I want to know, and what I need to know.'*

If one were able to see the way things are, that is, all of the way things are, all at once, it would be very difficult for one to handle. The full truth, if seen all at once, would be devastating to one in one's present condition, for there is such a great divergence between the way we believe things to be and the way they are.

We, as a human race, are now at the threshold of finding out more about the way things are. But it is important to note that **the *new* way of perceiving the way things are, that is, the new way of *seeing* the way things are, is as different from the way in which truth has been made known in the past, as the way things are is different from the way we have believed them to be.**

What happens in this 'Time of Transition'?

Thus, there is needed a time of transition – a time of personal *Awareness in Transition* – in which one sees a little bit and accepts it, and then sees a little bit more. It is a new attitude that enables one to see more of the way things are, then to enquire more into the way things are, and then to handle that which one sees as a result of the enquiry.

Genuine inspiration not only comes from the inside out, but it brings with it that which is genuinely new. When stimulated from without, we can pretty well predict in the physical world the shape of things to come, given the nature of the tools we have to work with and the repertoire of ways in which we use those tools. We can even speculate on different ways to use the tools and then prognosticate on the eventual result.

But this predictability loses its credentials and its effectiveness when one attempts to apply it to something that comes from the inside out, and to recognise this gives one the ability to take the first step towards changing the attitude. *It is important to recognise that what comes from the inside out and is carried by genuine inspiration is genuinely new, different, original, and positive.*

Can this be compared with anything already known?

That which one sees when one first has a glimpse of the way things are is not like anything. It is not like anything one has seen before, for if it were, it would be something that one might have seen before. It is this change of attitude –

which is so important – that enables one to sort out one of these from the other, and even to open to the possibility that this may be the way things are.

This change of attitude is rather necessary to be able to accept its own concept, so that one may begin to bring the way one has believed things to be into harmony with the way one is now beginning to see the way things are; and it is absolutely necessary for one to be able to handle that which one sees thereafter, for one will soon begin to see that true change, true growth, and truth itself come not from what is observable or from what has already been expressed and created: true change, true growth, and truth itself come from the inside out.

22   The Dawning of an Inner Discipline

There is a special discipline, an Inner Discipline, that one must develop for one to work with the inspiration that comes from the inside out and the purpose of which is to bring with it that which is new and to manifest the way things are and the way things are changing.

Where does this Inner Discipline come from?

This Inner Discipline too must come from the inside out, but its foundations must be developed from the outside.

There are two ways to do this: one can do it for oneself, or one can submit to the imposed discipline of another. In either case, the initial process is the same: that is, the building of a foundation for the practice and application of Inner Discipline. This is the training of the mind, the emotions, the body and the personality to act on that which is seen to be needed to be done.

Discrimination is the essential ingredient in seeing what needs to be done; Inner Discipline is the essential ingredient in doing it.

When one is first born and when one is very young, there is very little discipline that one can implement in one's bodies. In fact, there is little to suggest that there is any need for discipline or self-control when one is still an infant. There is, further, little need or ability to reason or to make a decision as to what needs to be done or what controls need to be imposed on one's bodies so that they will refrain from doing that which must not be done. In these early days, one has little need for any self-imposed discipline, because parental care directs and restrains one's actions. Such direction is imposed by the interweaving of sanctions, rewards and punishments that enforce and reinforce one's actions and restraints.

How does Inner Discipline relate to our true purpose?

There is but one purpose in taking human birth: the living out of the part that one plays in evolution and the realisation of the true nature of the Self: that is, answering the question, 'Who am I, and why am I here?' *The first part of this purpose is infinite and the second part is eternal.* The first continues until the second begins. The first part is regulated largely from without, the second part is regulated from within; that is, the first part is regulated largely by discipline imposed from outside, and the second part is regulated from an Inner Discipline that comes from within.

So long as one is merely moving with evolution, that is, one's own evolution and the evolution of the place one occupies in the scheme of the way things are, many decisions are made by others, or by consequences and circumstances, on one's behalf. This is the case when one is very young. This is also the case for someone who moves through life and never grows up, evolutionarily speaking.

How does Inner Discipline differ from 'imposed discipline'?

When one's evolutionary development moves to such a point that one begins to grow up, one has begun to open in awareness. Part of this opening of awareness is that one will begin to see the need for the development of this Inner Discipline.

One will wish to begin to make one's own decisions: this is the beginning of discrimination. And one will wish to begin to regulate one's own direction and the course of one's life. To do this requires an Inner Discipline that will enable one to do that which one has decided through discrimination must be done.

Inner discipline is different from imposed discipline. It is different from the discipline or the concept of discipline to which one has become accustomed from the time when one was very little and had discipline imposed by a parent or other authority figure or by society. It is also different from the discipline imposed by the inevitable consequences that we all have created and must face. This latter is an imposed discipline; it happens without our wish or our control. Imposed discipline is part of the way things are, and it happens even though we may believe things to be other than the way they are, and it happens even when we wish for things to be other than the way they are.

Once creation is expressed and manifested in the phenomenal world, it regulates itself by imposed discipline. There is an orderliness that must be maintained, and there are rules to maintain that orderliness. These rules are implemented by imposed discipline. Such rules, orderliness, and imposed discipline then enable what has been created to proliferate outwardly, to multiply, to rearrange itself, to play, to enjoy and to be enjoyed.

At the outermost rim of the wheel of creation, where the enjoyment takes place, things are fairly predictable. In the enjoyment, if things are going well, it is natural for one to wish that things continue to be predictable, and the development of rules and the imposed discipline to implement these rules would seem to offer assurance that one could then continue to predict that things would go well, and that one could continue to enjoy things.

Somewhere in here, there is a funny little grey area where the way things are changes to become the way one believes things to be or the way one wishes things to be. Somewhere in here, desire, peering outward and bolstered by aspiration, devises how to change things so that there can be more enjoyment.

Imposed discipline in this realm of predictable enjoyment can serve the purpose of assuring continued enjoyment. If one is enjoying a time or a space that one finds less than enjoyable, it is natural for one to wish things were other than as they are, or for one, in an attempt to find escape from the unenjoyable state of things, to believe that things are other than as they are. In the case of one who wishes things to be other than as they are, it is natural for one to wish to change the rules so that things can be more enjoyable and then to impose those new rules so that the new-found enjoyment can be assured to be more predictable.

What is the conflict between imposed discipline and change?

But in the midst of all of this, one may have forgotten how things are, and that the way things are is *change*. Change continues to come forth from the inside out, adding new ingredients to the pot that one is stirring with imposed discipline, even when one has attempted to tighten the lid and keep things in a condition where one can continue to enjoy them.

There is a conflict here. Outside, where the enjoyment takes place, there is a wish to keep things the way they are then, that is, without change. But when one begins to see and to know that the way things are is *change*, and that change must come, and that change comes from the inside out, there is a conflict.

The way things have become is often the way one would wish them to be. Wishes can then become beliefs, which give rise to superstition, which in turn gives rise to rules, which again in turn must be enforced by an imposed discipline. This discipline is most often imposed by someone who wishes for things to remain as they are, and now we have a full circle of confusion; for the way things are is not to remain as they are but to change.

Can we compromise imposed discipline and change?

Sometimes there is an attempt at a compromise. It happens when someone who is enjoying the way things are and wishes them to remain as they are perceives that there is a change coming that cannot be avoided. Such a change, of course, is just another example of a rearrangement that is also imposed from without. One who wishes for things to remain as they are may agree to accept some change, but one may try to stipulate that the change to be accepted must be minimal, and even in the acceptance, it is likely that the one reluctantly accepting the change will be, even then, devising ways to circumvent the change or minimise its consequences. This part of one can become very strong and well developed, especially in a world where present thinking processes are designed and refined to maintain the status quo at all costs.

How does this change when one does begin to 'see' within?

When one begins to see, all of this too begins to change, and there can be massive inner upheaval as well as outer conflict. The conflict arises, of course, not merely when one realises that change is inevitable, but when one recognises, through a dawning discrimination, that the change that comes from the inside out is not only inevitable but also desirable.

Another part of one's already developed discipline resists even the change that is desirable. Ultimately, that part of one which perceives the desirability of change will prevail over the resistance; but at this point, it will not prevail over the keenly developed and extremely powerful ability to impose the discipline of resistance.

In the beginning, the imposed discipline is in control and the Inner Discipline that would welcome and express the new that comes from change is literally non-existent. It is this Inner Discipline which is in harmony with that part of one's awareness that is opening, and which is beginning to see and welcome change and wishes to express the genuine inspiration that is now to be developed.

This is done by transforming the vehicles. But first, it is done by developing a foundational discipline to obey orders, whether those orders come from outside or inside. One who is evolutionarily ready can develop this Inner Discipline from within after the development of the foundations of the imposed discipline. It is a rare person who can develop the Inner Discipline without the need to build the externally imposed foundational discipline, and anyone who is not evolutionarily ready must submit to imposed discipline from without.

We will explore this concept in more depth later in this Material. But if one can now grasp and put into practice the concepts that have been described in this chapter, one is well and truly established on the Path of Self-discovery and ready for the transition towards a **New Consciousness.**

23 Self-transformation of the Ego

Impatience at a time when one feels a pressure – from either within or without – can be unnerving at the least and at the outside dangerous and even devastating, for it is at such a time that one can become most vulnerable to an attack by the ego.

What is so necessary now is a level temperament; and impatience not only invites but can often actually induce the fear that one will not 'succeed' in attaining that which is 'sought'. In the extreme, fear may be exceeded by the relative realisation that failure is either imminent or present, and then all is lost: confidence, control, and most importantly, the actual assimilation into one's very being of those desirable traits to which one has aspired.

Why is 'patience' so important?

Attendant to impatience – the desire to 'get on with it' – one will also find the ubiquitous (although erroneous) notion that constant action on one's own part and by one's own efforts must physically and actively be put forth. While it is true that the exhortation is often made that one should keep busy and find something to do with one's hands, the time does come – and it must be determined with great discrimination – when all action must *stop*!

There is a tendency to do everything within one's power to exhaust all efforts at one's disposal to aid and further the impetus which is in fact self-perpetuating, but which, deceptively, induces one to action, precipitated by the notion that the more energy is expended through action, the greater will be the progress.

Stop! Just as the flow of energy and instruction from without may abate, so must one's own flow of input be stemmed. This of course does allow one to assimilate the fruits of one's efforts, but there is an even more important reason.

At a certain point, one's own efforts become a source of distraction and diversion rather than a source of strength and sustenance. The exact location of this point is as deceptive as the location of the 'line' over which one must step when the time is right. But with some reflection and discrimination, one can discern its presence; and to acknowledge its presence prematurely is preferable to a belated recognition.

Practically speaking, the situation can arise when one finds oneself in a position where one is relieved of most worldly concerns, well fed, cared for, and with virtually 'nothing' to do. Now what?

Now what? What to do? Such an excellent 'opportunity' to further one's progress, but what to do?

What is the function of the 'ego'?

Here it would do well to have another look at that part of us often referred to as the 'ego' – or more properly, one of the more desirable functions of the ego. So often the ego is spoken of derogatorily or with scorn. But it should be remembered or recognised that without the ego there is nothing but consciousness.

True, this is the state which one, in the beginning, aspires to reach; but the nature of the game and the challenge is that *the ego must be used on itself to transform itself*, and without it, it itself can do nothing. This sounds confusing at first, but it would be well for one to also remember a definition of 'yoga' often offered to one embarking on the path: an operation performed on the mind, by the mind, with the mind. The word 'ego' could be substituted for 'mind'.

How does the ego work?

The desirable function of the ego above mentioned is that, once pointed in a certain direction, and given a 'shove', the ego will perform its mission with a vigour and zeal found in no other manifestation of any kind.

There is nothing that can stop its motion and direction – except its own effort to change its own direction – and this is the 'operation' referred to in the above definition.

As well, it is helpful to remember here that the ego, exercising this function of 'perpetual motion', so often comes in for criticism on the part of the aspirant – essentially for just doing its job.

One may cry, whine and curse the ego, while close examination will reveal that what is really the object of scorn is not the ego itself, and this desirable function of the ego, but the direction of the ego and, one could say, the '*attitude*' of the ego.

For example, 'attitude' in aeronautical terms is the speed, direction, and mode which an aircraft assumes to be able to fly straight ahead. Similarly, one has the discretion to place the ego in an attitude, or mode. The ego has been placed in an attitude by the aspirant during the years of this lifetime, before one puts forth a conscious effort towards spiritual growth, as well as in many other thousands of lifetimes through which one has romped, joyfully and sadly, up and down, allowing the ego to play to the demands of the senses, reacting to the stimuli of the phenomenal world.

And now the aspirant, pursuing the newly found potential state of bliss or enlightenment of which one hears and reads, expresses perplexion at the problem at hand.

Why is the ego causing so much trouble?'

The ego is merely doing the very job for which it was designed in the manner which has been self-determined. It is the most faithful of servants, the most loyal of soldiers – serving and fighting the battle into which it has been placed, never questioning, never stopping, never resting, never re-examining its course or direction.

When one has gained a true perspective of the desirable function of the ego – that it can be made to *serve* the aspirant – then there is only one thing to do: *Stop, Rest, Question* and re-examine the course and direction on which the ego is set. But this may prove to be more difficult than would appear at first glance; for the ego is set on course, direction and speed, and will now vigorously resist all efforts of or towards change.

How is this resistance manifested?

Firstly, one may assume that some change of the ego has been accomplished in the practice of spiritual discipline to date, and some has come about by the natural maturation process effected by evolution.

In this regard, the ego may have assumed some new direction and purpose, that is, movement on or towards the 'spiritual path'; but chances are that little has been done towards arresting the speed and vigour with which it is attempting to do its work. One will see unbounded enthusiasm in the aspirant, especially one new to the path, and such a condition and situation really mean that, for the ego, only the nature of the toy has changed, not the play itself.

In other words, only the goal has changed; and instead of material progress, academic prowess or intellectual progress, the goal is now 'spiritual progress'. And the ego will pursue this new 'goal' with just as much determination as it has all of the others. If meditation is the selected mode for the moment, the meditation may be done, at least at first, with the eyes tightly shut, lips pursed, and concentration so tight that its purpose could not possibly be fulfilled even if it were known.

If hatha yoga is the mode, the overenthusiasm proceeding from the vigour with which the ego attempts to do the job assigned results in the stiff muscles, sore joints, and oft-times a resolution to return to the more familiar grounds of academic, material or intellectual endeavours. And so it goes.

Another, and perhaps the most paradoxical, pursuit, is that of reading and study. During the early days on the path, one will find, or will be found by, some item of written material which is so exciting and stimulating that, with newly discovered circuits meticulously connected and charged with flowing current, the ego – even more invigorated now by some 'gain' or 'progress' – blasts forth with the erroneous notion that all can now be accomplished by reading everything one can accumulate on or concerning this new venture.

We hear one exclaim that this book or that pamphlet or a particular writer 'changed my life'. What is this? Sadly, for most, it is an activity which adds impetus to the course and direction already determined for and by the ego, and the aspirant is led even further astray on a search for *'the book'* or *'the writer'* or *'the guru'* that will certainly present all of the rest of the answers to all problems so far presented.

Just what are the real dangers presented here?

Firstly, and probably most important, is the fact that the eternal search for truth and enlightenment becomes self-defeating, in that what is actually accomplished is *not* further accumulation of 'knowledge', but one actually becomes diverted from the true enquiry of importance; one is distracted and seeks without what *can only be found within.*

Here again it is well to remember the definition of 'yoga', and to remember that the operation must be performed by the mind *on itself, using its own substance.* True knowledge is only self-knowledge, and this is the crux: one must find that point in time at which one must cease exterior enquiry and *stop*, then turn the mind, *and the ego*, in upon itself. Further action merely perpetuates the distraction.

But to do this may be very difficult. The ego is set on course and speed and mode of operation and it is determined to hold so. Now, to be told to *stop, the mind looks at the mind with the mind and wonders if the mind is out of its mind…*

This concern is all but confirmed for the mind when it then remembers that most, if not all, of the enquiry heretofore has been external, and this notion that actual knowledge can be gained from any place other than the written or spoken word, and without putting forth concerted action, is totally foreign to anything yet considered. Even if such a thought has been considered intellectually, the ego here is being asked to venture into new ground, unfamiliar and unlighted.

Previous action was at least active and busy, if not comfortable and familiar, and besides, this new pursuit is frightening. It is now ordered that activity be ceased. The very nature of this request made by the aspirant of the ego brings us to the second of the dangers presented.

How does the ego react to this?

The mind, now being faced with an entirely new and unfamiliar concept of enquiry into itself to learn about itself, will now draw upon all that it has learned and stored in its arsenal in preparation for engaging in that very battle which is now before it: *the defence of its own existence and purpose* – at least (and this is important) as that existence and purpose have heretofore been known and defined by it.

Here, now, can begin perhaps the most important process to be set in motion by the spiritual aspirant if handled properly; for, as the mind, with its ally the ego, now looks to its trove of accumulated arguments and concepts to put forth in defence of its own activity and existence, if identification can be so controlled as to be with the substance of the argument rather than the form, the process can cause the efforts by the ego to set in motion an activity which could be said to be one of 'self-transformation', in which the ego will or may effectively destroy itself in attempting to justify and defend its own existence.

To attempt to understand or grasp such a notion, one must first make some enquiry into the nature of the mind and how it stores its 'defence-of-existence' weapons for the ego, and then make enquiry into the nature of the difference between the substance and form of the weapons or argument, and finally enquiry into how one can control the identification so as to set in motion this process of *Self-transformation of the Ego*.

24 Self-reflection and Self-discovery

Self-reflection is an essential part of Self-discovery. This essay describes how to start the process of self-reflection and what to watch for.

Self-reflection is a very practical process by which one can begin to harmonise one's life with one's own unique set of inevitable consequences and the purpose of one's life. Self-reflection is a medium- to long-term project, but it will have short-term effects and consequences as well.

How does one begin the process of Self-reflection?

There are six steps or points to the beginning process and an infinite number of practices in between. One can become familiar with these six points and begin to use them even if they have some language that is unfamiliar, and even if one does not understand them. Each step is explained in detail. One can begin immediately to work with the processes. These steps are not necessarily steps to be taken in the order listed, but rather they can and should be worked with simultaneously.

The six steps are:

1   become aware of the 'point of becoming' just above the top of one's head.

2   focus the awareness at this point of becoming.

3   as the awareness is focused at the point of becoming, watch what happens

   - in the thoughts: the nature and function of one's thought processes;
   - in daily life: day to day and minute-to-minute – especially the coincidences in the life vehicles: the mind, the emotions, the physical body.

4   become one with what happens within as it manifests without.

5   as one becomes one with the process, ask the question: 'Who is the I that says "my"?'

6   relax and be prepared for anything to happen.

How does Self-reflection differ from other disciplines?

Now let's look at an orientation of what one is going to do with each of these steps. To do this, we will first talk about how self-reflection differs from other forms of meditation and other practices.

No matter what other practices one has worked with or what paths one may have explored or followed, when one first begins to practise self-reflection, one will open one's self to a Positive Presence.

This is probably different from the others with which one has been working or to which one may have been exposed. It can be very disorienting at first, but as one becomes familiar with how to work with it, one will become more comfortable with it.

The discovery of the Positive Presence is part of the process of self-discovery. It is something of a double-catch situation in that one needs to tap the Positive Presence before one can enter the path of self-discovery, and one needs to embark on the Path of Self-discovery before one can tap the Positive Presence.

What are the *'phenomenal'* and *'aphenomenal'* realms?

The Positive Presence carries a positive 'energy' as opposed to the negative energy. The negative energy is that energy which drives our life at the level to which one relates on a day-to-day basis: the earth level or the phenomenal realm.

The *phenomenal* realm is that realm below the Point of Becoming mentioned in the first step of the process. Above the Point of Becoming is the *aphenomenal* realm, and it contains those parts of one's life and one's being that have not yet been made *phenomenal*: that is, which have not yet materialised or manifested in our life.

An analogy would be the way the mind works with the mouth: one gets an idea in the mind and then one speaks of it with one's mouth. We could say that when the idea comes into the mind, it is still *aphenomenal*, and when one verbalises it, it becomes *phenomenal*.

The difference is that the idea and the verbalisation are still both in the negative or phenomenal realm, while the Positive Presence is in the aphenomenal realm until it enters the phenomenal realm through the Point of Becoming at the top of one's head.

If this sounds confusing, it is probably only because one may not yet be familiar with the terminology of this Material.

If one begins to work with self-reflection, the concept and the process will become clear and very real. Although working with this process is very personal, there are guidelines and explanations elsewhere in this Material which may help.

The phenomenal realm is built of energy that originally came from the aphenomenal realm or the realm where the Positive Presence resides. We could say that the Positive Presence or the positive energy in that realm is the raw material of creation, and the negative energy in the phenomenal realm is the energy after it has become 'visible' or 'workable'.

In the phenomenal realm, the amount of energy is finite except as it is replenished or added to by an injection, so to speak, of positive energy from the aphenomenal realm. This means that all of the energy in the phenomenal realm is recycled from matter to energy and back again, and nothing is lost. This is the essence of Einstein's theory of relativity between energy and matter.

Almost all of the spiritual disciplines and practices on the earth, today, work with the negative energy of the phenomenal realm. Most of these disciplines are designed to compress or concentrate this phenomenal energy and make new things and ideas from this energy.

There is enough negative energy to keep our universe going for a long time; in fact, such a long time that even hundreds or perhaps thousands of generations of our human family may not exhaust the seemingly endless limits of the ideas and things that can be made from this negative energy. But it is limited in both supply and in the scope of what it can do.

For instance, although this negative energy gives us the wherewithal to create new things like hybrid tomatoes, fast computers and nuclear bombs, still it is unable to transform its own consciousness without an injection of the Positive Presence from the aphenomenal realm. Lots of things that we create appear new to us. Some of them are indeed new to the realm, but most of them are made out of the same old energy that we have used for thousands of years to make and do everything else.

Even a rudimentary understanding of this concept is enough to enable one to begin to work with self-reflection. One should now review the six steps mentioned above and begin to employ them in one's life.

Further explanations of these concepts appear in other sections of this book in this Material.

Our New Human Consciousness

Our Awareness in Transition

An Overview

With the advent of a change of consciousness imminent on this planet, there is a new generation of embodied souls whose awareness is opening very rapidly. They harbour a different attitude towards the antiquated customs, disciplines, and rules previously employed in a now outdated method of search for truth and enlightenment – an attitude of suspicion, or perhaps rebellion. Thus, with **Our Opening of Awareness**, as one finds, within, the need to repudiate and reject outdated practices, concepts and disciplines, one may also find, to one's dismay, that there is no fulfilling and satisfying mode of activity which feels right. As those opening in awareness begin to question and reject the old ways, they will place **Discrimination in Action**. As one becomes aware of the need to discriminate, there is one very important fundamental concept which must, if possible, be recognised and understood in the beginning: it is that the process of discrimination itself is what is important – and essential – and not those decisions, conclusions or ideas that are arrived at or separated out by the process or as a result of the process. The discrimination spoken of here is basically foreign to a Western culture that encourages the seeking of results, satisfaction, comfort, gain and security – and even survival – at the expense of truth. Another aspect of our awareness in transition is the need for **Accepting True Responsibility**. On opening one may be suspicious, not knowing where to turn for help; for it might seem that nowhere that one has turned thus far has yielded any true peace or satisfaction. One asking for help in a time of *need* cannot afford to be proud; and one who is opening in awareness in a troubled time of transition is in perhaps the greatest *need* that can be experienced.

It will be remembered that in the old way of seeking truth, the *'onus'* or responsibility for going forward rested upon the one who sought knowledge to seek out another who could teach. But in this new era, we are **Shifting The Onus**. The responsibility, which formerly rested on the one who sought knowledge and respected a well-developed and structured system in which life moved slowly, now shifts – it moves – to the one who knows; and it is the one who knows – the one who can help – who must now go forward or be there – available – to the one who yearns. One who is opening is keenly intuitive and will not be deceived by claims or rhetoric. One who would offer help must be genuine, truthful, and supremely confident of their own knowledge as it has thus far become manifest within. Having been called upon to help perhaps only a short time after having oneself received some kind of assistance, one may feel vulnerable in that precarious new equilibrium. One of the keys to the maintenance of that precious balance is discrimination. Another key to the maintenance of this balance is a **Making the Commitment** within the Self. This is not a commitment to a leader, a group, a movement, a religion, a teaching or a philosophy. It is rather a commitment within the Self to make a shift, or perhaps rather to accept a continuing shift, that allows and enables one to remain totally free to stand ready to offer help, whenever and however it may be needed, by a brother, a sister, a nation, a planet or a universe.

Refining The Communication is an important step in making oneself available to help. An exchange involving proof, argument, reasoning, and attempts to convince are obsolete aspects of a passing and outdated method of enquiry after truth. The material communicated cannot be 'understood' by the one in need. There is no way that its essence, substance or form can be 'understood' by another to whom it is presented – at least in the way that such a one is accustomed to 'understanding' thus far. This communication operates both *between or among* two or more opening individual souls and within each opening individual soul. The communication between or among individual souls is merely a less refined manifestation of the communication of the Soul *within* the Self. It should be acknowledged at this point that one opening in awareness might be in a fragile and vulnerable state or condition. For a need to be properly met and fulfilled, it must be mature and ripe. A need prematurely appeased is never fully satisfied; the appetite may be placated, but the hunger remains.

On opening, one must put forth some effort in **Resolving the Dilemma**. At this time, one opening may find that activities and relationships of just a short time earlier now seem to be unimportant or irrelevant – devoid of any meaning, but still anachronistically existent. One may feel a loss of direction, a perception of the unimportance of prior pursuits. Memory may begin to falter or fail, interrupting some activity in midstream. Incomplete thoughts may be interspersed with illuminative flashes of revealing insight. Emotions may rage temporarily out of control; formerly reliable reasoning or decision-making processes may begin to miscarry and prove deficient. One may cringe with a new perception of the inconsideration, cruelty, and selfishness rampant throughout creation – and especially in one's own conduct. One may even begin to feel that one is 'different', cosmically misplaced, alone or 'strange'. Depression may set in, followed by unbounded joy attendant to an exhilarating release – and all this perhaps accompanied by alternating elation, self-enquiry, doubt, perception and so on. This dilemma must be resolved from within. It cannot be directed from without; and it cannot be resolved rationally.

This dilemma can be resolved only by **Recognising inner Discipline**. Inner discipline enables one to move, to act, to manifest a positive response. The absence of Inner Discipline leaves one who is opening susceptible and vulnerable to influences from without – influences which plant the seeds of doubt and which may, even from an early moment, discourage one from engaging in a search for answers for which there do not appear to be any questions. The pull is powerful to turn back, and many do – at least for the present. And so it goes. The question one must now ask is, 'To what degree has one effectively developed the ability to determine a purpose or course of action and thence to proceed on that chosen path?'

After one recognises the current state of one's own Inner Discipline, one must then put effort into **Developing Inner Discipline**. As layers of concepts, sheaths of conduct, and the burden and weight of redundant conclusions, assumptions, emotions and activities fall away, one will lose whatever moment-to-moment awareness one may have had, as well as whatever one may have previously developed in the way of an ability to exercise a moment-to-moment discipline.

With the increasing positive presence of Light, the opening of an awareness within, the emergence of an ability to move within in strength, and the Grace of Liberation from the Wheel of Bondage which is shared at the proper time, likewise, as mentioned above, there will occur an increase in one's ability to cognitively and intentionally examine and deal with each event of inevitable consequence. The Inner Discipline called for to be developed now is that which enables one to act, or initiate action, called forth by some experience, event, or change without one being able to comprehend the purpose of that action, and – further – without being able to perceive how it may be relevant to the subsequent change, action, experience or consequence. This requires **Access** to the Light Within. The implementation of Light depends on the expression of a disciplined will to completely, instantaneously, unquestioningly and continuously adapt to change. Conventionally or traditionally, growth is generally viewed to be a progressing or moving from one point to another, during which various accoutrements are gathered and accumulated. This view of growth can never be truly positive or evolutionarily creative, for it refuses or restricts the introduction of Light and resists and denies the possibility of true change. *'True Growth'*, as is it described in this Material, refers initially to the continuous and effective shedding of unnecessary and/or obsolete encumbrances and the expansion and manifestation of a New Awareness. True Growth suggests first, then, an initial and complete identification with the True Self focused at the Point of Becoming within the level of the Soul.

To accomplish this transition, one gains a new perspective of **Attitude and Understanding**, for at this time, one may encounter a new resistance. This resistance is one of which one must be constantly vigilant; it is the same one that causes one at the very outset to question the inner urging to humbly seek help and to open to that which is known within and is emerging from the True

Self. This resistance thrives on pride, resists change, shuns any notion of self-denial and humility, and lives in the fiction of a reflected self-sufficiency. Its main characteristic is dissipation, directly contravening all efforts towards discipline and action. It is essential that one who is opening should build a solid base and foundation of disciplined action from which to move towards a transformation of this undermining tendency. *'Understanding'*, as it is generally conceived, denotes a process by which a concept is either encountered or formulated and thence assimilated into one's being. This knowingness begins with that which Is and then that which is known by *direct perception* – within the True Self – and it is then accepted as and for what it is *without reference to past experience or understanding*.

Following then the development of an Inner Discipline, one will appreciate the importance of **Effort and Action**. How does one travel this path without becoming psychologically disoriented? The psychological disorientation with which we are here concerned is a syndrome that can develop in one who is opening because of one's inability to reconcile and integrate all of the various dimensions of one's existence. This syndrome is not unique to this new path; indeed, it is present in all paths towards enlightenment. However, there are two important distinctions to note that differentiate the present opening of awareness in this new path. Firstly: absence of the 'faith gap'. One who is opening on this new path is denied a comforting facility that was available to one who is opening in other times and in other cultures. This facility could be called a 'faith gap'.

This term describes a quiet but disquieting 'no-mind' area, in the passing systems of old, between that which one *knows* and that which one is asked to *accept* – *on faith*. Secondly: the absence of the 'guru'. One opening on this new path is denied the vehicle by which one in other cultures and times could bridge that 'faith gap': a leader, teacher, or guru in whom one opening could place the faith required.

On this new Path of Self-discovery, faith has been replaced by an *'objective trust'*, and the leader or guru has been replaced by another opening in awareness who may have found a path across that quagmire and through those tunnels, and who may now be willing to share the benefits of that search and effort: that is, *One Who Can Help. The key to dissolving this syndrome, then, is to trust that which is seen and act on that which is trusted.* This key can enable one who is opening to bridge the 'faith gap' and to complete the *'credibility circle'* by adding those final essential elements: *experience and realisation*. If one has related well to that which has thus far been presented and has traversed the transition, one may be ready to explore the possibility of Self-determination and a New Consciousness.

25 Our Awareness in Transition

With the advent of a change of consciousness imminent on this planet, there is a new generation of embodied souls whose awareness is opening very rapidly. They occupy physical bodies of all ages from early childhood to elderly adulthood. They are bright, alive and well; spontaneous, fresh and 'now'. They harbour a different attitude towards the antiquated customs, disciplines, and rules previously employed in a now outdated method of search for truth and enlightenment; an attitude of suspicion – or perhaps rebellion. They seem to have a sense of urgency. They are impatient, and they are seldom silent.

At the outset, it is very important to recognise that, in the passing system of the search for knowledge and truth, the onus or responsibility was on the seeker to initiate the search and to go forward seeking a teacher. Once in the presence of a teacher, the seeker was expected to wait – patiently, humbly and respectfully silent.

How is this new generation of seekers for spiritual truth different?

For the embodied souls of this new generation, unlike the seekers of other times and cultures, there seems to be another possibility open, and they are well aware of it. This other possibility is one of apparent rebellion. One of this new generation of embodied souls may have been impatient and rebellious in other matters and now is apparently rebelling against the disciplines of old. One may demand knowledge or enlightenment but be unwilling to accept practices of austerity or rigorous and arduous discipline.

Rebellion has become almost a way of life in the modern age from which humanity on this planet is now emerging, and this attitude of rebellion can be found in many aspects of society, from global politics to individual personality. Indeed, it seems to be part of the transition in which human society presently finds itself.

What is spoken of here, however, is not necessarily political or social rebellion, although many have mistaken it to be so. On opening, regardless of one's physical age, one will recognise that one's true destiny is not to rebelliously destroy the old systems but to help build a new one.

One will endeavour to do this by grasping an understanding of the old ways, and blending the best from the past into the new by rejecting the outdated in a gentle, humble way, according to it the respect that it deserves. One would then forge the new in ways that would be unimaginable in the old system.

The rebellion which the opening soul may find growing within rather refers to the inner will to release and let go of outdated and obsolete disciplines and practices which have been followed and which have served well in traditional pathways of the past and which have survived to the present in the absence of any acceptable and viable alternative.

When one finds, within, the need to repudiate and reject outdated practices, concepts and disciplines, one may also find, to one's dismay, that there is no fulfilling and satisfying mode of activity which feels right, and one may thence turn, in frustration, to political or social rebellion.

It could also be observed that the instances of political rebellion which are being seen in the world are merely the result of this void, and it is inevitable that such political and social unrest will begin to subside as a different and satisfying mode of opening to knowledge, enlightenment and truth begins to become manifest and be implemented in daily life.

What is the nature of this 'transition'?

An embodied soul now opening and feeling discontent or rebellion would seem to occupy a position or responsibility of being a *'transition vehicle'*, so to speak – that is, one being presented with the opportunity to undergo and experience certain changes or transitions in awareness within for the benefit of those to follow in years and generations to come. One gropes for a way to cope with problems of the present and future generations, and it will be seen that the peace of the future must start with the harmony of the present. It can also be recognised that steps to achieve this harmony of the present must be taken in all levels of life, in all aspects of society, in all races and creeds, in all religions and beliefs, in all political, social and economic activity, and by persons of all physical ages. It is a harmony that must transcend diversity.

Rebellion was not open to those who followed the disciplines and methods of other times and cultures, and it is still not open to those who follow such outdated disciplines that have survived the paring process of time. The modes of search in times past were fairly restricted, and very restrictive, and most often it was a case of either accept what was available or resign from the search. This is still evident in the practices of obsolete systems. The traditions that they have followed and which have served well in the past have now stagnated, and there is no movement within them, forward, to the changing present.

The influence of these outdated traditions and disciplines is now spreading in voluminous export, and finding wide initial acceptance in the void and absence of any different and innovative alternative. However, there may be dissatisfaction deep within anyone who attempts to follow them and find solace in the teachings imparted from outdated systems, distant cultures or other times. There is a rumbling of uneasiness, as one who has apparently been offered or given everything that is available knows that they have not received what they are seeking to satisfy the inner hunger.

One may become further impatient when one's discontent and rebellion find companionship among that of one's fellows. Together, they find the strength to reject the traditional and outdated; but in favour of what, they do not know.

The accumulation of physical or intellectual knowledge has not satisfied the yearning, and now the transition is carrying humankind into an inner search, and there is a feeling of urgency to grow towards a new balance.

Unlike a seeker of other cultures, other times, or foreign paths, one who is now opening in a time of transition may have started with a rejection of any and all kinds of authority and discipline. In one's suspicion, there is a '*Neo-Sophistication*', and one with Awareness in Transition will probably not allow the old style authoritarian ways, autocratic methods, and arbitrary rules to gain a foothold now. Often they are rejected before they are allowed to be presented.

What is the dilemma faced by a seeker in transition?

Frustration can then begin to plague a confused soul, for one must face the pressure of a dilemma: that is,

> **that which would be acceptable to satisfy the hunger within appears to be unavailable; and that which is available, in the form of outmoded teachings, practices and disciplines, is not acceptable.**

Confronted, then, with outdated and unacceptable systems, (the essence of which has already been rejected), but not knowing where to put forth the required effort to satisfy that hunger within, the one opening is faced with a stalemate or a stand-off; that is,

> **the obsolete teachings and systems cannot offer; and a neo-sophisticated rebel refuses to ask!**

What results, then, is a demand, not yet fully voiced, for a *different system and method that cuts through the ritualistic trivia and leaves no room for egos*. The changes that have given rise to that demand are the results of desires, for as desires and wishes have been fulfilled, Humankind on this planet has not accepted the inevitable consequences that proceed from decisions made in response to desires.

One may accept enjoyments but attempt to avoid resulting responsibilities.

Thus, as a result of the demand for a different system which would enable one to cope with the results of desires and enjoyments, change is becoming more and more evident in the contemporary upheavals of society, and the world, as consciousness begins to expand, awareness begins to open, and pressure begins to grow for an acknowledgement and acceptance of responsibility.

In the recent past, much effort has been expended in the search for alternative lifestyles, philosophies and approaches, and these have produced only temporary satisfaction resulting from yet another attempt to avoid responsibility and consequence.

For one opening and sincerely intending to participate in the transition, linking a now outdated traditional system with a new stage of evolution by implementing a different system (the outlines of which are just now emerging), it would seem helpful for one to at least become familiar with the outdated and outmoded systems that are being rejected, and to retain the most desirable aspects of those systems for future reference and use – perhaps to keep the 'flowers' from the garden of humankind's experience, while discarding the weeds.

At least a cursory knowledge of the obsolescent ways may be useful for one wishing to lend heart, hand and mind to do whatever might be done to help develop whatever it is that is coming next.

It may be helpful if one can say, 'I have been there – I understand.' But, one who is opening to a new time and a different way will not claim to rely on the past but will know – *within* – of the present – and hence, of the past and of the future.

One may be able to absorb in a few moments or months, or a few short years, what might previously have required decades or lifetimes to acquire and digest. One may now wish to trust and believe that which is felt within, and this may conflict with the present way of a system, which assumes that one is ignorant until proven learned by its own obsolete standards, and which considers one empty until proven filled with its own now irrelevant and unworkable teachings.

On opening, one knows that something is known within – something that was not imparted by, nor learned from, one's culture or society – something that is inherently true and unquestionable; but, at this stage, one will probably not know what it is. The obsolescent aspects of a passing culture cannot accept that there can be such confident knowledge based on something other than that which was accumulated before. On opening, one will thus be well advised to acknowledge and accept that which is known, within, from where one stands when first the light begins to dawn. One will look in vain to find proof of its existence in the teachings of a passing culture and society.

How will this new generation reject the old ways?

The rejection of an outmoded system that is based on accumulated physical and intellectual knowledge will follow naturally the rebellious rejection of established, but outmoded, moral patterns and material values. The value of retaining some of the 'flowers' or desirable aspects, however, can be seen when certain traits of character or behaviour – namely impatience, recklessness, impetuosity – and, in the extreme, cynicism and audacity – are exhibited by one exercising rejection in a rebellious manner. These traits are often condemned, as is the process of rebellious rejection with which they are identified. But they are merely characteristics, often prompted by emotion or overenthusiasm. One who proceeds in such a characteristic manner can delay or inhibit the purpose of the process. By retaining certain desirable traits of character salvaged from a passing culture, the process can take place more smoothly and effectively. And even these desirable traits may themselves become rejected.

One presently embodied and opening in a time of transition may demand instant enlightenment and feels justified in doing so. Our indulgent culture and society has generally, in the past, granted and fulfilled most demands for instant comfort, attention and satisfaction. Anyone spoiled by such a system has neither the patience nor the inclination to humbly await the dawning of a higher state of consciousness, taught and carried by outmoded systems and disciplines that served well in other times and cultures. This impatient attitude may have contributed to the appearance of many of the abusive methods currently employed in a search for truth, or an attempted escape from untruth.

If one will but recognise that rash and reckless behaviour, and rejection without discrimination, can be self-defeating, harming or destroying one's articles of expression – that is, the physical, emotional, and mental bodies – then it will be seen that a precious state of patient balance must be maintained for the transition operation to be a success – for a completed new awareness to emerge.

What aspects of the old culture and disciplines will be retained?

What would appear to be desirable and helpful, then, in this time of transition, is the emergence of a way in which one who is opening – fresh, spontaneous, and sometimes impatient, sceptical, confused, or even suspicious and desperate

Our New Human Consciousness

– one who is rejecting an obsolete system – can be effectively shown that the system being rejected may contain some of the very ingredients necessary to allow a new and expanded awareness to grow from within.

How is this to be seen – or shown? Great discrimination is required. If entire systems of manifested wisdom, knowledge or discipline are allowed to be discarded without discrimination, then preservation and maintenance of that precious state of balance may be lost or destroyed.

Discrimination is one of the qualities that must be nurtured and developed by one who is opening so that its benefits may then be imparted to those who follow.

26 Discrimination in Action

> As one becomes aware of the need to discriminate, there is one very important fundamental concept which must, if possible, be recognised and understood in the beginning. It is that the process of discrimination itself is what is important – and essential – and not those decisions, conclusions or ideas that are arrived at or separated out by the process or as a result of the process. Constant vigilance is necessary to avoid the pitfall of attaching an undue amount of significance to the results or conclusions reached, for conclusions can bind the intellect and cause it to cling to and defend that which it erroneously claims as its own.

It could be said that what is important is the activity of gardening itself, with the flowers and weeds collected from the garden of experience being of relative significance only; the flowers only until they are wilted by continuing evolution, and even the weeds can redeem themselves and become useful for the future when placed on the compost pile of the present. It is the development of the process of evolutionary discrimination that enables the opening soul to recognise one from the other.

What is 'evolutionary discrimination'?

The discrimination spoken of here is basically foreign to a Western culture, which encourages the seeking of results, satisfaction, comfort, gain and security, and even survival at the expense of truth. In building, within, a foundation of discrimination, one serving to build the new in a time of transition will encounter trials and tests that hone and temper and mellowly refine one's ability to discriminate and select that which is to be carried forward, discarding in the process that which is to be left behind. Such trials and tests may mount a conflict between pressure to retain the traditional and an inner urging to formulate the new. Such trials ultimately lend strength to a growing confidence to believe in, and rely upon, that which one knows within the Self.

This concept of *'newness'* may be somewhat temporarily troublesome, for what is generally considered to be new is often merely a restatement or reformulation of the old – lacking any truly innovative ingredients – and that which is truly new often encounters resistance from the traditional. A blending of the best of each engenders respect and cooperation from both.

In gleaning from the raw material of transition the beneficial aspects to be moulded for the future, the trials, tests and resistance may cause the opening soul to place too much stress on what are believed to be mistakes and failures. While it is true that mistakes will be made, more often they will be more correctly seen to be merely experiences previously untried, and necessarily traversed now for the benefit of the natural path of evolution, or experiences being finally undergone in preparation for evolutionary displacement. Undue concern is not necessarily warranted if, as a result of such experiences, one temporarily reverts to a mode of conduct already discarded.

This will inevitably occur naturally as the process of discrimination begins to enable one to perceive that actions for the present and future are guided by criteria formulated by the moment, and there is a laying aside of a method of decision-making that has been employed by one's physical ancestors for hundreds of generations – that of drawing a conclusion from past experience in order to formulate present or future conduct. One who is participating in the transition must have the latitude to try, fail, accept, reject, and make decisions that will affect not only one's contemporaries, but humankind for generations – both in the future and in the past.

What are the 'rules' for using Discrimination?

The rapidity with which matters are changing and moving requires one to be so open and discriminating that seemingly similar questions can be faced only moments apart, producing what may appear to be conflicting results or decisions – *each correct at the time the decision is made*.

As a preliminary, then, it might be comfortably said that there are *no rules*.

That is, there is nothing that one is compelled to do or practise, or prohibited from doing – with only one exception: one must be truly and thoroughly considerate of others, respecting their space, and refraining from entering that space without permission and consideration. In short, the only prescribed conduct is that of common decency. There is no required conduct or diet – physical, emotional, mental, or spiritual.

One who is opening may thus be put at ease, for in an uneasy time of change and rebellion, both internal and external, it is quite likely that there has been an attempt to reject – or at least question – most rules anyway. If one can rely on the emerging truth of the moment (even as that truth appears to change and transform itself from one instant to the next), all will develop and unfold naturally.

As the opening soul begins to recognise that there is an absence of rules, and that moment-to-moment discrimination and consideration are the emerging guiding principles, the sudden realisation of the resulting freedom can be a thrilling experience, but it may be somewhat unnerving for someone who still clings to or retains the need for a strictly structured life pattern. If one becomes disturbed by such freedom, perhaps one has not yet truly begun to open; for deep within the structure may be hidden a fear of finding the answers that one has professed to be seeking! In such a case of finding the answers in the freedom, one would be deprived of the search – an activity upon which one's course may be firmly set, to which one may be almost unfalteringly committed, and to which one can become very attached.

Within one who is truly opening to truth, there will be engendered in the apparent vacuum of this freedom a sense of responsibility and a need to develop and assume a posture of personal integrity and dignity. There will be a sense of duty. If, in one's exuberance and new freedom, one fails to recognise this presence of responsibility, it will not escape attention for long. It will be a responsibility which proceeds from sacrifice – even of one's own comfort and security – rather than from a charity that might remain after fulfilment of one's own wants is assured.

It is perhaps now, for the first time, with this realisation of freedom, responsibility and duty that the attitude of the opening soul will begin to transform from one of *revolution* – to one of *evolution*.

What can be salvaged from the old systems?

What is it, then, that might be salvaged from rejected or obsolete systems, practices, and disciplines to be combined with the new principles for use by embodied souls opening in awareness during a time of transition?

It has been wisely said that there are only two kinds of people in the world: those who know, and those who do not know. It could further be said that this applies at all levels of evolution. Even as one begins to open in awareness, the distinction between these two kinds of people will remain hidden, and they will for some considerable time continue to appear identical one with the other.

It is within the 'one who knows' that the seed of discrimination will begin to grow, and it is that quality of discrimination that will gradually enable one opening to distinguish one kind from the other. However, before that quality is developed, the opening soul will, on more than one occasion, mistakenly assume (in one's yearning to find and relate to another who knows), that one can safely determine one kind from another, for early on, both kinds will appear identical not only to one who is opening, but also to one with an indiscriminate eye.

One who does not yet know – that is, one who is not yet fertile enough to have the seed of discrimination germinated within – may perhaps be in need of stronger external discipline and will yet feel more comfortable within a defined, ordered and regulated structure – a structure and framework already established and operating. This is understandable, and many will feel this way.

There are many teachers, masters and disciplines in the world to whom such a one can turn and from whom one can, and will, receive the stronger external guidance, authoritarian control and stricter discipline.

Until the need for such structured guidance is exhausted, one will continue to seek and follow it in one form or another. As discrimination begins to grow, the need for stricter imposed discipline will fall away naturally as one moves from one aspect of evolutionary unfoldment to another.

As the inevitable and imminent Change of Consciousness begins to become manifest on this planet, all will gradually begin to discriminate, to one degree or another; thence, all will begin to know. However, there will then arise a distinction between those who know, on the one hand, and on the other hand, those who know and can place into action what they know. The one who knows, who can discriminate, and who can take action on what is known, is one – the Pathfinder – who participates in the transition – helps clear the way, find and prepare the path, and assist in building the new for the next stage of evolutionary development.

There is a distinguishing characteristic in one opening in awareness in a time of transition: there is a gleaming in the eye, and a glimmering in the heart. There is a cry for help – a cry to be lifted and encouraged to accept Responsibility and fulfil one's evolutionary duty; but it must be done gently.

27 *Accepting True Responsibility*

One who has perhaps already rejected (or at least questioned) the authority of parents, government, society and its leaders, and religion and conventional teachings, may not yet be able to accept suggestions for personal direction or discipline at this time from any authority or influence.

Indeed, on opening one may have no idea or concept that what one is embarking upon is the unfolding of awareness, discrimination, and personal discipline: that is, *Accepting True Responsibility*. One knows only that the heart harbours a secret, unsettled yearning. One may be suspicious, not knowing where to turn for help, for it might seem that nowhere that one has turned thus far has yielded any true peace or satisfaction.

At such a time, however, one probably knows one thing deep inside, (even if it cannot or will not be acknowledged openly thus far): *whatever needs to be done, it cannot be done alone – one knows that help is needed, and that help is needed soon; and one may recognise that if help is not forthcoming soon, one may be in trouble.*

What happens when one feels the need for help?

This knowledge of the need for help may not even be a conscious knowledge, but it is there, deep inside. This knowledge of the need for help is in itself not enough, even if it is consciously recognised; for on opening one is approaching a point in personal evolution, where, after recognising and acknowledging the need for help, one must then exercise one's own will to ask for and accept help, thereby voluntarily opening to an essential and positive flow of energy and help, and possibly some external influence.

This gesture of asking for help may be difficult for one who has found from past experience that one can, for the most part, remain complacently passive, expecting that, in almost any predicament, help will be at least offered if not actually thrust upon one by an overly protective and indulgent society that stifles the growth potential lying dormant in one's needs by rushing to accommodate those needs often before they are fully matured.

Someone living in and opening in such a protecting and providing society has thus also been deprived of the opportunity of a profound experience available only to one who sincerely asks for help – an experience and characteristic that is still basically foreign to most cultures on this planet, and that could be salvaged from other times and cultures – that of *humility*.

> **One asking for help in a time of need cannot afford to be proud; and one opening in awareness in a troubled time of transition is in perhaps the greatest *need* that one can experience.**

One who is proud cannot be receptive; one in need must be humble when asking for help. But even one humble enough to ask for help, even if able to receive it, may remain confused as to whom or where to ask.

What is very important to recognise is that it is this one essential characteristic trait – *the ability to recognise one's own need and to ask for help* – that may enable one to accept – and be receptive to – the first ray of hope available in a time of confusion.

> **It will be found again and again, literally from beginning to end, that this ability to recognise one's own need for help, then ask for help, and humbly accept help, is the one saving grace and differentiating trait that can dispel confusion; for it will allow – and prompt – one to open to that which is truly new.**

Where was the 'onus' in the old culture and disciplines?

In this era, encompassing for this discussion the past several thousand years, knowledge and wisdom have been imparted from one, (an accomplished and adept teacher) to another who sought to learn, and who then, when considered fully learned, became the teacher, and so on.

It will be remembered that the *'onus'* or responsibility for going forward rested upon the one who sought knowledge to seek out another who could teach.

Teachers, for the most part, remained fairly remote, well hidden, and reluctant to discuss much of anything at all with one who wished to learn, until such a one had passed the test of genuineness, sincerity and humility.

The age of present Eastern civilisations, versus the relatively late appearance of present Western civilisations, suggest that much of these exchanges took place in what is commonly called 'the East'. This may be largely true, for the younger civilisations and cultures, lacking a system of imparting knowledge that suited their own requirements (a system which must eventually emerge by necessity) looked to that which had developed before.

But even before the emergence of the present Eastern cultures many thousands of years ago, other cultures, geographically located in ancient

Western lands, carried the coveted knowledge forward to the then younger civilisations now located in the East.

In these older cultures and civilisations (where the responsibility for going forward was on the one who needed to learn), all were reared with, and steeped in, a reverence for the unknown, and there was an inherent cultural respect for one who bore knowledge; one who could help and teach.

This was generally true even though a teacher might appear reluctant to teach, content to exist in a blissful state, and oblivious to the outside world. Impetuosity would never have been exhibited by one who sought to learn, nor would it have been tolerated by one who could teach.

How is evolution changing the search for truth and enlightenment?

Although the essence of the need for the passing of the coveted knowledge remains unchanged from age to age, evolution continually and continuously modifies the substance of that wisdom called forth by the needs of an era, and the unique problems to be encountered and dealt with by any given era.

Evolution also modifies the processes, methods and forms by which, and through which, knowledge is transferred from one to another. Such processes, methods and so on are tailored to suit the capabilities and characteristics of those who inhabit those times and cultures.

Although the embodied carrier of knowledge (or teacher, call it whatever one will) and the embodied soul opening to receive that knowledge may alter their costumes, style, dialogue and material, still the most basic nature of the drama remains the same from age to age. This fact is hidden from one just opening, but it has, in times past, been obvious to the one who became the teacher and who could help another.

What is the essence of this knowledge that is passed from one to another? What are its purposes? What are its characteristics?

There are many aspects of this knowledge.

One of these aspects is to correct an imbalance.

Firstly, it is helpful to recognise that there is, within each embodied creation – be it an individual soul, a tribe, group, nation, or a universe – a Point; or a space; where one is in Total Peace, complete harmony and absolute Balance. Some have experienced this Point or Space; others have not. Even one who has not seen or experienced it, still, on reflection, will probably know that it is there. It does exist.

If an individual, a tribe, a group, nation and so on, should lose its balance, if it cannot find its balance, or even if it forgets that its Point of Balance exists, then, when the time is right, when the proper gesture has been made, when the entity is receptive, an occurrence or an event will manifest in some way – or some form – to the one which has lost its Balance or equilibrium.

This occurrence or event to regain the Balance or equilibrium can take the form of anything that can be helpful to the entity; it can manifest in any way essential to correct the imbalance.

If one looks to the past, to another age – or another day – to another time of imbalance, one will see only the form of the manifestation that occurred to correct the imbalance at that time. In the desperation and frustration of imbalance, one may search the past, groping and grasping, hoping to find something which may have corrected an apparently similar imbalance in the past; and hoping that such a form or materialisation from the past can now be adapted to correct a present imbalance. In an attempt to use a form or manifestation from the past, and tailor it to the present, reference is made to *yesterday*'s words, teachings, rules, structures, forms or manifestations to try to correct *today*'s imbalance. Conclusions are drawn or reached; rules are formulated and imposed, and the imbalance can grow more intense as it crystallises in its own stagnation.

What distinguishes this new 'manifestation' from those of the past?

There are at least two basic elements that distinguish the presently emerging form or manifestation of this occurrence to correct the present imbalance.

Firstly, the urgency. Humankind on this planet has wrought upon itself, by desire, a flood of inventive and innovative physical accomplishments that has left in its wake a lagging inability to cope with the consequences of what has been created and developed. It has paused to enjoy, ignoring the attendant responsibility to evolve.

Contrary to common and erroneous contemporary belief, evolution is not limited in operation to this planet, nor even to this plane of existence. Not only does a complacent and selfishly indulgent attitude retard the growth of this present physical plane of life, but it unfairly restrains and restricts the evolutionary movement and growth of those phases of evolution that seek to move forward in their growth from other adjacent planes of existence.

> **They must, for some short time, also inhabit and learn from this plane, and from this planet, which is becoming overcrowded with those who refuse to relinquish an attachment to the fruits of their creation, enjoyment and indulgence.**

This urgency necessitates that a different and innovative system for the dissemination of a currently essential aspect of the coveted knowledge must emerge and develop rather quickly, in order that an occurrence to commence the correction of a present imbalance may proceed as rapidly as is evolutionarily possible. This urgency renders obsolete the cumbersome and time-consuming process whereby knowledge was imparted from a teacher to a student who, when considered fully learned, then became teacher. This urgency also renders obsolete much of the substance of the teaching so passed in that now outdated system.

A new system or process now necessarily begins with a common awareness of a few (eventually to be shared by all) emerging from within to be placed into practice by those who carry this awareness and accept the responsibility.

Secondly, the rebellion. The second factor that characterises and distinguishes the presently emerging occurrence is that possibility apparently available to those opening in this time of transition: that of a destructive display of rebellious repudiation of an antiquated, cumbersome and obsolete system.

One who is opening in this time of transition senses the urgency and stands now, hard of shell, but crying within, that some kind of grace will be shed to relieve the aching and yearning in the heart.

And hence, the onus shifts.

The responsibility that formerly rested on the one who sought knowledge, and respected a well-developed and structured system in which life moved slowly, now shifts; it moves – to the one who knows – and it is the one who knows who must now go forward or be there – available – to the one who yearns. And this challenge to go forward must be accepted even in the face of apparent opposition erected by a self-serving and complacent culture that selfishly resists change.

One who is opening may initially resist acceptance of that for which one yearns. The external pressures exerted by one's society or culture may be so strongly entrenched that one may lag behind, even though one is prompted from within to help forge a new way. It is the one who knows who will recognise the need and urgency, and it is now the one in need who may appear less than concerned, and even perhaps oblivious to the outside world. Even in the depth of disillusionment one in need knows within that there must be some help forthcoming to enable one to open to that which is known within.

The one upon whom True Responsibility now rests, however, is not some old venerable sage hidden somewhere in a remote cave or monastery, but rather it is one who was oneself recently opening to an expanded awareness – perhaps only moments before. One who accepts the True Responsibility and makes an approach to one in need may find that an offer is rebuffed or rejected.

But if the offer is not made by one who knows, then one may properly feel that one has unfairly neglected a responsibility.

What is the Responsibility of 'one who knows'?

Now the plot of the drama begins to thicken, and the one who knows and can offer help faces a perplexing question: how to make an approach – *indeed, **whether** to make an approach* – to one in need, one confused and distressed, but perhaps at the same time sceptical or even cynical? How is one to suggest that what is needed may be found by placing some trust in another – another who may help one to believe in and rely upon that which is known within?

28 Shifting the Onus

An embodied soul opening within to truth and enlightenment, and simultaneously facing the opportunity to be of help to another, has had a dual responsibility thrust upon their path. The thrilling experience of opening within the Self carries quickly upon its heels the duty to share that experience where it is needed. The knowledge received and the freedom that ensues cannot be selfishly hoarded; they must be shared, and a refusal to accept one's responsibility to share and to help will dangerously restrict the evolutionary flow and increase the urgency.

What happens when one asks: 'Why is this happening to me'?

One facing such an opportunity and responsibility may experience a feeling of intense and embarrassing humility. One is now being called upon to help – both by an inner prompting and by a groping from another opening soul. One may ask, 'Who, me? Why me?'

This is but the essence of a new system of the dissemination of the initial traces of Light in a time of transition from an era of darkness, selfishness and ignorance. The urgency of the present requires that one who has received must impart at least some of that received as soon as the need arises and as soon as the necessary gesture is made by the one in need.

How does 'one who knows' offer help to another?

One who is opening is keenly intuitive and will not be deceived by claims or rhetoric. If one is to offer help, then, one must be genuine, truthful, and supremely confident of one's own knowledge as it has thus far become manifest within. One must remain, as much as possible, carefully balanced within the Self, and, above all, gently but unrelentingly positive in the approach.

However, one who could be of help may also become exasperated, for the needs of one opening are evident and apparent to one who has only recently experienced anguish and anxiety. Many of these matters discussed in this Material will begin to become meaningful to one who wishes to offer help, namely: the urgency; the obsolescence of the old systems; and how the onus shifts.

In a time of urgency and transition, then, the roles are apparently reversed; that is, it is now the one who knows and can help who has the onus of responsibility of going forward and finding a way to impart what is needed; and it is the one opening and in need who may appear passive, complacent, uninterested, and even perhaps oblivious to the outside world, even while knowing deep within that help is desperately needed.

Strangely, it may be just such a one – an acquaintance, a friend, a peer, a spouse – who now begins to emerge as the one who can help, and this can be almost embarrassingly unacceptable, for respect is often lacking for one so close. The degree of the intensity of one's need may now determine one's ability to engender, within, the necessary attitude of respect so as to be receptive to the help about to be offered.

And hence, the onus has truly shifted.

It rests now on the one who would or could offer help, not only to go forward but also to be truly genuine, sincere, and deserving of the respect which must be rendered before one in need can be receptive.

Only now is it beginning to occur to those opening in a time of transition that respect and reverence may be due and properly placed in one's peer, companion, spouse, brother or sister. On close examination it will be seen that what is emerging now, in one in need, is this *attitude of respect*. It may be sprinkled with some disbelief, but this attitude is the first sprouting of the seed of a relationship between and among those opening and seeking to aid each other and in turn to help humankind. It is the sprouting of a seed of relationship that one day will allow a prophet to have honour and respect – but without worship – in his or her own 'country', so to speak – among one's companions and peers.

It is the seed that will enable one to stand in need and be receptive one moment and the next moment to be of help to another – and perhaps only moments later to accept help from the one to whom help has just been given. It is the seed of true and ultimate consideration, unselfish understanding, trust, and unbounded universal love. This seed of a new relationship may enable one opening, and in need, to shift from a stance of sceptical resistance to that of respectful receptivity.

Who makes the first 'overture'?

Initially, it may appear to one in need that contact with one who can help was coincidental, but the one eager to offer help knows better. It was only recently that help was offered in just such a manner to one now standing ready to offer. Even though the one now capable of offering help knows that the contact is not due to coincidence, it is better to refrain from saying so.

It is better to remain ready, prepared to help, and assume a waiting and patient attitude, because – and this is absolutely essential:

the first overture must come from the one in need of help, not only in the initial contact, but also in every subsequent instance in which new material is broached. Until such overture or gesture is made, the necessary and proper flow of communicative energy has not been established.

A great burden of self-control to restrain one's own eagerness and enthusiasm rests on the one who can offer help now. Any premature attempt to broach the subject – any attempt to officiously intermeddle – can reduce or delay the receptiveness of one in need.

The initial relationship of respect will grow to become one of trust towards a time when this essential overture or gesture is made by the one in need – be it an opening soul, a tribe, nation, planet or universe – towards the moment of reaching out, in humility – in true need – to ask for help, and be receptive.

The key to the precious balance of this opening relationship is *discrimination*. The responsibility (not only to await the overture and to go forward when it is made), but also the responsibility for what happens when the communication begins to flow rests on the one now able to offer help.

With such an injunction in mind, how is the one who can offer help to conduct oneself? If one is to pass the essential test of genuineness and sincerity and to engender the proper respect, there must be a *truth-in-being* that manifests in a perfect expression of that which is known within the Self. One who can offer help will appear initially indistinguishable from one in need, and (notwithstanding the growth of the Light within) will continue in humility to be so. Any attempt to build any facade of apparent veneration, or display any knowledge or superiority, will be instantly transparent to the one opening, who will find such an attempt as humorous as it is contemptible. There will be no respect engendered in any act of condescension.

One who is opening cannot and will not be deceived. One opening is one who 'knows' and is looking for another who 'knows' – not one who claims to know.

29 *Making the Commitment*

One who is capable of responding to an overture from one in need of help must stand preciously balanced in that which is known within. Having been called upon to help perhaps only a short time after having oneself received some kind of assistance, one may feel vulnerable in that precarious new equilibrium.

What are the keys to maintaining this new equilibrium?

One of the keys to the maintenance of that precious balance is discrimination – moment-to-moment evolutionary discrimination – in this case at hand, the discrimination to distinguish and recognise a genuine enquiry from one in need as well as the discrimination to recognise when the necessary overture has been made so that one in need may truly be receptive.

Another key to the maintenance of this balance is a Commitment, made within the self. Simply to know is not enough; one must first develop a solid reliance on that which is known, and then that knowledge must be brought forth and placed into action in one's daily life.

What is the nature of the 'Commitment'?

Just as one of the first keys to the maintenance of balance is discrimination, one of the first keys to placing knowledge into action is a Commitment within.

This is not a commitment to a leader, a group, a movement, a religion, a teaching or a philosophy. It is rather a commitment within the Self to make a shift, or perhaps rather to accept a continuing shift, that allows and enables one to remain totally free to stand ready to offer help whenever and however it may be needed by a brother, a sister, a nation, a planet or a universe.

It is also the acknowledgement within that this Commitment takes precedence over all else. It is only such a commitment or shift that renders one completely free of restrictions, rules and structures, for then one can begin to move in the realm of creation and expression, tempered only by the gentle awareness to be considerate of others.

It is not for one called upon for help to determine whether one is capable of helping. That determination has already been made: firstly, by the fact that help has been received by the one now being called upon, thereby creating an obligation to carry on that help to the optimum of one's ability (which also now will be ever increasing); and secondly, that determination of capability has been made by the one seeking help, one who will be very discriminating and selective as to where help is allowed to come from.

But it is within the spectrum of one's own determination and decision to make this Commitment (which must be made voluntarily and without coercion) – that is, to gratefully and humbly accept True Responsibility and commit one's energies and abilities to a readiness of participation in the transition towards a New Consciousness, and, if need be, of sacrifice – without limitation – whenever and however one is called upon.

What is the nature of the 'sacrifice' in the Commitment?

It may do well at this point to examine a different concept of 'sacrifice'.

The sacrifice described here is a gesture of open, selfless recognition and respect for the needs of another and a commitment of willingness to be there when the essential overture is made; that is, when the one in need becomes receptive. This sacrifice is one of choice: the choice of releasing a binding attachment to a selfish enjoyment in favour of the responsibility to mercifully and generously pass on to one in need at least a portion of what one has – or has received.

What is not being described here is a path of sacrifice through renunciation or ascetic self-denial or deprivation, for such an activity is unnecessary and irrelevant for one who relates to this Material and who wishes to participate in the transition. The path of renunciation and self-denial is a vestige of an obsolete discipline; it is an anachronism in a time of imminent abundance of light and energy that must be manifested, expressed and implemented to be fulfilled; and such a path of renunciation and self-denial will be followed now only by one in need of stronger external disciplines.

> **What is essential now is a voluntary, positive commitment to a freedom in which one can offer one's own abundant energies – in any way – when called upon. Such freedom cannot be restricted by the limitations of one's own renunciation or self-denial.**

If there is a renunciation now, it is the renunciation of selfishness in favour of harmony that transcends diversity; if there is a denial, it is a denial of bondage or separateness in favour of a new freedom in oneness; and if there is a sacrifice, it is the sacrifice and loss of negativity, self-concern, private security and fear, in favour of an abundance of joy, kindness and elation to be shared by all. *But* – there is a commitment to be made within.

To refuse such a commitment is to deny the presence and the value of that which one has already received. To humbly, but confidently, make such a commitment is to effectively open to a flow of energy and light that is far more than adequate and capable of meeting any demand or enquiry placed forth by one in need. Such flow of energy and light is likewise totally without limitation in ability to manifest positively – in force or form – to correct an imbalance or establish a new harmonious equilibrium.

What are the universal principles of 'receptivity' and 'abundance'?

A universal principle of receptivity requires one in need to recognise and acknowledge one's own need and exercise one's own will in making an initial overture to ask for help. Likewise, a universal principle of abundance requires one capable of being of service or help to first manifest – within – an initial gesture of commitment of humble readiness to manifest the help to one in need.

Such a positive Commitment neutralises and obliterates the stagnation and the selfish tendency to gather and hoard – anything. One who discriminates will know that what is important now is not that which has been or can be received, but rather the continuous and unlimited, unrestrictive and unrestricted flow of receiving – and giving – which can be for universal benefit.

As well, it is essential for one to make a humble – but firm – commitment within to freely express a continuous manifestation and visibly apparent unwavering adherence to a moment-to-moment practical application of the principles emerging in one's own life from within – even as those principles seem to change, evolve and transform with the flow of an ever-increasing awareness.

It is by this expression – this living – this being – that the first communication will be made. These words of suggestion are offered, then, to one who is opening and who has asked in gratitude and humility, 'What can one do to help?'

How does 'one who can help' conduct oneself?

One who can offer help must remain balanced, steady, unmoved, detached, gentle and joyful under the testing, scrutinising gaze of one in need but who is perhaps frustrated by scepticism. One will meet and pass the test of genuineness and sincerity by remaining firmly established in one's daily disciplined work – whatever it may be – and by remaining balanced within the Self, available for observation, utilising the greatest care to avoid any hint of separation or condescension.

These are lofty words to be sure. How are they to be practically exhibited, implemented, expressed and communicated?

A learned or acquired intellectual understanding is not enough. Before respect will be engendered, and before the necessary gesture or overture can be made, one in need must see and feel in the one who can help a knowledge, a confidence, and a depth that can reside only in one who has been through 'it' – whatever 'it' may be – survived it, and come out the other side – preferably laughing, joyful, and at peace within.

It is only then that one in need may extend a trembling hand to ask for help – to make that initial and essential advance or overture; and it is when that overture is made that one who can help will truly recognise – within – the necessity to move with the moment, the responsibility to 'be there' when needed, and the fact that the 'onus' has indeed shifted, and that, truly, only a brother or sister of the heart can offer help to another in need.

This initial reaching out by one in need will be most probably of a very subtle kind, broaching, at first perhaps, subjects only of a worldly or mundane nature, for scepticism and trepidation are still commingled with pride; humility is only just beginning to dawn in one who needs help, as that need begins to approach a state of desperation.

The one approached for help, while gentle and warm, and patient and ready in the comfort and peace of self-knowledge, must be unrelentingly positive in the exchange. Any response to an overture at this stage must be limited to the query put forth, for any effort now by one who can help to exhibit any authoritative knowledge will be instantly detected by one in need who is only just beginning to precariously emerge from a protective shell. At the slightest overreaching, one in need will probably return in hasty retreat to the security of the world previously known – however unacceptable it may seem.

One opening in awareness will avoid one who is overeager to help or who might be floating forth for export some idea designed to either confirm one's own insecure position or to gauge the reactions of others. At this time, one in need is far more interested in – and attracted by – what one is, and how one lives, and conducts oneself, rather than what one says, or knows, or says one knows. And one asking for help at such a time is essentially interested in being offered only so much as is in direct response to the query put forth – only so much as can be presently digested and assimilated.

The overture will inevitably be made! One in need is moved and prompted by an inner and higher compulsion – one that drives one to know, to find another who knows, to place one's heart next to another who knows, to gain from and grow with another who knows – and who openly places into everyday practice what is known, and who can share with one in need.

The initial trust can be developed by the sharing of information and practice on subjects and matters other than those of the vital and essential interest. The first queries, questions and enquiries will be ones to test – more to see *how* rather than with what they are answered.

As trust begins to develop, the light of humility overcomes the dark haughtiness of pride or fear, and respect replaces a perhaps too familiar 'camaraderie' or friendship. The query becomes deeper and more genuine, broaching subjects of real concern, and, as the fruits of the help received are digested into practice and found to survive the tests of daily life, the essential flow is strengthened, and a harmonious balance may begin to be felt as well as seen.

The one in need – and now experiencing some relief – probably is not aware of what is happening, but such a one knows within that a welcome sigh of relief is imminent.

As the intellect also must be satisfied as to the genuineness of the material becoming available – and of the one offering it – this testing, scrutinising process will proceed as the one in need asks, listens, watches, accepts and deliberates.

These words of caution addressed to one who can help do not imply that one should shrink from answering or responding to probing questions put forth. On the contrary! The True Responsibility that one feels, and the Commitment within one who can help, have established an attractive and sympathetic relative vibration that can be felt – sometimes consciously – by one in need. It is a vibration that says – almost overtly – 'I can help'; and when the overture is made, there is then created the obligation to respond. A refusal to respond to a sincere query can be just as disconcerting to one in need as a response or answer at the other extreme – that is, one that is overly responsive.

How does one who can help respond to a genuine 'overture'?

The response given must be with candour and truth – and this is important: it must be in accord with truth, *as it is then perceived* by the one responding. Any attempt to excuse one's reticence, or refusal to respond on the grounds that one has not yet reached a state of so-called 'full enlightenment', or has not yet perceived what one has preconceived to be some so-called 'ultimate truth', is in disharmony with the True Responsibility established upon one's own receipt of help.

It is also in disharmony with a universal principle of abundance, and such an attempt to avoid the responsibility to respond is unfair, unnerving, and unacceptable to one who not only needs help, but who has earned the right to that help by making an overture.

30 Refining the Communication

In the early stages when one who can offer help is approached by another who is opening in awareness and asks for help, and effort is put forth to respond to that overture, the gesture or answer offered in response may be in excess of that calm action or concise and tidy statement which, on reflection, would appear to have been sufficient.

How does the communication process work?

The response may, in fact, have been so apparently excessive in either content or enthusiasm that the one offering help may experience regret and self-recrimination for even having attempted to respond to the enquiry. It may even have happened that the exchange became heated, argumentative or demonstrative, as the one responding to the enquiry and trying to offer help fell prey to the temptation to attempt to convince another, either by 'proof' or reasoning, of the credibility of matters and points which, to the one responding, seemed blatantly obvious.

If it will be remembered that an exchange involving proof, argument, reasoning, and attempts to convince are obsolete aspects of a passing and outdated method of enquiry after truth, then it will also be seen that if one employs such devices in a discussion, as is under consideration here, one places oneself in a very precarious position: that is, of attempting to argue about matters of which there can be discussion but no argument; or of attempting to prove the truth of matters that need manifestation but no proof; and of attempting to convince another of the existence of matters that are already present within, but which one in need of help will not, or cannot, yet accept as being self-evident or self-existent.

Again, anyone who seeks to be convinced of that which is already beginning to be known within is still following a structured and obsolescent path and will seek in vain. And anyone who attempts to convince another of something that can be known only by one's own acceptance of what is known within wastes one's own energy and another's time.

How does 'perception' differ from 'understanding'?

Early on, it will be helpful to one responding to the needs of another to recognise another important key. This one is a key to the communication of the vital material and help to be imparted; that is,

> **no matter how the requested material is presented – even in response to a sincere and proper enquiry – there is no way that its essence, substance, or form can be 'understood' by another to whom it is presented – at least in the way that such a one is accustomed to 'understanding' thus far. It may be grasped; it may be seen; it may be perceived; or it may be felt; but it will not be 'understood'.**

The passing systems and methods of the quest for truth and enlightenment employ a force or a power that energises the devices of proof and argument. Contemporary 'understanding' of ideas, concepts, methods or philosophies is built and developed basically upon one of two procedures.

The first consists of subjugating, or replacing, that which is understood to be real or true in a responsive surrender to the impact of a presentation employing a stronger force or power.

The second consists of accepting a presentation based on a faith, often emotional and irrational, and the consequent abandonment of that which one previously understood to be real or true. This second procedure, when employed, necessarily supersedes and replaces the first, insofar as they disagree, and it is still basically foreign to and in conflict with most prevailing methods of contemporary learning and understanding.

Neither of these procedures is employed in the communication and acceptance of the vital and essential Material with which we are here concerned, for the Material presented herein does not deal with nor contain provable ideas, mental concepts or abstract philosophies; nor is this Material to be accepted like a creed that often asks one to accept or believe what one understands to be otherwise.

Rather, concern herein is with a communication that calls forth – harmoniously and gently – into external awareness and manifestation in everyday life that which is beginning to be known within – absent proof or faith – and which grows and expands in direct response and proportion to one's acceptance of its presence and vitality.

Such acceptance and manifestation transcend both proof and faith and are based upon a freedom to receive or reject in accordance only with that which is known within, and governed only by those criteria that are presently and momentarily constructed and personally uniquely essential at that time and for that purpose.

Further, this acceptance is evidenced by a doing – a doing of what is known; an externalisation of that which appears and is known within.

How does Communication work with the 'Soul within the Self'?

This communication operates both *between or among* two or more opening individual souls and *within* each opening individual soul.

Detailed comment on the latter aspect of this communication – that of the Soul within the Self – will be dealt with in a later chapter, but two observations are appropriate here concerning that aspect.

Firstly, the communication between or among individual souls through the physical, emotional or mental vehicles is merely a less refined manifestation of the communication of the Soul within the Self.

Secondly, as one begins to accept, work with, refine and manifest the communicative process of the Soul within the Self (including both the active manifestation of that which is communicated and the taking of responsibility for that which is manifested), then the protective (but fictitious) distinction of the Soul within the Self will begin to dissipate as morning mist in the sunlight of a new day. It is then that one can, and will, begin to dismantle the metaphors of separation or division in favour of the truth of oneness, including the disregard of the concept that one is a channel in favour of identification with the Source. More on these points later.

What happens when the Communication 'fails'?

Attention is now turned to communication between two opening souls: one who needs help, who has acknowledged that need, and who is receptive; and one who can help, who is now committed to do so, and who has been approached. More particularly, concern is now given to the possible discomfort experienced by one who has responded to the enquiry of another as carefully and correctly as is presently possible, but who is now disconcerted by the possibility that the exchange may apparently have failed. Excess concern, however, is not warranted, for the very nature of this encounter is such that neither its form, nature, nor outcome could have been anticipated.

Just as the responsive answer or action could not be 'understood' by one in need of help (so to speak), when received, neither could that response have been adequately 'prepared' (as it were) before it was given, at least in these early stages: such is the awesome price – and the delicate beauty – of spontaneity.

To be able to maintain constant preparedness and still respond spontaneously will require considerable effort, experience and control. Also, it requires an approach that may differ radically from that mode of operation to which one may have been accustomed.

When one who can help does respond to an enquiry which has arisen (perhaps unexpectedly), and does so with spontaneity, then discretion and discrimination may be lost for the moment. The response may exceed the bounds of propriety, candour and balance which one has previously defined for one's own conduct. If one responding to a query believes the exchange has 'failed' (so to speak) then, in the absence of self-control, great consternation or disturbance can arise within, precipitating or causing harsh self-criticism or even depression. Alas, detachment may also have been lost (if it were in fact ever present), else all could have been saved. But, as with evolutionary discrimination, detachment is still foreign to contemporary ways of most cultures on this planet, and to many who inhabit those cultures.

On reflection, one may become determined to become more watchful and aware and careful of what one says and does; and one thus embarks upon a path of mental and emotional rehabilitation which may occupy anything from a few seconds (in the most desirable instance) to days, weeks, or even months in the extreme. But let it be said in consolation that such self-criticism and dejection are unnecessary when even just a small amount of detached, objective analysis and resolve would suffice to enable one to regain at least a foothold on that essential balance.

Even in the most blatant or obtuse instance, it will be seen, in retrospect, that generally speaking, an answer that is excessive in either candour or length, or both, is preferable to the anguish that can result from leaving a sincere question or overture unanswered.

Only an unalterable and unshakeable confidence in that which is emerging from within the Self, coupled with the substantiating experience of manifestation – that is, the placing into practice that which is known within – can disintegrate this seed of potential doubt or discomfort that seems to sprout at each encounter or exchange.

How does one remain 'unrelentingly positive'?

Especially now, it is essential that one maintain a positive position, a position of unrelenting positivity, and a firm and steadfast (but gentle) reliance on that which is known within – *even as it appears to change and transform from moment-to-moment.*

It is by the adherence to the principles emerging from within and their practical application that the frequency and degree of such disturbing situations will be decreased. It is important to recognise now that the slightest wavering from such principles (or rather from the positive continuous flowing with life according to those emerging principles) will open the chance for one seeking help to question – and demand – answers according to procedures of understanding and explanation, to which such a one has been accustomed and which are now becoming evolutionarily obsolete and inoperable in such an exchange.

One who has been called upon for help will be well advised to carefully balance one's enthusiastic eagerness to impart help with a conservative reluctance to be compromised. It is well at this point to once again be reminded that the key is balance. The key to health, help, strength, expansion, harmony and communication is *balance*.

How does one develop 'balance and confidence within the Self'?

From a balanced and tranquil living with the flow of evolutionary principles emerging from within, there will emerge a growing self-confidence – *a true confidence in the Self* – that one will be well advised to preserve, protect and maintain at all costs.

Such confidence in the Self is nurtured with discrimination and tested by application, and its strength is in the knowingness that flows continuously from within the Self rather than from any results produced or conclusions drawn from the application.

> **It is this confidence in the Self and within the Self that serves as the true basis of communication from one to another – that is, either from one individual soul to another, or from the Source within the Self to the focal point of expression within the individual soul; for this self-confidence is a true manifestation of what one is – and is becoming – rather than what one says or does. It is thus in the being that real and complete communication is first made.**

How does one refine the ability to respond?

The refinement of the ability to respond – that is, the refinement of the ability to communicate precisely what is called for at any given moment by one in need (an individual soul, a tribe, a nation, a planet, or a universe) – is a process which is detailed and lengthy and actually forms a vital and integral part of one's evolutionary unfoldment. By its very nature, the refinement of this ability to respond cannot begin until there is an overture from one in need. It is at such a time that one being approached for help may recognise the responsibility to respond and communicate.

The first few occasions when one is approached and attempts to rise to the occasion can bring one quickly to the realisation that the ability to respond does indeed require refinement and deserve some positive effort and attention.

The assumption of the True Responsibility (with confidence and humility) is evolutionarily essential now in a time of transition, when a different process of imparting of the vital knowledge is emerging to correct an imbalance and offer a way of opening to truth and enlightenment uniquely adaptive to contemporary needs.

If one who can help takes such a step, that is, the assumption of True Responsibility (a step that can have some dynamic effects) a new dimension is experienced and a transition stage is entered. This is a time of particularly unique unfoldment and refinement of the ability to respond and communicate, and each one who voluntarily takes that step must manifest a way of Communication according to one's own unique role in the emergence of a new consciousness. This is a time when an abundance of exuberance, eagerness – and impatience – may be felt.

It is a time when one will be well and wisely advised to keep the hands and mind well occupied in some gentle and creative activity to divert some of the enthusiasm felt in the desire to share the awakening with others, lest one fall prey to the temptation to proselytise or evangelise, or perhaps meddle or intrude where one has not been invited.

It is true that what is growing within is to be shared, but it should be remembered that it is to be shared only when the proper overture has been made. Gentle creative manual activity will at this time help one to be patient and assist one to open and unfold at a comfortable pace and in a balanced manner. A radical alteration in lifestyle, such as ascetic withdrawal or impatient attempts to accelerate expansion, may precipitate a disturbance in that precious equilibrium which must be maintained to fulfil not only one's own purpose, but also the responsibility to those with whom one must communicate what one is carrying and manifesting.

It will be in observing such a day-to-day activity or occupation of one who is opening and can offer help that will afford to one who may need help some of the most effective and essential assistance, suggestions and example that one can encounter.

If it is recognised and remembered that the one in need of help may be desperate, frustrated and confused, it can be seen that what may be bestowed on such a one by observing the activities of one who can help is, rather than knowledge itself, an opening of an attitude – an essential attitude – one precursing respect, and engendering a kind of identification. And it is from just such an attitude that the first cautious – and perhaps trembling – overture will be made.

Communication can then begin.

31   Resolving the Dilemma

It is now appropriate to discuss the nature of the relationship between the one opening and the one who can help; to mention some of the dynamic consequences of the initiation and evolution of such a relationship; and to acquire some perception of the nature of the constant change, redirection and redefinition to which those consequences will be subjected. Attention will then be turned to matters concerning the Inner Discipline necessary to express and implement various aspects of a new consciousness.

How does one opening avoid 'immature influences'?

At this point, it should first be acknowledged that one who is opening in awareness might be in a fragile and vulnerable state or condition. It is both natural and necessary for one opening to exercise great care and caution in the acceptance of any help which is offered or which becomes available, especially suggestions, direction or so-called 'guidance' which appear to come from 'within'.

There do exist immature energies, manifestations of energies, entities and channels which seek the opportunities found in the vulnerability of one opening, and which are eager to take advantage of that vulnerability. These energies and entities may attempt to undermine a growing but tenuous confidence in that which is known within, in order to enlist one to purposes other than those which are in complete harmony with the optimum possibilities to which one is opening.

For a need to be properly met and fulfilled, it must be mature and ripe. One opening who attempts to assuage one's own need prematurely may inadvertently open to such immature or self-serving influences. One opening is wise to refrain, insofar as possible, from engaging or indulging in conjecture, speculation or assumption. If a need is allowed to fully mature, one can experience an objective knowing as well as a subjective feeling of true need opening to be fulfilled to its optimum potential.

A need prematurely appeased is never fully satisfied; the appetite may be placated, but the hunger remains. An objective knowing, which emerges from restraint, enables the need to peak and to open to total fulfilment in humble receptiveness. This knowing also precludes or minimises the possibility of interference or intrusion by immature influences or entities which may seek to serve a motive or a purpose other than that residing in and expressed from within the True Self. That which manifests to fulfil a mature need from within the True Self is replete with the Ring of Perfection found in genuineness – free of any shadow or shallow complacence found in mere reflection.

How does one balance the offer to help without being intrusive?

One who is opening in awareness – who is frustrated by desperate need – must also refrain from rashly concluding that another can help simply because of the possession of, or display, of qualifications that may seem impressive, or accomplishments that allegedly empower one to be of help to another. One who can truly help in the really vital matters will impress not with the display of past accomplishments, or even present abilities, but rather with a radiance of integrity. Such a one will be characterised by the calmness to await the first overture from one in true need and will not forcefully evangelise a position or a belief.

One who can truly help will not ask or advise that anything offered be accepted blindly in faith or trust, but will encourage one opening to rely solely on that which is known and felt and sensed, and seen deep within the Self.

Following the initial contact or exchange between the one opening and the one who can help, there will most probably be little, if any, recognition or acknowledgement by one opening that the exchange has in any way been extraordinary. But, with the exchange, a seed has been planted; an attraction may begin to grow. One opening may have a realisation that this new source of help may certainly have or know something which one opening must soon acquire.

This realisation may have important and far-reaching consequences that one opening could not possibly anticipate. By such a realisation, the one opening and initially characterised by an attitude of suspicion, eccentricity, desperation or scepticism, may overcome these obstacles and the blindness of a self-sufficiency grounded or based in a mere reflection, and acknowledge the exchange as an event of significance.

> **Now, all is in readiness. What happens now – at this point – to one whose awareness is opening is perhaps one of the most dynamic experiences that one may ever have.**

The nature of the enquiry forming within one opening is much more than a mere casual fleeting whim or fancy. It is different from any other question or venture ever put forth.

Mere contact with the one who can help, the conscious acknowledgement that a new and different relationship is to be formed as a result of the initial exchange, an emerging awareness that a continued exchange may precipitate a complete transformation – all of these may cause one's mental, emotional and even physical location to shift involuntarily and even, perhaps, traumatically.

That which authority, argument, faith, analysis, desperation, discipline, desire – and even love – have thus far failed to accomplish, has happened in the flash of an instant due to mere contact or exchange with one who can help.

This is a very delicate time for one opening, and a different sensation may begin to descend – a feeling of some disconcertion or discomfort, yet, concurrently, a feeling of a strange pleasantness.

What is now happening to one opening is beyond the realm of one's present confines of comprehension: any attempt to analyse or understand it at this time will be totally lost and in vain. All efforts and energies are now expended solely in experiencing and expanding, and there is precious little left available for deliberation or comprehension. That which is being expressed and experienced is beyond anything in the circuits of learned knowledge or the recorded memory of events or analysis.

One is being swept forth on a growing wave of an unfolding awareness, devoid of any relevance to a remembered past and not yet projectable into an unformed and as yet undetailed and unpredictable future: an awareness meaningful only to the eternal present.

How will one who needs help relate to one who can help?

On opening, one may feel an indefinable and thrilling attraction to this new contact – the one who can help. Such a feeling may be in stark contrast to that which one may have experienced in the initial contact. The feeling may be one of near obsession prompting one to be irresistibly drawn to be in close proximity to the one who can help – in physical presence, emotional rapport or mental communication.

Then, just as a tenuous trust begins to form, one may experience a strange sensation of reactionary disbelief – or ambivalence – and all this in a relatively short time, as one may begin to lose one's delicate grip on one's own previously defined and jealously guarded concept of a nebulous and unreal reality.

What is the 'dilemma' which one will face?

At this time, on opening one may find that activities and relationships of just a short time earlier now seem to be unimportant or irrelevant – devoid of any meaning, but still anachronistically existent. One may feel a loss of direction, a perception of the unimportance of prior pursuits. There may occur a spontaneous and abrupt change of sustenance – physical, emotional or mental – a craving for some previously undesired experience or an alteration in procreative drive or practices.

There may occur a period of intense sorrow, or guilt, or depression or of inadequacy – and many more manifestations and phenomena of change and transformation of awareness as space begins to assume new dimension, and time begins to warp and lose its meaning. Memory may begin to falter or fail, interrupting some activity in mid-stream. Incomplete thoughts may be interspersed with illuminative flashes of revealing insight. Emotions may rage temporarily out of control; formerly reliable reasoning or decision-making processes may begin to miscarry and prove deficient. One may cringe with a new perception of the inconsideration, cruelty and selfishness rampant throughout creation – and especially in one's own conduct.

One may even begin to feel that one is 'different', cosmically misplaced, alone, or 'strange'. Depression may set in, followed by unbounded joy attendant on an exhilarating release – and all this perhaps accompanied by alternating elation, self-enquiry, doubt, perception, and so on.

How can one opening resolve this dilemma?

One may attempt to relieve some anxiety by engaging in a distraction or pursuing a diversion, and in all probability this will be effective for a time: some new extracurricular activity, some new exploration or creation, some renewed dedication to one's work or profession. Each of these will delay or divert for a time, but when one looks (and inevitably one must look), the dilemma is still there. One knows that one must eventually take notice of its existence.

Following a series of attempted moves, inside or out, towards something more satisfying, challenging or comfortable, one may turn to the condemnation of one's creation, culture or values – or lack of them. This process of search can occupy an extended period, sometimes agonising, and seemingly endless.

This syndrome of reaction may be initial, but it will most probably also be cyclical or recurring in its nature – that is, one may feel that which is described above all in a flash or in a very short time, or over a period of time; but it may also be experienced in an ever-expanding and reappearing pattern, as one continues to burst and break free of ever-surfacing obsolete physical practices, emotional habits and mental concepts.

If one can recognise this simple syndrome or process at an early juncture, it will help facilitate easier release and detached expansion at other moments of opening.

On opening, one may or may not place a connection between these experiences or phenomena and the one who can help with whom contact, re-contact or an exchange has taken place. If one fails to perceive a connection, one may seek understanding, comfort or help from any of several sources or devices – including immature energies or entities – many of which will respond with empty or irrelevant explanations.

There may follow an experience of acute frustration, or even anger or fear, for one is entering a space totally unfamiliar, ground personally untrodden. All attempts to associate such experience with anything at all previously familiar – relationships, feelings, sensations, or knowledge of any kind – will be totally in vain. It may seem that there is no consolation available, no help forthcoming, no remnant remaining of that which was formerly considered to be concrete, familiar and real.

While it may be that one blessed with the grace of detachment may negotiate the assimilation of this new awareness or adapt to a transformation unscathed, still, for one experiencing these more traumatic circumstances, it can all be terribly frightening, as each and every bastion of support appears to crumble and fall away. Possibly, health or stability may also become shaky or deteriorate. A vision or fear of insanity or incapacity may descend upon one who was once haughty, proud, or secure in rebellion, eccentricity or fictitious self-sufficiency, but who is now humble and contrite and perhaps desperate in a depressing quandary of seemingly inexplicable solitude.

What is it that has happened to one opening and now perhaps facing a perplexing predicament? One has not yet lost one's capacity to maintain stability, but as a result of the operation of a number of evolutionary factors and opportunities, one's external consciousness has been subjected to a radical and involuntary shift. One has been temporarily, but emphatically, deprived of one's balance that was previously focused comfortably, though tenuously, in a familiar venue, where the swirl of one's personal evolution coursed in relatively predictable patterns. The balance has now displaced to a field of higher and finer vibrations, rendering the former venue, and the activities therein, empty and listless. The move was in fact predictable, in essence if not in detail; but anyone tenaciously clinging to the familiar would be blinded to the indications.

What happens when one faces the dilemma?

One is now at a juncture facing several possibilities, the selection or determination of which can be of momentous consequence. It is at this point that one opening can voluntarily exercise an important option: to introduce a positive flow to extract one from a seemingly interminable or recurring torturous dilemma.

The dilemma: one must face the decision whether to flow forth with an elusive equilibrium or to rely on one's own present abilities, one's own devices, manufactured and grounded in a fictitious self-sufficiency now only a remnant from a past balance rendered empty by evolutionary necessity.

If one acknowledges an inability to cope with the shifting circumstance with available devices and humbly determines to open to the flow, then the Presence which can manifest in force or form to correct an imbalance or establish a new equilibrium can be available on solicitous request.

The decision to seek help can virtually determine one's immediate future and direction, as well as the termination of one's obligation to labour under the burden of infinite inevitable consequences, and it can determine the positive unfoldment of one's contractual destiny.

As one is facing this dilemma, it is possible that one may experience a temporary remission, a spontaneous diminishing of the pressure, a respite from the dilemma. The situation may appear to simplify as the initial burst of confusion abates, leaving one with the relatively comfortable, but totally erroneous, idea that the entire experience is – and has been – nothing but a disagreeable and temporary fantasy.

Such, of course, unfortunately, is not the case.

As a consequence of this temporary remission, one may recover – or devise – enough stability, based on the still available echoing reverberations of a former balance, to encounter yet another aspect of the dilemma; that is, whether to probe further and to try to determine if in fact there do exist any answers and reasonable explanations for what one has recently experienced.

The apparent alternative is to more comfortably, if possible, ignore what has transpired and make an attempt to recapture a former balance by actively pursuing what was formerly considered to be a 'normal' existence. From the created realm of one's existence (that realm which seeks to enjoy the present state and resists change), one may be encouraged to follow this latter course; that is, to attempt to disregard what has happened.

This resistance is merely a manifestation of fear on the part of one who cannot yet see, who does not yet know, and who regards the inclination to probe further as a threat to a present condition which, although somewhat or sometimes uncomfortable, is still familiar and preferable to some allegedly improved, but as yet unimaginable and indescribable, alternative.

From within, however, the prompting may be otherwise: one opening may feel the urging to forge ahead; to pursue the elusive equilibrium; to open to the Positive flow; to seek the *answer*.

This dilemma must be resolved *from within*; it cannot be directed from without; and it cannot be resolved rationally.

This determination to resolve the dilemma may well be the first instance of a decision based on what is known within the Self.

32   *Recognising Inner Discipline*

> Inner Discipline enables one to move, to act, to manifest a positive response. The absence of Inner Discipline leaves one opening susceptible and vulnerable to influences from without – influences which plant the seeds of doubt and which may, even from an early moment, discourage one from engaging in a search for answers for which there do not appear to be any questions.

Although an early 'alternative reality' experience may be authentic in its occurrence, still, the memory of it may fade, and one may feel that further search will lend credence and substance to the fear that indeed there may not be any answers.

A small hidden voice from the silence within may ask gently, 'But what of that momentary elation? What of that glimpse of the unexplored – that thrilling and awesome glance at the unfamiliar?'

Only one of strong resolve and discipline will listen – one free of distraction, one able to move at the most subtle suggestion. The pull is powerful to turn back, and many do – at least for the present. And so it goes.

Anyone opening who does turn back in an attempt to reassemble from a fragmented memory an antiquated and stagnant former state of balance will find the respite short-lived. As one evolves in one's personal time-span spectrum, the vitality of the energy of an opening awareness increases, further reducing the significance of obsolete prior pursuits. Any attempt to restrict the opening – either from within or without – will enlarge and aggravate the imbalance.

If one does effectively refuse to open to the flow from within and delay acknowledgement of that which is emerging, one may experience the descent of a silent but disquieting inertia, during which existence assumes the form of a trite and insipid regularity and repetitive meaninglessness. The ability to delay the opening and restrict the flow will be influenced and determined by one's own personal time-span spectrum, by universal evolutionary events, and by the needs of others opening in awareness, who must eventually turn for help to the very one now attempting to delay one's own opening, growth, availability, and acceptance of responsibility.

One who does, however, resolve to commit effort and energy towards opening to the Positive flow will recognise that Inner Discipline is essential – a primary and elementary step – before one can proceed upon the path upon which one is now embarking.

How does one combine Discrimination with Discipline?

Early on, as one's awareness began to open and expand, one may have developed quite some acute ability to discard something to which one could no longer relate – something that may have become personally obsolete. Such items may have become distasteful as well as unnecessary, and discarding them was painless, effortless and perhaps vigorous. Rejection and release at such moments are almost automatic, requiring little, if any, will or discipline. Such action is characteristic of one whose awareness is opening but still immature.

In contrast, one whose awareness is opening and maturing – one in transition – will become increasingly able to emotionlessly and objectively part with something or terminate a relationship to which one still has some attachment. One is thus beginning to apply discrimination and develop some Inner Discipline.

Further, one whose awareness, discrimination, and discipline are mature can intentionally initiate a severance or departure, with detachment – and compassion.

What are the 'abilities' one must develop in this Transition?

As one's awareness opens and grows and matures in transition, there are two abilities that one will develop.

- **The first** of these is the ability to recognise and acknowledge that the time has arrived for a release.
- **The second** is the ability to exercise the discipline to undertake the release or engage in any positive action.

It is this second of these abilities that we will now discuss.

When one's opening awareness is still relatively immature, one's behaviour may be rebellious, demonstrative and disturbing. One's rejection of items or matters deemed to be disdainful or disagreeable is often violent. To an unopened or untrained eye, such behaviour is apparently chaotic and unrestrained. Such performance may, however, actually be systematic, in a primitive or 'negative' way.

What is denoted here by 'negative' is conduct that is primarily destructive or disruptive concerning the object of the conduct, but which may be positive or constructive in the nature of the conduct itself: a chaos in which there is in fact some order. Therein, one may find the first seeds of the trait of discipline that one may wish to cultivate.

Following any resolve or determination of purpose must come discipline, if purpose is to be placed into action. One opening in awareness in a time of transition must continuously, through discrimination, clear away existing but obsolescent frameworks, concepts, references, ideas, beliefs and practices, as well as manifestations thereof.

In the most desirable instance, one will do so gently, systematically, and purposefully; although this may be too much to expect of one in whom the opening has just begun. On opening, one is cultivating the ability to place resolve, determination and purpose into action. Therefore, concern is now not so much with what one's conduct has been, but rather with how effectively one has gone about doing what has been done.

What is the essential ingredient in developing Inner Discipline?

The question one must ask oneself is:

To what degree has one effectively developed the ability to determine a purpose or course of action and thence to proceed on that chosen path?

This is the essence of a continuing self-enquiry by one opening to accept responsibility, as well as of the enquiry asked by one who can help of one in need. In other words, without regard to the object of the action, *how strongly has one developed any Inner Discipline that is available for any intended purpose*?

If one has developed this discipline well, then it is possible that one need only gently redirect it towards new purpose.

If one has overdeveloped this discipline, that in itself may become a distraction, especially when one moves to action with rigidity or with military severity; or when one's circuits of action are so crystallised as to prevent one from exercising the flexibility needed for one to be discriminating.

More often, on opening one may have allowed whatever discipline one might have had to lapse into dormancy or to degenerate into inactive oblivion. One might expect little else when one feels to be in imminent danger of losing contact with the familiar and the comfortable. At such time, all one's available energy and effort is expended towards maintaining a precarious handhold on some sort of nebulous reality, leaving very little to be utilised in any manner intentionally chosen. Indeed, that which one has believed to be one's self is literally fighting, and apparently losing, a battle for survival itself. One has, at such time, abandoned action and is engaged in reaction.

What happens when one cannot muster discipline into action?

There are other instances in which one will have little discipline available for positive action.

One is where, on opening, one is acutely perceptive and rebellious and identifies the quality of discipline with what one wishes to reject. In such an event, discipline itself may have been rejected in favour of a slothful and unregulated style of existence.

Another is where one has chosen a path in which one is urged to surrender one's will to another, and in so doing, one descends into a lethargic state of inaction.

While it is necessary and desirable for one opening to relinquish those motives and actions that proceed from selfish personal ambition, still the emerging and growing identification with the source within the Self will call forth a mature blending of lower motive with higher will. One's resulting transformation of purpose and ultimate potential, then, will rest gently above, awaiting the exercise of concerted disciplined action to manifest them in service to an evolving omniverse.

Even to someone with an unopened or untrained eye, it should appear obvious that resolution without discipline is an empty gesture, and the inevitable consequence will be inaction and frustration at the inability to carry forth that which one has determined to do. For one opening in awareness, the path is fraught with ubiquitous distraction, as the grip and pull of past fruitless ventures and attachments seem to compete with more current and important pursuits.

How is determination without discipline an 'empty gesture'?

The absence of discipline within deprives one opening of one of the most basic foundations upon which any movement or action will be based, and one will be assured of extensive delay and frustration from the outset.

Even if one is graced with a degree of humility and has found the way to one who can help, still, any suggestions offered, even if accepted, will fall unused in the absence of the discipline to place them into action – and the efforts of both will be for naught.

If one is to be of help, then, it is essential that one candidly and honestly recognise the degree to which this characteristic of discipline is present in one opening in awareness and who is in need of help.

This essential quality of discipline – the ability to move; to *do* – can come only from within one opening; it cannot be imparted by another. It can be demonstrated, encouraged and strengthened, but it cannot be imparted.

The discipline discussed in these notes is not a hard line, authoritarian restraint which seeks to dominate and control, but rather it is an orderly and harmonious blending of potential with will in the devoted service of manifesting what is needed and called forth by one in need – whether that one in need be an opening soul, a tribe, a nation, a planet or a universe.

How does one who can help assist in the development of Inner Discipline?

One who can help can only point out the need for recognition, presence, and development of discipline, but the effort must come from one opening who aspires to discriminatingly place resolve into action. Once one has made a firm and complete commitment within, resolved the dilemma, and made a determination to flow with the positive unfolding to accept responsibility, then importance will be accorded only to that which one is able to manifest into action. No amount of resolve can replace the smallest amount of disciplined action.

How then is such a quality of Discriminatory Discipline to be nurtured and developed?

- **Firstly**, on opening one must candidly recognise the necessity and importance of Inner Discipline and honestly self-assess one's present ability to place resolve into action.
- **Secondly**, one must then be prepared to set forth at least the required resolve or declaration of intent and purpose to unfold and amplify and cultivate one's Inner Discipline in its fullness.

Are there any short cuts?

These points may seem elementary, but there may be a latent tendency which, if allowed to grow, will encourage one aspiring to great heights to attempt to locate or construct methods or devices whereby an end can be accomplished without the expenditure of the required effort. This tendency towards seeking a shorter path may serve one well in the pursuit of former activities and matters *other* than those to which one is opening and which form the core and substance of this Material.

For one seeking short cuts, or for one attempting to divide one's efforts or attention between the matters of an opening awareness and matters of distraction, there are available methods devised by those who claim to have found or constructed means which allegedly will produce desired results without the need for the disciplined expenditure of the required effort, or which means are employed for purposes other than those which are in harmony with a complete unfolding. Anyone seeking such means or methods should seek the company in which they are found.

However, one committed to a complete unfolding need apply only slight, honest and truthful introspection to perceive that in what is to be a complete and thorough opening to and manifestation of what is known within, the nature and degree of this undertaking leave no leeway to expect any results from methods which deviate in any manner from a full and proper expenditure of effort and disciplined action.

The essence of this Material gives no sway to any such methods of short cut, short circuit or distraction, nor to one who would seek or practise any way other than one in which the unfolding is totally thorough and complete.

33 *Developing Inner Discipline*

> One who is opening in awareness, and who has determined to develop the Inner Discipline to place resolve into action, but whose self-reliance is less than complete, and whose confidence is less than secure, may recognise the present state of one's own discipline, acknowledge the need for help, and humbly seek assistance from one who can help; that is, one whose own discipline is sufficiently developed and stable as to be an example to one seeking to develop discipline.

How does one move from 'reaction' to 'creation'?

On opening and experiencing the changes and transformation in this time of transition, one may have been – or may be – encased in a cyclical syndrome of negative reaction and inevitable consequence. That is, rather than being able to discriminatingly create and manifest a positive course of action, one may be at the mercy of events, at the mercy of one's circuits, buffeted about by changes which arise and transpire seemingly beyond the reach of positive conscious control.

So long as one is at the mercy of events, one can do little but react to the events or inevitable consequences as they arise. Perhaps, the only positive aspect of these reactions has been the positive consistency by and with which one almost obliviously discarded items that had become personally obsolete.

In this consistency of rejective reaction, there lies dormant a subtle suggestion of a positive approach that forms a basis for the development of a positive and creative Inner Discipline. The first emergence of this positive approach will still be one of repudiation, but it can begin to be positive in form even if it is negative in substance; that is, even though it is still negative, in that it is one of rejection, disassociation or disintegration, it may begin to be positive in that it becomes *intentional* rather than instinctively reactive.

Confusion and frustration may still predominate. The order found in natural degeneration and rejection, as well as a view of any assertive approach, will be lost to the untrained and naive eye that is just beginning to open. The present unavailability of obsolete emotional reactions in which one may formerly have found comfort and taken refuge may leave one numbed by its abysmal vacuum.

As layers of concepts, sheaths of conduct, and the burden and weight of redundant conclusions, assumptions, emotions and activities fall away, one will lose whatever moment-to-moment awareness one may have had, as well as whatever one may have previously developed in the way of an ability to exercise a moment-to-moment discipline.

One who has determined to complete the transition, become self-determining, and participate in the change of consciousness is approaching the completion of a particular cycle of personal evolutionary development and will be influenced by the approach of the completion of this personal cycle, as well as by the approaching end of a planetary and universal cycle and by the approaching implementation of a change of consciousness.

How does one increase the ability to deal with inevitable consequences?

In the early opening and unfoldment of awareness, during which one almost certainly still relates to time and space, the growing Positive Presence of light brings forth both an acceleration of events and, as will be described later, the increasingly growing ability to meet and deal with these events.

In this early opening, one may be experiencing that which appears to be a personal time compression; that is, a period of the expansion and upliftment of awareness during which one's personal evolutionary inevitable consequences and events seem to occur or be presented more rapidly than had previously been experienced.

To state the matter differently, as one begins to open in awareness and experience this personal time compression, the events of personal evolutionary inevitable consequence may arise, educe a personal reactive change or adjustment, and then be dispatched with an increasingly greater rapidity than that to which one may have previously been accustomed.

At this time, one may not be afforded the luxury of time or opportunity to assess or assimilate the results or lessons of such events, even if one had the abilities to make such an assessment.

Life and existence in the transition, in this period when time seems to be compressed, may be completely occupied and filled, ruled and controlled by the fulfilment of the baser desires and needs attendant to caring for the physical vehicles of expression. Even their needs may arise and evaporate before they can be accommodated. Or, once a craving or a need is served, enjoyment or satisfaction may still remain empty or elusive.

There may be suggestions that a natural corrective healing process is beginning to emerge from within the Self: a process of true healing that not only corrects and cures, but which also restores full soundness and establishes a new equilibrium.

On opening one is called upon to simultaneously attend to the more basic needs as they are, or have been known for the physical bodies, and to cope with newly arising needs, and the constant surfacing of new or heretofore latent emotions, and the presentation of new concepts, possibilities and realities not previously considered or even available.

Some of the experiences and changes that occur involve alterations in blood chemistry, endocrine gland secretions, and the general physiological and evolutionary modifications precipitated by the introduction of light and the necessity for one to assimilate and implement the dawning of a new and expanded awareness in transition towards the advent of a new consciousness.

With the increasing positive presence of light, the opening of an awareness within, the emergence of an ability to move within in strength, and the Grace of Liberation from the Wheel of Bondage which is shared at the proper time, likewise, as mentioned above, there will occur an increase in one's ability to cognitively and intentionally examine and deal with each event of inevitable consequence. Further, there will occur an increase in one's ability to directly perceive, assess and assimilate the subtler meanings and consequences of each event and its disposition, as one is ever more able to view those events with detachment.

How does one adapt to the increasing flow of events?

One is now approaching a juncture at which a matter of importance may be observed. It is a simple but subtle matter to which allusion has been made, and it is sufficient if one only glimpses the essence of what is now to be described.

As restraints fall away, one may recognise, as described above, that one is being swept along by a flow of cosmic events which seems to be moving at an ever-accelerating pace quite beyond one's conscious or intentional control.

At this point, it is sufficient if one can recognise only this much of the principle. If one can see this much, one may be able to perceive the purpose towards which one is moving; that is, the increasingly conscious and intentional development of an Inner Discipline that enables one first to accept, acquiesce in, and adapt to this flow, and thence to convert and transform this flow of evolutionary events and inevitable consequences from a flow along and upon which one is being swept, and which is characterised by negative and involuntary reaction, to one of *positive and intentional creativity*.

At this point, it is sufficient only to glimpse this principle; it is not necessary, nor perhaps possible, to grasp it, retain it or analyse it.

How does one convert 'involuntary reaction' to 'intentional creative action'?

It will be useful now to examine some steps that can be taken to enable one to convert involuntary reaction to intentional creative action.

The Inner Discipline called for to be developed now is that which enables one to act, or initiate action, called forth by some experience, event, or change without one being able to comprehend the purpose of that action, and – further – without being able to perceive how it may be relevant to the subsequent change, action, or experience or consequence.

Although the desired action is, in the beginning, elicited by an event, it is intended that the action should become *responsive* rather than *reactive*. As the Inner Discipline is maturing, the action will be elicited by a need rather than an event. When it is mature, one can move to creative action, free of stimulus.

Previously, when facing an imminent change, one may have employed a process loosely referred to as 'reason' or 'rationalisation' in an attempt to anticipate events and consequences, and to plot and decide upon a course of action. The dismantling of this antiquated decision-making process will be discussed and examined in detail later.

At this time however, one may recognise that what have previously been reliable guidelines for moving to action, and processes for introspection, deliberation, thought, memory, and decision-making are becoming unreliable, or are disintegrating, or have simply become non-existent. They have not as yet been replaced, and anyone who waits for them to be replaced from anywhere except from within, and with anything except with that which is truly new – that is, devoid of any resemblance to or reference to any previously employed guidelines or the limitations found therein – waits in vain.

In contrast to previous personal procedures, one is unable, it seems, to justify actions by anticipating consequences, for the consequences themselves, even if apparently correctly foreseen, may transform even as the actions, if undertaken, are placed into operation. An obsolete reality, once stable, concrete and reliable, has suddenly become fluid and uncomfortably impermanent. Hence, this obsolescent reasoning process that has only the values and structure of a system no longer personally operable begins to fail, and perhaps surrenders in despair.

With this deterioration of rationalisation, a new process and new criteria are demanded, for one may be encountering answers to which there are as yet no questions; concepts for which there are as yet no meanings; actions for which there are as yet no reasons. One may grope for direction looking perhaps to discrimination – *Evolutionary Discrimination* – a new and different process now emerging from within, but which is still largely abstract, immature and incomplete. Discrimination is thus largely ineffectual of and by itself, as no framework or pattern can be found upon which to build or establish any bases of reference from which to move, or foundations to which one can relate; and one in transition probably still moves to action from frameworks, patterns, bases or foundations.

Being unable to quickly and effectively complete the transition from rationalisation to discrimination, one looks to some procedure, some approach, some discipline as it has been known. Once again, one looks in vain, for any previously employed discipline system may have been coupled with the obsolete process of rationalisation. Or it may have been formulated by environment. Or it may have been imposed by intimidation or pressure from some external authority. Any such system will now be foreign to one's present needs; but any new and emerging Inner Discipline is as yet immature and incomplete.

How does this move one towards a new reality?

One's opening and growth are now truly moving towards a new, different, and unimaginable reality. One is blossoming through a cosmic adolescence, as it were. One is pressed to accept a new and different value system, filled with unfamiliar criteria. It may appear to one who temporarily slips into the viewing of matters in an obsolete way that, until a new system or approach becomes settled, there is nothing upon which to act, and that attempts to develop a discipline will be empty gestures.

As guidelines and references are changing from moment-to-moment, the very nature of the present state of fluid uncertainty invites discouragement, depression, inaction and lethargy. One may feel at a complete loss how to even choose a course of action or conduct, let alone muster the wherewithal to follow it. For one in such a state of confusion, or perhaps even chaos or derangement, a self-discipline, an *Inner Discipline*, may offer the only prospect of relief, and that relief is not available until that first step is taken, even as irrational or '*arational*' as it may appear.

Until the first step is taken, that is until the first step is taken in each instance in which one encounters the confusion, even the purpose of the necessity of the first step itself will not become visible or evident.

Although this first step can be encouraged by one who can help, it cannot be determined, ordered, formulated or imposed from without. One must alone, from within, determine and initiate the first step of Inner Discipline.

If one views the first step of Inner Discipline from where one stands in confusion and attempts to justify it in a conventional way, the step to be taken will appear irrational and futile. Its purpose will not be perceived until after it is taken or set in motion – perhaps long after. Understandably, one can become discouraged and lethargic, as constantly fluctuating demands are being made upon one's awareness and judgement. New standards, criteria and concepts present themselves and perhaps then remove themselves at seemingly accelerating intervals, and one is pressed to keep abreast of the rapid pace of change.

If one can express the will to take this first step of initiating a seemingly purposeless disciplined action in each instance where one encounters confusion, one may perceive that it is Inner Discipline itself now which must develop and regulate itself, prompting and executing immediately and without question or analysis that action called forth from within at any given moment, even though opposite and apparently contradictory action may be called for the very next moment, and even if one can predict, anticipate or directly perceive and foresee the nature of the imminent contradictory action.

It is important to see now that what is essential is *action* which proceeds from an Inner Discipline able to initiate that action independently; that is, from within, free of external influence, including the influence of one's own circuits, and especially the influence of the circuits of the rationalisation process of the mind.

How can 'acknowledgement' initiate the necessary changes?

If one views the matter rationally or conventionally, the wiser course may appear to be a suspension of action or activity, a delay, in a seeming anticipation of the availability of a new and settled set of standards or permanent criteria. Thus, one may vacillate from one approach to the other; that is, at one moment one may move from a restrained and calculating rational approach, which is breaking down despite the attempt on the part of the rational mind to justify it. To one opening, this approach will correctly appear to be cumbersome, undependable and obsolescent.

At another moment, one may begin to move from disciplined action which proceeds from a 'knowingness' within the Self, constantly moving from an ever-new first step which refuses to be shaped or determined exclusively by prior events or crystallised circuits.

Inherent in this ability to move with the first step of disciplined action, is that first step taken long ago: that of acknowledging the need for help and opening to the help given now facilitating a constantly increasing flow of positive and transformative light energy, which expands one's awareness as it is accepted and manifested into action.

It is that moment, that instant, when what is known within the Self flashes through with its *ring of truth*, that the unquestioning Inner Discipline must be present and strong, ready to move, to act. With that flash that carries the *ring of genuineness* will come an instantaneous determination and resolve, with which all parts and dimensions of the integrated being are in harmony.

One who is opening, and whose awareness, discrimination, and discipline are maturing, will become increasingly able to act upon what is perceived in that instant, as it becomes manifest from deep within the Self.

34 Access

One who is opening in awareness and developing discipline, and in whom detachment is also beginning to emerge and mature, will perceive that the action called for, although disciplined, is not necessarily impulsive.

To integrate effectively the knowing, the perception and the action, and harmoniously orchestrate the timing of the manifestation to fulfil a need, one must be perfectly balanced within and confident that mature – or maturing – discrimination and discipline will be constantly and comfortably present.

Effective timing will develop with increased application of discipline as one transcends the apparent time-warp syndrome and its attendant problems.

What is the difference between 'intentional action' and 'impulsive reaction'?

Present concern is primarily placed on the ability to deliberately and intentionally act upon that which is perceived in the moment of insight, rather than the ability to impulsively react within the moment. In the first instance, discrimination is always comfortably present; in the latter it is disconcertingly absent.

Action proceeding from Inner Discipline is therefore deliberate, inspired, intentional and genuinely spontaneous. Impulsive reaction is involuntary, instinctive and automatic – even defensive, or fearful. Hence, an immovable and unassailable foundation of Inner Discipline must be established. If it is not, one opening will be challenged at every turn, and one's demeanour and perspective may become stagnant, inert and inflexible.

The implementation of light depends on the expression of a disciplined will to keep moving with that ever-important first step, and to do this,

> *the one most important ingredient that one must develop is the ability and the Inner Discipline to completely, instantaneously, unquestioningly and continuously adapt to change.*

An increasing and ever-widening constant awareness gives rise to ever-increasing ability to perceive the changes to which one must adapt. And an attitude of detachment gives rise to an ever-increasing ability to adapt to those changes. If one can express the Inner Discipline, discrimination, and detachment to adapt constantly, continuously, and gently, the ensuing adjustments are easily and harmoniously synchronised and assimilated. To do this, one must be firmly set on a path of self-obedience, self-control, self-reliance and self-determination; but, if viewed rationally and conventionally, it may appear to be a path of confusion, frustration, and, apparently, one of imminent self-destruction.

Such a course requires the emergence and development of a personal system of total, airtight, ironclad Inner Discipline which is constantly being refined, redefined, and reformulated to regulate its own growth and development. With the development of an Inner Discipline, there can be disciplined action; and with disciplined action there can be true growth. And the deliberate and truly spontaneous application of this developing Inner Discipline can be effective only if employed within the concept of true growth.

How has the concept of 'growth' become obsolete?

It will be helpful at this point to examine this concept of true growth. But firstly, let us take a look at that conventional view of growth which is to be laid aside.

Conventionally or traditionally, growth is generally viewed to be a progressing or moving from one point to another, during which various accoutrements are gathered and accumulated. In this context, someone growing is expected, often by the imposition of some pre-defined or externally imposed control, to progress towards a goal or a state or a desired end. Such so-called 'growth' is expected to take place in the face of certain odds and in the midst of a competitive atmosphere and environment.

Such a view of growth is considered 'progressive' by those ensconced in a system that exemplifies it and which accepts its definitions and limitations. So-called 'progress' within such a system, that is, working towards the goal or desired end state, is worthy of commendation in this system if it is judged laudable by the values of the system or by another in the system supposedly capable of making such a determination.

This antiquated approach to growth that materialises among competition, imposed controls and external value judgements, is actually negative in its nature in that it is retrogressive. As it moves, such growth creates, gathers and accumulates various goods and accomplishments presupposed to be desirable. Its movement is outward and its fruits are physical, emotional or mental acquisitions, abilities or agilities.

Such a view of growth perpetrates a basic deception on one who accepts it and practises it, for it is self-generating, and self-perpetuating. It endlessly creates one goal after another, deluding the person held in its grip into believing that upon reaching a certain point, conquering a certain emotional obstacle, or understanding some obscure mental abstraction, one will have either arrived at or achieved some state of accomplishment in which one will be satisfied, placated or enlightened – or a combination thereof.

This continuous negative creation feeds on its own continuous and circuitous expansion. It thrives on an infinite refusal to accept the present, and encourages – indeed, often demands – that one judge or assess future goals or activities by reference to activities and accomplishments from the past, or by externally imposed standards – or both.

This view of growth can never be truly positive or evolutionarily creative, for it refuses or restricts the introduction of light and resists and denies the possibility of true change. It also deludes one into identifying with the vehicle employed in the search or pursuit of the goal, or even into identifying with the state or goal being sought – all of which are of temporary or transitory existence at best.

The phenomenal or negative realm into which this materialistic creativity expands anaesthetises one's inherent sensitivity and innate access to the inner knowingness by satiating the desires, satisfying the senses, enticing one to drop one's focus from the Point of Becoming into that which one has become. It treats the ever-appearing goals as stimuli to action and thus elicits reaction. The result is an endless wheel of recurring encounters, attachments, and inevitable consequences in search of a nebulous and elusive end goal to end all goals.

How does 'True Growth' differ from the concept of conventional 'growth'?

'*True growth*' as is it described in this Material refers, initially, to the continuous and effective shedding of unnecessary and/or obsolete encumbrances and the expansion and manifestation of a *new awareness*.

One opening must constantly be aware of, and secure in, an attitude that is harmonious with this position. This proper attitude is one in which one allows and even, with the application of Inner Discipline, *initiates and perpetuates the shedding*.

If one loses sight of the proper attitude, one may become distracted and view the shedding itself as a goal – or series of goals – towards which one must strive, or through which one must work or towards which one must aspire in order to successfully win or gain some putative victory of enlightenment, happiness, or whatever one views as the end result or goal of the process.

Any such goal orientation is disharmonious with true growth, in that any applied discipline employed with the purpose of achieving a goal causes the goal to be prematurely defined.

This in turn closes off access to the True Self and denies the presence of light. It attempts to restrict change and shape events according to the limitations of the prematurely defined end result. Further, such goal orientation engenders an attitude that is at odds with the acceptance of true responsibility.

Goal fixation provides a vehicle for the pursuit of and the fulfilment of desire, and it can cause one to call forth and encourage the employment of energies whose sole purpose is self-gratification, self-satisfaction and self-protection, and whose base is a reflected self-sufficiency.

Such energies employ guile and cunning to reach or accomplish a desired end, and can seduce one opening – and still vulnerable – into a misdirection and misapplication of that with which one may have been entrusted. Even successful accomplishment of a worthy and laudable goal by such means is an empty victory, in that it can leave one with the distorted perspective as to the worth of the goals or the accomplishments as they may be relative to the real needs of an evolving omniverse.

The buoyant effect of such an empty victory is to cause one to feel pride in the accomplishment in supposedly having won or succeeded in the face of obstacles or resistance. This pride can then prod one to further define another goal, and another, and embark upon a crusading delusion, the end result of which is massive distraction and ultimate frustration.

An Inner Discipline which is developed in harmony with discrimination, renders goal orientation itself obsolete. It renders the position that one must assume to accomplish the goal disharmonious with complete identification with the True Self and the expression of that which is known within the Self.

How does one make the transition towards True Growth?

Hence, it will be seen that true growth and the attendant shedding that transpire initially in the transition are not goals to be attained, or even obstacles to be overcome or worked through; but they are rather steps to be taken in the unfoldment after one initiates the shift to identification with the True Self. True growth allows and even enables the light of the Self to shine through, permeating and illuminating the vehicles of expression into which and through which the True Self is projecting.

True growth suggests instead an initial and complete identification with the True Self focused at the Point of Becoming within the level of the soul. After one makes this identification, there follows a period of apparently paradoxical transitional unfoldment in which the accumulated trivia of phenomenal negative creation are discriminatively rejected and discarded, preferably in a gentle and harmonious process — out of, rather than into, the bondage of attachment.

In the transition process, attachments are recognised and released, including attachments to any desired states or goals or any fruits, spoils or accomplishments supposedly available upon attaining such a state or goal, and *even any attachment to the search itself towards such a state or goal*. To complete the paradox, one may be called upon to retain possession of the fruits created or accomplishments gained, holding them in trust with a dedication to a different purpose.

One who is embarking on the path of true growth will, first, then affirm complete identification with the True Self, even if complete realisation of that affirmation or identification seems elusive or less than instantaneous.

Upon initiating this shift, one will commence a continuous transformation, during which one's awareness will open and expand, ever bringing to view or perception those items attachment to which is in disharmony with the true expression of that which one *is*, with which one has now identified, and the purpose into which one is unfolding.

The ease with which this positive expression occurs and unfolds is largely dependent on the exercise of the Inner Discipline being developed. This is a continuous and continual self-testing, self-evaluating, and self-refining process. The development and exercise of this discipline is not in and of itself growth. Its development is a formative transitional activity, a precursor or precondition to the true growth that will begin to emerge as discipline and discrimination are maturing when one's commitment is so firm as to be voluntarily irreversible, and when one has accepted complete and true responsibility in its ultimate and broadest context.

Is True Growth the final 'goal'?

One must not be deluded into assuming or believing that what is happening is all preparation.

> **That which one is experiencing is not preparation for the unfoldment:** *this is the unfoldment; this is next.*

If one regards that which is happening as preparation, then one will be deluded into the pursuit of the goal of the end of the preparation.

The very experiences that one may view as preparation are the very items carried to enable one to generate the back-pressure in order to manifest that which fulfils a need and, in turn, enables one to traverse the relative experiences and to shed the fetters and transcend those limitations which surface during, and as a result of, the experiences.

The discipline to be developed, then, is that which enables one to manifest and positively express what is coming to be known within the Self in harmony with true growth. This discipline cannot be developed according to ways or methods already in existence, for real Inner Discipline emerges from true change and the introduction of light: from positive creativity by the True Self as it projects into matter of negative or phenomenal creation at the Point of Becoming.

Inner discipline is a vehicle of will tempered with wisdom and applied with discrimination. The wisdom required emanates from within and emerges with the development and implementation of an Inner Discipline.

If one looks to another for help, how is that help evaluated?

If one who is opening and developing discipline does turn to another for help, it is very important that the one seeking help be discriminating and selective in determining to whom one will turn. Indeed, in the selection of the one who can help, one who is opening must employ that very discrimination which one seeks to develop. It is essential that the help offered and received be carefully evaluated. One who has been approached for help, but whose own discrimination and discipline are less than fully mature and developed, may offer help which is based on observation or on intellectual conclusions, or on that which emanates from emotional experiences, rather than from insight from which light is gleaned to meet the need of the moment.

The help offered must carry the *ring of genuineness*, rather than being the kind exported merely to confirm preconceived notions or beliefs, or to strengthen an insecure position or to attempt to bolster one's own ability to influence another.

Help that carries the ring of genuineness, the essence of light, and the depth of pure reason will complement and harmonise with that which is known within by the one receiving it. And it will be easily assimilated and incorporated into what one opening seeks to manifest. Such help must, as well, be received with genuineness by one in need who must scrutinise one's own motives and purpose with meticulous integrity so as to ensure that the help received is placed to its highest potential.

After one opening and asking for help has made a positive evaluation and determination, then one should proceed to follow the suggestions received in the communication and begin to act on them without further question, for a new resistance to the developing discipline and disciplined action may soon begin to make its presence known and felt.

What happens if one feels this resistance?

If this new resistance is allowed to gain even the slightest foothold at the outset, it can insidiously and surreptitiously undermine and prematurely abort even the strongest determination, resolve, and attempts to establish discipline.

This resistance is not obvious, nor is its attack frontal so as to make its presence easily detectable. Rather, it is much more basic in nature. It is allied with fear and feeds on doubt. It craves and clings to security; it avoids and evades freedom; it refuses to openly confront and resist, but follows a path of specious and sophistic subterfuge.

The only defence to this resistance is openness, courageous adaptability and positive action which proceed from an Inner Discipline that enables one to move with that which emerges from within the Self.

This resistance will attempt to make its presence felt throughout the traversing of this path until one's physical vehicles are finally, safely and completely permeated with the essence of the light of the True Self with which one has identified, and until harmonisation and co-operation of those vehicles is assured.

It is the essence of the True Self present in those vehicles which desires freedom, and only the reflection of the Self that avoids and deplores it. When one has irreversibly and irrevocably aligned with the True Self, and has accepted what can be offered and shared when the time is right, and has determined to manifest the essence of its light through the application of a strong Inner Discipline, one can then stand on the threshold of a new freedom and a true expression of that which is known within the Self.

35   *Attitude and Understanding*

At this point, it will be helpful to raise some issues which we will examine in more detail in the next section on Self-determination. It is sufficient at this point to become aware of these issues.

The development of Inner Discipline calls for unequivocal commitment and unswerving dedication to purpose. The distractions to be encountered assume classic form and proportion, and a unique resistance may be felt expressing itself from deep within the phenomenal realms of one's own created universe.

What is the nature of this 'unique resistance'?

This resistance is one for which one must be constantly vigilant; it is the same one that causes someone at the very outset to question the inner urging to humbly seek help and to open to that which is known within and emerging from the True Self.

It is this resistance which causes one to believe that one must 'understand' what is happening before one will accept the need for action.

How can one 'understand' what is going on?

It will be helpful if one can have some view of the action to be disciplined, the nature of the performance that one seeks to express, and the attitude that one must develop to express the performance.

One whose awareness is expanding in True Growth will find that early on much effort is expended in resolving doubt, attempting to rationalise the probable consequences, causes and effects of the events which transpire, and the pursuit of enquiry. Although one may have come to perceive knowledge as something acquired by learning, the knowledge for which one now yearns while opening is not a learned knowledge.

Someone oriented to a belief that knowledge is learned may mistakenly assume, that what one seeks to acquire must and can be learned. One may thus mistakenly approach that which is happening within as a series of events, the essence or lessons of which are to be studied, learned and understood.

Those employing this antiquated process are often reluctant or unwilling to take any new concept or experience encountered into action, except for the purpose of experimentation to prove or disprove some aspect of the concept, or to confirm some facet of the concept, until it is thus tested, accepted, learned and understood according to the fashion and rules of the antiquated process, and until the necessary and proper conclusions are drawn, proposed or postulated.

How is Attitude related to 'knowingness'?

The knowingness to which one is opening is different. It is approached and assimilated in a way that is in direct contravention to this antiquated and obsolete process of so-called learning and understanding. This knowingness begins with that which *is* and then that which is known by *direct perception* – within the True Self – and it is then accepted as and for what it is *without reference to past experience or understanding*.

Unresolved or un-manifested determination creates its own fertile ground for the cultivation of doubt, and it perpetuates its own cycle of dilemma and confusion in that someone locked into an obsolete decision-making process refuses to act until the nature of the action, consequences thereof, and reasons therefore are understood.

Where then does one begin?

How does one shift to a position of acceptance of that which is emerging from within?

Anyone approaching what is *new* in a way that is *old* will experience increasing frustration at the inability to reconcile the two matters. But one is invited to try – to attempt to effect a reconciliation: one is in fact encouraged to do so – to exhaust the circuitous process in a futile attempt to rationalise and understand what is happening. Only when one completes this search within the mind – satisfying that part which seeks to understand that it cannot understand what is happening, thence acknowledging that what is emerging cannot be understood before action is taken on it – can one transcend the reservation and dissolve the barrier between perceptual rationalisation and *pure reason*. In essence, one must be prepared to act – without knowing why!

Until that point is reached, the seed of doubt rests on fertile ground: the seed of doubt which suggests that action taken without a perception of consequences or reasons would be either foolish, or futile, or both.

Will 'ignorance' degenerate and disappear naturally with evolution?

Items of the phenomenal or manifested universe decompose or degenerate when left in a state of inaction. One may erroneously believe that the items of the aphenomenal universe, that is, those consequential traits that require attention and development, will also degenerate, decompose, and eventually fall away if treated with a similar passive inaction.

This erroneous belief can cause one to ignore or refrain from taking the essential action or making the essential effort. If one so refrains from positive disciplined action and effort, the individual soul – even while seeking liberation – binds itself to a process by which it perpetuates its own bondage to a continuous cycle of a series of incarnations until one puts forth the positive effort and action in an active gesture towards self-liberation.

The condition of 'ignorance' – that state of human existence which perpetuates one's bondage to the wheel of seemingly infinite birth, death and rebirth, will not, contrary to this erroneous belief, simply go away if ignored and left alone. Effort is essential.

For someone whose evolutionary perception has not yet approached this threshold of understanding, and even in someone who has perceived this truth but has not yet undertaken the necessary action and begun to put forth the necessary effort, the belief may persist that simple and passive inaction on one's part can provide an effective avenue towards self-development, self-discovery, personal evolution, and enlightenment.

This belief is a vestige of a passing and now obsolete method of seeking truth and enlightenment. In that passing system, the responsibility for the liberation of the soul from the wheel of reincarnation was assumed by another who also had the ability to vicariously assume the effort and action for the soul eligible for liberation.

While it is true – at least in this period of transition – that an initiating event is still essential to effect complete eligibility for liberation, the imparting of that event no longer exonerates the embodied soul from asserting its own effort and action.

This is an exciting evolutionary development, for it brings closer the possibility of self-determination and self-liberation to the condition of human existence, and shifts the onus for one's own personal evolutionary growth on to the one seeking liberation.

Further, it brings the dawning of the possibility that one can accept and assimilate a new dimension of one's own divine nature, and manifest aspects of that new dimension into the phenomenal realm for the benefit of all. And one can – actually, *one must* – do this while still in the physical articles of expression – the physical bodies.

We will explore these issues in depth in the next section of this book.

36   Effort and Action

Humankind has entered a new stage of its evolutionary development. We are no longer preparing for the descent of this new consciousness: it is now imminent – it is upon us. In this new era, one can no longer simply accept gratuitous liberation; one must assume the responsibility and assert the Effort and Action to manifest those aspects of a new consciousness that one carries. These aspects are there – deep within each of us – and have been created by our own inevitable consequences and the creative back-pressure inherent in those consequences.

How do Effort and Action dispel 'ignorance'?

If one ignores or refuses to accept the responsibility and put forth the necessary effort and action, that is if one neglects the cultivation of the availability to place resolve into action, one thus places the opposite ends of one's own personal existential spectrum into opposition and antagonism with each other. This ultimately allows natural degeneration and discard of the physical bodies – to be sure – but it also inhibits and frustrates one's own spiritual evolution, in that one may miss the evolutionary opportunity to manifest certain aspects of this new dimension of consciousness.

If one accepts the opportunity, assumes the responsibility, and asserts the effort and action, the benefits accrue not only to the one who makes this move, but also to one's culture, the planet, and the evolutionary process itself.

A full understanding and comprehension of all of the concepts related to these matters requires an extensive investigation into basic metaphysics and related matters. A discussion of those matters at this juncture would be necessarily abbreviated, but it would also be premature, as it would assume that one already has knowledge of some of that for which one now searches and to which one is now opening.

It is sufficient to state at this juncture that to refrain from concerted effort and disciplined action towards refinement of the implementation process will deprive one opening of the full benefit of this new path.

So, how does one travel this path without becoming psychologically disoriented?

To realise fully one's potential in the opening, effort and action along the way are as essential as the opening realisations themselves. It is the process itself that is important, and some of the actions undertaken along the way may be altered or abandoned at a later time.

Without action and refinement in the application of what one sees as one opens, not only does one deprive oneself of those dimensions that are available, but one may inadvertently sprout the seeds of mental decay and degeneration, as well as psychological disorientation.

The psychological disorientation with which we are here concerned is a syndrome that can develop in one who is opening because of one's inability to reconcile and integrate all of the various dimensions of one's existence.

As the opening of awareness progresses, one becomes more aware of these dimensions and of one's activities on these dimensions. This in itself is a natural process and does not cause problems. The problem of this particular 'psychological disorientation' syndrome stems from one's inability to integrate and understand all the steps and facets of the growing awareness as one opens.

This syndrome is not unique to this new path that is being manifested for Western culture; indeed, it is present in all paths towards enlightenment. However, there are two important distinctions to note that differentiate the present opening of awareness in this new path.

What is the 'faith gap'?

Firstly: absence of the 'faith gap'. One who is opening on this new path is denied a comforting facility that was available to those opening in other times and in other cultures. This facility could be called a 'faith gap'. This term describes a quiet but disquieting 'no-mind' area, in the passing systems of old, between that which one *knows* and that which one is asked to *believe – on faith*. This means that in the passing systems there were certain aspects of the path opening ahead that one was asked to accept on faith, and, at this point in the opening, faith could be defined as the mental action of *believing* something which one *knows* is not *true* – at least not true by the process now used by the human mind to define truth.

What happened to the 'guru'?

Secondly: the absence of the 'guru'. One who is opening on this new path is denied the vehicle by which one in other cultures and times could bridge that 'faith gap': a leader, teacher or guru, in whom one opening could place the faith required.

So, rather than having the comfort of faith itself and someone in whom one could place that faith, one is, so to speak, left to one's own devices to work out the puzzles, paradoxes, contradictions, dichotomies and intricacies of the various aspects of an opening awareness inherent in the new consciousness.

This is a task of major proportions, especially as one must make one's own bricks of belief without the straw of faith.

It becomes evident on reflection that some new tools must become available, and they are available to one who is opening on a new path. But to find these tools, one must find one's own way through an infinite labyrinth of tunnels in the mind and across a quagmire of a 'no-mind' land without the benefit of someone to lead the way and the faith that one previously would have placed in that leader.

So, what has replaced 'faith' and the 'guru'?

On this new Path of Self-discovery, faith has been replaced by an *'objective trust'*, and the leader or guru has been replaced by another opening in awareness who may have found a path across that quagmire and through those tunnels and who may now be willing to share the benefits of that search and effort: that is, *one who can help.*

The syndrome of psychological disorientation with which we are here concerned, arises in one who is opening who knows that simple faith is not enough. One opening knows that if faith were available, there is (for various reasons already discussed in depth) no one in whom one could comfortably place that faith.

The syndrome of concern arises when one opening refuses to place an *'objective trust'* in that which one sees and knows within the Self and, further, refuses to act on that objective trust.

What is the key to dissolving this 'psychological disorientation syndrome'?

The key to dissolving this syndrome, then, is to trust that which is seen and act on that which is trusted. This key can enable one who is opening to bridge the 'faith gap' and to complete the **'credibility circle'** by adding those final essential elements: *experience and realisation.*

The syndrome of psychological disorientation that can threaten one's mental stability in the opening process is literally created by the one opening who refuses to trust that which is seen within and who refuses to act on that trust. This can break the tenuous circle of self-credibility and can send one off on an infinite chase through the labyrinth of mental and emotional dead-end dimensions.

> **This can be a very dangerous chase, because the overactive mind and the immature ego can form a deadly team and conjure up incalculable mischief. One opening who is led astray by this miscreant duo can spiral outward and downward in a futile attempt to assert control by calculating the possibilities, the probabilities, the certainties, and the uncertainties that self-create and perpetuate themselves for no other purpose than to keep the game alive. And there is little humour in a game that can induce paranoia, engender fear, precipitate breakdown, disintegrate self-esteem and destroy self-confidence.**

In an attempt to regain control, one may resurrect an elusive faith or search for someone or something in which to place that faith. But it soon becomes clear that one long ago passed that post, and such attempts to grasp a wispy line of faith are now as redundant as the objects they seek.

So, what began as a mischievous romp by the mind and the ego now becomes a trip of fear and trepidation, as one attempts to traverse an uncharted sea of empty conclusions and suppositions by using an obsolete portfolio of now undependable mind-tricks. It is only when one stops and acknowledges that one is hopelessly lost and dangerously close to the precipice of personal breakdown that one can access that source of light, and climb out of the labyrinth, and begin to build a new attitude and a bridge of belief – that is, *objective trust* – on which to act.

How does one use the steps of Acknowledgement, Access, Attitude, and Action?

There are four practical steps one can take to dissolve this syndrome: Acknowledgement, Access, Attitude and Action.

1 As soon as one realises that 'something is wrong' or that 'something has changed', one must *acknowledge* and trust that feeling.
2 As soon as one acknowledges that feeling – or 'knowingness' – one must *access* the intuitive insight.
3 As soon as access to intuitive insight is available, one must immediately shift the *attitude* to one of objective trust.
4 As soon as that attitude is established, one must move to *action*, for it can be fatal to stop, '*think*' and try to '*understand*'.

It is this temptation to stop, think, analyse and understand the action that is prompted from within and is about to be taken that can, at the outset, abort the action itself, or, at the least, cause one to miss the opportunity to execute the action with appropriate ease and proper timing.

What is the new 'mentation process'?

At this stage, one is educating the mind to a new mode of mental action – *a new 'mentation' process*, if you will – and the mind is the key to bridging the gap between knowledge and *'knowingness'*. The mind actually will educate itself to this new mode of action by observing the benefits of acting on that which is seen within versus analysing that which is believed.

As one becomes more adept at reaching this point of acknowledgement, one will begin to perceive that one must refrain from attempting to determine what it is that is 'wrong' or has 'changed'. The essential step is to acknowledge the feeling that something needs attention, or that one is about to move in a tangential direction that could initiate further distraction.

Thus, these four essential steps – *acknowledgement, access, attitude, action* – provide a viable approach for one to dissolve the crystallised circuits of the mind through which one can spiral downward on the wings of analysis. Once one breaks the grip that analysis has on the mind, one becomes eligible to extend the benefits of action into the more physical or phenomenal areas of one's being.

What must one do to implement this in everyday life?

It is time now to consider the condition, care, maintenance and development of these physical areas of one's being: the physical bodies. It would seem obvious that general physical health and well-being are essential to manifest fully that which is here under consideration. Hence, extended discussion of physical development will here be avoided, as undue attention to such matters at this point would appear unnecessary.

However, attention is now due to some of the more subtle consequences of physical action. We will consider this subject at this point, even though discussion of the most subtle and sublime aspects of this topic must be delayed and await a fuller prerequisite treatment of other elementary items covered hereafter.

Of particular concern at this moment is the effect of certain physical actions upon physiological functions and their interplay and inter-relationship with certain mental processes and personal psychological and spiritual development. Attention and interest here are with the care and lubrication, if you will, of that portal at which the incorporeal (that is, the aphenomenal or spiritual dimension) blends with the corporeal (that is, the phenomenal or physical dimension of one's being).

What is the 'Point of Becoming'?

The exact location at which this blending occurs is vague and elusive at best. The location of this Point of Becoming is subject to two significant variables.

- **Firstly**, in one whose awareness has not yet opened and whose interests and inclinations are still of a more basic and instinctive nature, this junction is more tangible and stationary. It is more easily defined and recognised, for such a one has yet no voluntary access to the aphenomenal regions until one's personal development reaches the stage where the veil begins to dissolve. Generally, this stage is entered when the trove of one's own inevitable consequences is reduced by personal evolutionary growth or relieved by the presence – and acceptance – of *grace*.
- **Secondly**, in one whose awareness is opening and who becomes eligible to consciously enter into the enquiry of the more subtle subjects and areas or the true nature of things, although the junction becomes less tangible and definable, its nature also becomes more nebulous and elusive, for such a one begins to have an ever-increasing access to these more subtle regions. At first, this access is, of course, largely involuntary; that is, the occurrence of the flashes of insight and the onset of realisations are more gratuitous, sporadic and seemingly unpredictable. With the opening of awareness, the assertion of effort, the development of discipline, and, of course, the presence and acceptance of grace, one has, increasingly, more voluntary access to these regions.

How and where does the 'incorporeal' blend with the 'corporeal'?

With this access, this area of blending of the incorporeal with the corporeal, or the 'aphenomenal' with the phenomenal, expands to allow the physical dimensions of one's being to begin the process in which these physical dimensions are subsumed and transformed. With this expansion, the area of inner communication becomes wider and of a deeper and more infinite dimension.

Even as this area of blending opens, its depth is not static: it expands and contracts, and access to it is influenced by one's effort and by the acceptance and implementation of the insights and realisations, the frequency and occurrence of which will begin to grow.

The interpretation of these insights and realisations is a matter of some concern at this point. One may ask, 'What does one do with this new and exciting knowingness that is beginning to materialise within?'

This interpretation is, in the beginning, largely intellectual. One who is opening may initially attempt to reconcile the paradoxes by using the obsolete reasoning and thinking processes.

Some of this intellectual effort will be successful to some degree, for the intellect must be satisfied. But that success will be limited until certain other processes are initiated.

What are the physiological processes called into play here?

For one to begin to fully interpret and implement the essence and benefit of these new insights at the level of everyday, minute-to-minute waking awareness, certain essential physiological processes are called into play. These processes include, among others, the function and effect of the endocrine glands of the physical vehicles.

Current medical knowledge offers very little concerning the endocrine glands. In most cases, these glands lie dormant, and they perform some perfunctory services to the physical body. We are not concerned with these perfunctory services in this discussion.

As the awareness opens and one's personal evolutionary growth brings one to the threshold of voluntary aspiration towards higher knowledge, the latent activities of these glands are awakened. The secretions forthcoming from these glands enable one's awareness to expand and one's consciousness to change. In addition, they allow certain necessary physical tools to be implemented.

In short, it is impossible for one to consciously (as opposed to unconsciously, as in sleep) or subconsciously (as in mentation of which one is generally unaware) enter into the newly available alternative dimensions and tap the insights and realisations from what is commonly called 'intuition' without the aid of the heretofore latent functions of these glands.

To activate the latent functions of these glands, there are certain modes of actions that are effective. They have withstood the trials of time and have, in fact, become more refined. These modes of action become available to one who is opening when the time is right, and their use is essential to further facilitate the continued expansion of one's awareness.

One should once again recognise that mere knowledge of either the modes of action to be undertaken or their existence is useless unless they are placed into practice and action. Many of these practices are of an esoteric nature, and they are conveyed to one who is opening when one is ready.

If one has related well to that which has thus far been presented and has made the transition, one may be ready to explore the *Process of Self-determination* and a new consciousness.

Our New Human Consciousness

Our Process of Self-determination

An Overview

To enter the process of **Self-determination**, one will recognise the need for development of discrimination and an Inner Discipline. This requires a new way of thinking. The old process demands that one must know *why* before one takes action. Now, one must be prepared to act without knowing why! If one has acknowledged the need for help and has sought help from some outside source, authority, guide or teacher, it is possible that there may have developed a dependency on the one to whom one has turned for help. There is a significant shift which must take place within. This shift involves **Reducing Dependency** – the reduction of external dependence on one to whom one may have turned for help. There is a twofold integrity which one who is opening must develop: firstly, a quantitative integrity, that is, an integrity in which one is independent and free from external influence; and secondly, a qualitative integrity, that is, an integrity within by which one determines for oneself the rightness and wrongness of the matters of one's life.

Inherent in the relationship of dependency is the reservation of the privilege of *attribution*. This is helpful in the beginning but detrimental later on. Attribution occurs when one attributes to an external source the credit or the blame for what has transpired. It is at this time that one begins to deal with **Consequences, Ignorance, Action, and Destiny**. As one begins to discriminate between what is learned and what is *known*, there is an important distinction to be made between that which simply must play out and that which requires one to take action. The first of these relates to inevitable consequences, and the second relates to one's contractual destiny. Eventually, we will see that the items of inevitable consequence can be converted to items of action. It is at this time that one begins **Relating To The Aphenomenal**. The point at which the incorporeal becomes corporeal is at best vague and elusive; sometimes almost undefinable. And in the extreme, it is virtually invisible. This point is a relative place and can best be described as that grey area where idea becomes fact, where feeling becomes emotion, and impulse becomes action. It is also where aphenomenal becomes phenomenal, where spirit becomes soul, where soul becomes matter. Self-determination enables one to be at ease as one moves in and among the corridors of the inner structure. As one becomes more adept at moving in and through various dimensions, one then begins **Educating The Life Vehicles**. Discipline in the physical bodies is an empty gesture if there is no discrimination present in the application of such discipline. Similarly, if one has finely honed the ability to discriminate, the forthcoming wisdom is lost if there is no discipline present to place resolve into action.

To coordinate discipline on the one hand and discrimination on the other, a bridge between them is needed. The middle ground, spanned by this bridge, is the fine and subtle area of emotion. The bridge itself is control of this emotional middle ground, and the emotional extremes of desire and disdain. These are matters of which Western psychology really knows very little. One is now **Facing An Alternative Reality**. Thus far, the pressure for change may have been gentle. Moreover, the changes which one may have undergone have perhaps, for the most part, been gentle – changes which only slightly taxed one's ability and which have not yet really taxed one's credibility.

In this time of transition, one may still have been able to retain the ability to rationalise the changes which one has experienced; that is, to explain them to one's mind in terms which the mind understands and in concepts in which the mind is still working comfortably for the most part. In such case, there is still some separation, some divergence and contradiction in the coexistence of these two realms of experience. Now the two realms of this bifurcated existence will begin to converge. One now begins **Manifesting A New Personal Reality**. When one acknowledges the possibility of the existence of an alternative to what one has previously considered to be reality, one has then, for the first time, the opportunity of manifesting that new reality. This, of course, requires **Rejecting, Dismantling, And Discarding The Old**. As each step in the manifestation presents itself through each acknowledgement of the possibility of a new and different reality, relationships begin to alter and fade. To manifest this new personal reality, one must adopt a unique **Attitude In Transition**. When the awareness opens and begins to perceive the subtle signals which herald individual change, the precise definitions of a previously well-structured reality begin to become blurred around the edges, and the mental, emotional and physical components of one's being will begin to express their concern and consternation about the changes which are occurring.

Although action is important now – actually essential – it is not the factor which is controlling. The controlling factor is attitude, but even attitude is now to become only another phase of transition. We are faced with **Dismantling An Obsolete Belief System**. The process which one must undertake to reverse this deplorable condition is so dynamic in effect that it can be metamorphic, and so simple in application that it can be overlooked. One should be aware that what is now to be described, while apparently simple in form and nature, if applied, can and will have monumental effects on the emotional and mental composition of the individual personality. One should approach the following material with due respect and apprehension, but likewise, with courage and confidence.

The process begins with the ability to discard something which is no longer of use, that is **Questioning The Basic Assumption**. It is a relatively easy process when it is applied to items of a material nature for which we no longer have any need or affection. There are two problems which arise when we begin to apply this: firstly, the items to be examined are not of a material nature; secondly, the items to be discarded are often mistakenly assumed to be essential. The process of deductive reasoning and all of these ancillary processes of reaching conclusions on which to base action are deeply entrenched in Western thinking. They are so foundational as to be considered inviolable and almost sacred. It is this process, of course, on which the entire foundation of Western scientific thinking and investigation is based. To question the system, to ask even the first question, is considered by some to be personally, socially, and certainly scientifically at least indiscreet, if not almost blasphemous. But now, **It's Time For A Change**.

Such a time is now upon us individually as well as collectively. We have hesitated. We have waited. We have refused to acknowledge the need for change, and the change is now upon us, and it will soon be all around us. This change carries with it the essence of a reality which is so new and different that we will marvel at its innovation. The transformation which it carries is so deep and so widely consequential that its implications cannot be grasped from where we stand at the moment. There are many steps which we must take to move into it. There are many states of consciousness which we must experience before the new change of consciousness is fully manifested.

37   Self-determination

Self-determination is the ability to independently place into action that which emerges from what is known within without reference to external sources, external authorities or past experiences.

One whose awareness is opening and maturing in this time of transition will recognise the need for development of discrimination and of an Inner Discipline to enable one to become self-determining. The development of this discrimination requires a new way of thinking. The refinement of an Inner Discipline is a delicate process which, for a time, may require one's total available effort and energy and tax one's patience and stamina. It is truly a time to make haste... slowly. Invariably, one's ability to see will develop and expand more rapidly than one's ability to assimilate what one sees. Certainly, it will exceed one's ability to do what one has assimilated after it has been seen.

When one can see more than one can do, one may become impatient, and impatience will lead to imbalance. Balance is essential now, and it is easily lost and difficult to regain, for there is a fine intermingling of mental, emotional and physical reaction and adjustment occurring as this new awareness dawns and a new consciousness descends. Everything in its path will be transformed. At such time, one is again well advised to occupy one's time and one's hands with some creative manual activity which requires dexterity, attention and the expenditure of manual energy.

The development of discrimination and Inner Discipline calls for unequivocal commitment and unswerving dedication to purpose. That purpose is principally the acceptance of change. The distractions and resistance which one will encounter assume classic form and proportion. One of these items of resistance may be felt expressing itself strongly, and it deserves special attention.

This resistance, of which one must be constantly vigilant, is the same resistance which causes one at the very outset to question the inner urging to open to that which is coming to be known within and is emerging from the true Self.

This resistance thrives on pride; it resists change; it shuns any notion of self-denial and humility; it cultivates fear; and it lives in the fiction of a reflected self-sufficiency. Its main characteristic is dissipation. It directly contravenes all efforts towards discipline and action; it seeks to maintain the status quo. This resistance will be discussed in greater detail at a later note. At that time, we will examine a way by which one can develop the ability to transform this undermining resistance.

Just now, it will be helpful if one can have some idea of the action to be taken and the principles which govern this action.

The first of these principles is the importance of placing insights into action. If one is to truly benefit from the effort to be put forth and to avoid the traumas which one has previously encountered, resolve must be carried forth into disciplined action. Unresolved or un-manifest determination creates its own fertile ground for the cultivation of doubt. This doubt will cause one to speculate on the efficacy of the action which might have been undertaken, but which has now been delayed, set aside or abandoned.

This doubt is spawned by the desire to be able to predict consequences or results. As we will see, this doubt and this desire combine to effectively undermine positive action and true growth. The speculation engendered by doubt employs a mental process which attempts to foresee the results of action. This mental process is circuitous and ineffectual. The longer it is employed, the stronger it becomes; and the stronger it is, the more it then gives rise to further doubt and speculation.

If we assume that one has the necessary resolve and determination to do something, and if we assume further that one also has developed some discipline to at least be able to begin to place some resolve into action; and, further, if one has begun to refine the process of discrimination, where, then, does one begin? How does one deal with doubt and shift to a position of being able to place new insights into action?

The most important first step is to assess how one approaches the matters of life; that is, the attitude with which one determines the actions which one will take.

Someone who approaches something new in a way which is old will feel increasing frustration at the inability to reconcile the two matters. But one will inevitably try; one will attempt to effect reconciliation. One is in fact encouraged to do so. It is important to exhaust the circuitous process in a futile attempt to rationalise and understand what is happening. Only when one completes this search within, satisfying the intellect which seeks to understand, thence acknowledging that what is emerging cannot be understood before action is taken on it, can one transcend the doubts and dissolve the barrier between perceptual rationalisation and Pure Reason. In essence, one must be prepared to begin to take action on that which is known within without resorting to an obsolete and circuitous reasoning process which seldom, if ever, produces satisfactory results. The old process demands that one must know why before one takes action.

Now, one must be prepared to act without knowing why!

Until that point is reached, the seed of doubt rests on fertile ground. This seed of doubt suggests to one that it would be either foolish or futile for one to undertake any action until one knows the reasons for or the consequences of the action to be taken.

This seed of doubt is really just another form of a seed or process which exists in nature. It is not only useful but also essential. In its most basic and elemental form, it is constantly present, alive and waiting only for the slightest opportunity to sprout in all transactions of life.

This seed or process is in fact essential for the purposes of degeneration and disposal of the items which nature considers being unusable, undesirable and obsolete.

All matter is subject to the unavoidable relief of this reducing force, especially all matter left unattended, inactive and static. All material manifestations of the physical or phenomenal universe must ultimately succumb to this degeneration when their essential part of the drama of evolution has been completed and played out. All things must be set aside when they have been rendered obsolete by an emerging need which requires characteristics, attributes and traits absent in them in their present state.

All items of the physical universe are subject to this process: physical creation which has been abandoned, emotions which are no longer necessary or appropriate, and mental or reasoning processes which have outlived their usefulness and are no longer effective for the evolving human community.

Included in this degenerative process are physical bodies which are not quickened by constant adaptation to the changes of evolution. This requires a conversion accomplished by the True Self upon its own re-identification and consequent expression of its Positive Presence into and throughout the matter into which it has projected.

Improper identification, or misidentification, by the True Self with the matter into which it has projected has seduced its reflected essence into assuming and accepting the characteristics and attributes, and limitations and tendencies, of that matter into which it has projected. This much is well known, obvious, and accepted, and has been known to many generations of those who opened to truth and enlightenment. In fact, those who opened to truth through antiquated disciplines often, at the time of becoming enlightened, either rejected their physical bodies altogether or undertook to maintain them only to the extent needed to assure their minimal survival to a time when they would exist in a supposedly enlightened state. They assumed that they had no further use or need of the physical bodies. In such event, the discarded physical bodies were left in an inactive state to succumb to the degeneration and decomposition according to natural laws.

As part of the change of consciousness and the expansion of awareness now occurring, there is to be an awakening of a new dimension of evolutionary activity in which physical bodies may be transformed and converted. This will be inaugurated by an initial re-identification with the True Self by all aspects of the projected essence. Then, there will be a transformation of all of the physical processes in the physical bodies as well as all of the emotional and mental processes in the finer regions of physical existence.

That part of one's consciousness which has projected into the physical bodies is now seeking elevation, enlightenment and liberation. It may have perpetuated its own continued bondage by seeking to escape from the limitations of its misidentification by refusing to place enough importance on the need to integrate what one sees into the body, emotions, and mind and the activities of everyday life. It is by this integration that the bodies are enlightened. Without the enlightenment of the physical bodies, there can be no evolving adaptation and expression in the world in which the physical bodies live. Without the physical bodies themselves, there can be no expression at all. But even with the possession of a physical body, even with the possession of a physical body which is enlightened, there can be no expression without the acceptance of responsibility. Without the acceptance of responsibility, one simply delegates to the future that which one attempted to relegate to the past. This will virtually ensure continued bondage and ignorance.

The second principle is the development of an attitude by which one can transcend doubt. Early on, when the awareness begins to open, the effort which one expends in the resolution of doubt, the pursuit of enquiry, and the attempt to rationalise probable consequences, causes, and effects of an event, can be attributed to the way, or the attitude, with which one views knowledge. As a result of the teachings of the present culture, one probably views knowledge as something which is or can be learned.

One oriented towards knowledge which is acquired by learning may assume, mistakenly, that what one seeks to acquire within can be – or must be – learned in this conventional way. One may thus mistakenly approach that which is happening within as a series of events, the essence or lessons of which are to be studied, learned, and understood and remembered, and from which conclusions are to be drawn.

'Understanding', as it is generally viewed, denotes a process by which a concept is encountered or formulated and thence assimilated into one's being. This assimilation is accomplished by incorporating the concept either in its entirety or by steps by finding agreement between this new concept, or its facets, and other concepts which have previously been encountered, learned and assimilated by the same process in earlier stages of one's personal education and evolution. If a concept agrees with something one has already learned or understood, then it is accepted and incorporated according to this process: then it is said to be 'understood'.

Until a concept is thus learned, tested, accepted and understood in such a manner, and until the necessary and proper conclusions are drawn, anyone employing this 'learning' process is reluctant or unwilling to take any such encountered concept into action, except for experimentation to prove or disprove or confirm some facet of the concept. There is little room in the process for the assimilation of a concept or an experience which can find no agreement or reference among concepts already accepted, assimilated and accumulated by this antiquated 'learning' process.

The new 'knowingness' which one is experiencing now is approached and assimilated in a different way: a way which is in direct contravention to this antiquated and obsolete process of so-called 'learning' and 'understanding'. This knowingness begins with that which *is*: it begins with an experience or an idea which cannot find agreement or confirmation among concepts which are already understood. It then becomes something one 'knows'. But it seems to be held in a different part of the mind away from other things which have been learned in the old way. It is in this new way accepted as and for what it is. It is not and cannot be subjected to proof or any process which seeks to justify an acceptance of its form or essence according to agreement or disagreement with anything which has been learned. It cannot be tested against anything which is 'understood' according to the antiquated process which one has previously used, and which is probably still very much in use in one's daily life.

To test this new 'knowingness' requires bypassing 'understanding' and placing it into action in order to bring it to a level where it can be seen, comprehended, and finally assimilated in a new way of understanding. In order to perform that action, one's Inner Discipline must be keenly developed and sharply honed. It must be prepared to bypass intellectual analysis.

When this knowingness begins to be experienced, awareness is still focused in and controlled by the circuits of the intellect. These circuits have been created by an antiquated learning process which will almost inevitably approach the emerging 'knowingness' in the same manner to which one has become accustomed to approaching all questions: that is, with reservation or even with outright refusal to accept that which is known within, until some attempt is made to prove its validity or understand its content according to the antiquated learning and intellectual procedures described above.

This antiquated process encourages one to delay action until the proof is complete, and that which is known within must await this proof. If proof is not forthcoming, doubt appears. In its un-manifest state, it thus becomes vulnerable to the process of degeneration and may never be acted upon.

Such unresolved or un-manifest determination creates its own fertile ground for the cultivation of doubt. It perpetuates its own cycle of dilemma and confusion while one who is locked into an obsolete decision-making process refuses to act until the nature of the action, the consequences thereof, and reasons therefore are anticipated, scrutinised and understood. But since that which is beginning to grow within is quietly but constantly present and will not go away, one who is gingerly accepting its presence begins to see that one must first act so as to manifest that which is known within before it can be understood.

This positive disciplined action is not reaction proceeding from what one has experienced, learned and stored. Its consequences cannot be anticipated or understood in the old way. They cannot even be perceived until the idea is acted upon. Once action is taken, then one can see the consequences materialise, and then those consequences can be comprehended and understood in a new way.

38   Reducing Dependency

> **To become self-determining, one must ultimately begin to seek one's own help from within and forge a reliance on that which is known and seen within. The discipline which one must develop must emerge from within. Discrimination must be refined from within. If one has acknowledged the need for help and has sought help from some outside source, authority, guide or teacher, it is possible that there may have developed a dependency on the one to whom one has turned for help.**

Before one can embark on a serious development and refinement of Inner Discipline and discrimination, there is a significant shift which must take place within. This shift involves the reduction of external dependence on one to whom one may have turned for help. This shift marks the beginning of a reliance on that which is known within the Self.

Until this shift is begun, any dependence on one who can help may diminish the emergence of one's ability to directly perceive that which is known within and to act on that which may be seen by that *Inner Knowingness*. This dependency is a vestige of obsolete spiritual disciplines and religious beliefs which served well in their time and place. In such an antiquated relationship, where the seeker was so dependent on the teacher, the one who could help took full responsibility for the one seeking truth, who learned humility and respect through the dependency. In such a relationship, discipline was imposed from without and it was guided and shaped by the one who could help the one who is opening.

This relationship between one who needs help and one who can offer help can be very beneficial in the beginning. For some, it is absolutely essential. There may be invaluable guidance and assistance given when one first begins to open and to question. The length of time such a relationship should be allowed to exist is a matter individually unique to each one who opens. Formerly, the decision to reduce the dependency or terminate the relationship rested on the teacher; but now that decision ultimately rests on the one who is opening and evolving discrimination in such matters.

If this relationship of dependency is allowed to grow and exist for too long, it could create an emotional subjugation. It could stifle true expression, for excessive dependency encourages analysis, intellectual interpretation, speculation and emotional reaction, and these activities will do little to help in the beginning. Further, the help that one may receive from one on whom too much dependency rests may be limited in that it is not a full, pure and complete, original and genuine expression of one's own contractual destiny.

This shift, wherein the dependency is reduced, can dissolve the crystallisation of a relationship of dependency which may bind one soul to another. Just as the presence of the relationship may be essential in the beginning, so too is the reduction of such dependency essential as one begins to see within, and to be able to place into action what one sees and to be able to evaluate for oneself what one does.

There is a twofold integrity which one opening must develop: first, a quantitative integrity, that is, an integrity in which one is independent and free from external influence. This quantitative integrity is essential if one is to see for oneself. And secondly, a qualitative integrity, that is, an integrity within by which one determines for oneself the rightness and wrongness of the matters of one's life. This qualitative integrity is essential if one is to determine for oneself.

There is also a communication process which one must develop within. The communication between one who is opening and one to whom one may have turned for help is merely a less refined version of that inner communication to be developed – that of communication of the Soul within the Self. In the beginning, the communication between one who is opening and the one who can help (whatever form that help may be in) is necessary, for the one opening probably does not have the ability to see within and to communicate within the Self to find what one wishes to know. Additionally, the resistance, objections and scepticism which one may have in the beginning are perhaps more easily overcome when the answers come from a source of authority, knowledge or comfort from whom one is more accustomed to receiving help. Even as the opening continues and one begins to reduce the dependency on one who may be of help, one may find that from time to time one must return for additional assistance from this comfortable source.

But, as time moves on, the dependency will begin to diminish of its own accord, and one opening will do well to recognise that reduction and to flow with its release. It may be tempting to want to wait until one finds something within on which to rely before attempting to reduce the dependency, but this may not be possible. It is true that when one door closes another one will open, and it may be necessary to let go of one source of help before one can have access to another. One may even find that there is a series of sources of help to whom one turns before becoming reliant on that which is known within.

As the shift begins to occur, and a reduction of dependency ensues, there will likewise occur a natural redirection of the communication. Reduction of the dependency on an external source enhances reliance on that which is coming to be known and seen within. But even though the direction of the communication changes, the nature of the communicative effort remains the same. This is very important. The principle still applies that for one to be receptive there must be the recognition of a need within and then an overture, a request for help. One who begins to shift the communication effort within must still apply this principle: there must be a continuous overture so that one can remain receptive to the help which now is beginning to come from within.

This shift from outer dependency to *inner reliance* inaugurates a very exciting time. First, one will begin to feel the communication of the soul within the Self. As that communication develops, one will begin to see also the dissolution of the protective (but fictitious) distinction of the Soul apart from the Self. One can then begin to dismantle the metaphor of separation in favour of the *truth of oneness*. One may further perceive the dissolution of the veil of separateness which formerly existed between the Self Within and the self without.

When one recognises the dependency and knows that it must be reduced, how does one go about it? Very carefully. One should remember that this is a time of transition both for the culture in which many are opening and for each one who is opening within.

It is wisest then, as with all things spiritual, to make haste slowly, and one will be well advised to reduce the dependency on the one who can help, or who has been of help while retaining the exchange with the one who has been of help. The communication then becomes a bifurcated monologic exchange.

In many of the antiquated disciplines and religions, this exchange was not possible because of the relationship between the disciple and the one upon whose teachings the discipline was modelled. In the absence of a new approach, many of these foreign and obsolete disciplines were imported into the West. The new approach now emerging in the West has many characteristics, and this exchange is one of those traits. But one must allow time for this exchange to develop as it should.

There is action to be taken both on the part of the one who can help and the one who has sought help and who has become perhaps overly dependent on the other. The reduction of the dependency can be effectuated by the one who has been called upon to be of help, but that undermines several principles of this new approach. If the one who has been of help makes the decision to reduce the dependency, then matters are proceeding much as they did in the obsolete disciplines; that is, the onus is still within the one who can help to make certain decisions, and this move would simply be another such decision made by one on behalf of another. In matters such as the determination of the course which things are to take, this is not proper, because the onus in such matters has shifted to the one who is opening and the responsibility rests with the one who is opening, to discriminatingly recognise when such a shift should be made. For one who has been of help to direct that such a shift should occur is not in harmony with the assumption of responsibility by the one who is opening. The nature of the change of consciousness and the nature of the new approach by which one expresses what known within require that the burden of action, the disciplined action to reduce the dependency, is on the one who is opening. It is virtually out of the control of the one who has been of help.

There are, however, some important principles to be observed. First, while it is important to reduce the dependency, it is also important to retain access to the flow from one who can be of help. Secondly, it is important to reduce the dependency gradually. It can be very detrimental to dismantle it too quickly. Thirdly, by this time, the one who is opening should have recognised that there have been certain intangible matters imparted by the one who has been of help; that is, matters other than just advice, as it were. It is incumbent on the one opening in awareness and now reducing the dependency to do so very carefully, for some of the matters which have been imparted are very fine in nature, and require very delicate handling to be preserved.

If the one reducing the dependency does so in an abrupt or reckless manner, the benefit of these finer items can be lost. In the beginning of the relationship between one who needed help and the one who could be of help, there was probably a great relief for the one who is opening to have found some answers. At some point in the relationship, the one opening may believe that the one who can help may no longer be able to offer what is needed. This may be true, for the initial hunger has passed, and one who needed help is, to some degree, satiated, and there is not the urgency that there once was. This is a natural development. Additionally, it is a fact of such a relationship that one can carry or help another only so far. This too is natural, for even if the ability remains to be of help, there may be a divergence of direction.

If this divergence is dramatic, which it may be, the parting may be catalysed by a perception of differences, even a strong or violent disagreement. One opening and reducing dependency now must be very careful indeed. If there is the slightest disdain allowed to be felt in the one who is opening, there is a risk that some of the finer matters which may have been imparted will be lost. An attitude of disdain manufactures a separateness, and the resulting gap will destroy the availability of that which was imparted in the spirit of oneness.

ATTRIBUTION

This in itself poses a difficult dilemma for the one who is opening. Inherent in the relationship of dependency is the reservation of the privilege of *attribution*.

This is helpful in the beginning but detrimental later on. Attribution occurs when one attributes to an external source the credit for what has transpired which one considers to be fortunate or acceptable or the blame for that which has transpired which one considers to be unfortunate or less than acceptable.

Attribution is a characteristic of all the major religions of the world today and of most of the so-called spiritual disciplines. It certainly survives in any discipline where the faith, trust, dependency, or even hope, are placed anywhere other than within the Self.

Attribution cannot survive the assumption of responsibility. The two are inconsistent, incompatible and mutually exclusive. As the change of consciousness becomes more manifest, and the assumption of responsibility becomes more evident, the influence which religions and the leaders of many spiritual disciplines hold over their followers will begin to diminish.

Just as attribution cannot survive the assumption of responsibility, fear cannot survive the emergence of truth. It is a new phase of truth which is now becoming available to the human community. This is happening through a natural evolutionary opening, not only of the awareness of individuals but also of the human community as a whole.

We can see then that it is not just an individual opening to truth who must now reduce the dependency on one who has been of help, but *humankind as a whole* will now reduce the dependency on those aspects or forms of divine consciousness which, while formerly being of help, have now become crutches or even institutions which hinder the growth and opening of an individual, as well as the growth of the collective awareness of humankind and the acceptance of the next phase of human evolution: a true change of consciousness.

To some degree, once the dependency has begun to be reduced by the one now accepting responsibility for one's own personal past, present, and future, the onus shifts to the one who has been of help, whether it is an individual or an institution. Such a one must now certainly welcome the independence of one formerly dependent, and must now willingly accept this reduction of dependency. There is a danger, of course, if the one who has been of help has become attached to being in the position of being needed, for this is certainly a position of power. Many have fallen into the trap of becoming intoxicated by that power, especially when the need for the help passes and the desire to prolong the possession of power remains.

However, if the one who is opening and now reducing the dependency on another can be courageous enough to assume the responsibility for the consequences of one's own circumstance, there is little chance or opportunity for the relationship to be so perverted. In the assumption of responsibility, there is a neutrality which deprives the continuance of an obsolete relationship of its back-pressure. It simply cannot survive.

Just as the keys to opening to that which is emerging from within are discrimination and discipline, so then the key to the establishment of this neutrality is *detachment*. Detachment in the assumption of responsibility also dissolves the fear that continuously exists so long as one is blinded by the fiction of attribution: that is, the fiction that someone or something other than the oneself is responsible for a present, past, or future state of affairs.

In the section which follows this one in this series on Self-determination, we will further discuss this matter of disciplined action and how it can be refined. We will also discuss detachment. We will then move on to the brink of a new very exciting development: the recognition of and the adaptation to a new personal reality, the development of a new and different attitude, and how that new attitude can actually affect the quality of life.

39 Consequences, Ignorance, Action and Destiny

As one begins to discriminate between what is learned and what is *known*, there is an important distinction to be made between that which simply must play out and that which requires one to take action.

The first of these relates to inevitable consequences and the second relates to one's contractual destiny. Eventually, we will see that the items of inevitable consequence can be converted to items of action. But just now we are concerned with the distinction to be made on one particular matter and how one's action on that matter determines one's destiny.

As we have seen, the seed of degeneration is constantly present, waiting to sprout in all transactions of the phenomenal universe. In some matter it engenders decomposition; in some matters it engenders doubt. Both of these are essentially the result of the same thing: the reduction to the elements of something on which action has ceased or on which no action has been taken.

When one observes the sprouting of the seed of degeneration in physical matter, and if one is still employing an obsolete reasoning process which draws conclusions from such observations, then it is easy and tempting to conclude that anything left alone and unattended will degenerate and go away if no action is taken on it. This is a reasonable and proper conclusion, based on those observations.

There is one particular matter which will not go away if left alone. There is one particular matter which cannot be disposed of by the absence of activity. This exception to the rule, this item which eludes our grasp and deludes our mind is *ignorance*. Ignorance will not go away if left alone: to dispel ignorance requires action – disciplined action – and effort.

Today's knowledge becomes tomorrow's ignorance. Tomorrow's ignorance then becomes superstition. Refusal to take the necessary continuous positive action to dispel one's own ignorance is the one factor which binds one to the wheel of the phenomenal universe. Until one puts forth positive action to dispel one's ignorance, one regenerates and perpetuates one's own existence in a series of incarnations. In this cycle of rebirth, one must endlessly face and deal with inevitable consequences which arise from the past, distort one's perception of the present, and condemn one to continued bondage in the future.

The effort to be put forth to dispel ignorance is multifaceted. It can be very disconcerting to stand on the brink of this new journey and not know where to start. Perhaps it will help if one can have a glimpse of the state to which one presently aspires; but in order to glimpse this state now and not pollute one's perception of it, one must be very careful. This is a time of transition for one who is opening, and it is tempting to interpret what one sees by using the tools which one now possesses and employs in other matters.

Just now we will look at one facet of this new conduct. It is one aspect of Inner Discipline which one who is opening will need to define, and then redefine.

Inner discipline is defined, refined and developed more easily if there is a firm foundation of outer discipline. Anyone who has been exposed to some form of external discipline early in life and has accepted that external discipline is very fortunate. If one has perfected outer discipline to any appreciable degree, then one need only move to the refinement of Inner Discipline. Recognising and developing this outer discipline and the building of the foundations of outer discipline are matters discussed elsewhere in these notes.

If one is reasonably confident of one's ability to exercise outer discipline, then one can begin a refinement of Inner Discipline, knowing that what one sees within can be carried forth into action.

It is at this time that one will begin to combine and integrate various diverse aspects of the new awareness which is dawning within. Now, one will begin to take what one sees, however small it may appear, test it with discrimination, make a decision, and carry that decision into manifested action. One must now be careful to avoid the delusion that this is what one already does in everyday life. This process is different: it is *self-determining*. The seeing, the testing, the deciding and the acting will now be done in a new way without reference to external sources, external authorities or past experiences.

One of the effects of this process is the development of the ability to move the point in time at which decisions are made. Without this process, a decision on any matter might be made too late – perhaps even after the event had occurred. Even though one may still mistakenly believe that one had some choice in the matter, the decision at this point is only how to cope with an event which has already occurred. The glimpses and flashes which one has within are signals of forthcoming events, consequences and opportunities, and with practice one can begin to move towards the ability to make a decision which is earlier in time but later in effect on most matters which one will confront.

Now, just briefly, we will look at the nature of the decision which one makes in this way. At the moment, we are not concerned with the decisions themselves; those are matters of any given moment. And we are not concerned with the process; that will expand with practice.

The nature of the decision of any given moment is, however, a matter of some consequence; and when viewed in the time spectrum, it becomes a matter of great consequence.

The nature of any given decision is determined by when it is made in relation to the matters affected by that decision. By 'nature' here, we mean the form the decision takes; that is, if it is made late in time in relation to the matters which it affects, it is largely a decision designed to enable one to cope with matters or events which are already manifested phenomenal fact. If it is made early in time in relation to such matters, then it will both effect certain events which are to come (that is, cause them to happen), and it will affect certain events as well (that is, alter or change them).

For most persons, awareness is focused downwards and outwards in the circuits of outer physical existence, and there is little opportunity to make early decisions which would effect the manifestation of events or affect their destiny. Most decisions are thus reactive, and there can be little positive disciplined action.

For one whose awareness is opening within, there is at first the odd occasion on which to make a directive decision, and then there is the increasing opportunity to do so more and more. The more it is practised, the greater the increase of both depth and breadth of opportunity.

When the focus is downwards and outwards, the decision is, by necessity, self-serving, self-preserving, defensive, reactive, and made according to the antiquated decision-making process by which one selfishly seeks to anticipate consequences according to past experiences for the purpose of serving one's own ends.

As the focus of awareness opens and rises, the decision is not limited by such self-containing restrictions. Rather, the decision becomes an event in itself.

When one begins to make decisions of this nature, the focus of attention is not to the past asking, 'How was this done last time?'; nor is it in the future asking, 'How will things be if this is done?' Rather, the focus is upwards and the attention is placed on the question, *'What is now to be done?'*

> **This question, when asked, will elicit a response. That response will have a ring of genuineness, and all effort must be put forth to preserve its purity.**

In that moment of perception, the decision can be made and materialised. The matter is there and then decided and set forth. It is determined. The nature or form of the decision is thus a matter of action – determined, disciplined action. It is a positive step, even if it is a step which says that nothing is now to be done!

This is a capsule view of the form of the decision. It is different from the form of most decisions which one may now be making. There is also a significant difference in the way one deals with the decision after it is made, and we will look at that later in this series of notes.

It is, however, helpful to look at one thing in that regard just now. This new decision is the vehicle by which one will begin to integrate that which is known and seen within into one's everyday physical, emotional and mental existence and activity. It is by this integration that one will begin to enlighten the mind, change one's emotional structure, and raise the level of health and performance of the physical body.

And it is by this integration that one begins to put forth the effort by which one can begin to dispel ignorance.

One whose spiritual awareness is opening is faced with a choice: to keep this new awareness locked away in some secret part of one's being and to attempt to continue life as it has been as if nothing has changed, or to bring it into practice in everyday life. To maintain the separation, refusing to act and bring resolve into action, places the opposite ends of one's existential spectrum in antagonism to each other. This causes ultimate physical degeneration and condemns one to further circuitous travail, buried in ignorance on the wheel of human existence.

To fully comprehend these concepts requires a firm schooling in basic metaphysics and other matters. To discuss those subjects now would not only be premature, but it would assume already a knowledge of certain matters themselves which are to be seen as one opens to inner enlightenment.

Emphasis so far in this discussion of self-determination has been placed mainly on putting resolve into disciplined physical action. Actually, the importance here should be placed equally among perception, resolve and action. But when one begins to open, there is often too much attention given to the details of one's physical health, environment and well-being. With some, this attention grows far beyond the bounds of proper balance, and indeed approaches the threshold of overzealousness and even fanaticism.

Obsession with the physical details of one's life often becomes a distraction in itself, and it can generate its own circuitous syndrome of consequences. Too much concern with matters such as diet, physical health, physical exercise and exotic physical disciplines can create an imbalance. If such an obsession with the physical side of things is allowed to grow too strong, it can effectively block the inner communication and the flow of new material which generates from within the self. Furthermore, the practice of exotic physical disciplines, often imported from other cultures, can arouse and excite energies which may be antagonistic to the Presence to which one is opening within.

While physical well-being is, of course, important, attention to it should be balanced. It should be remembered that physical existence, including all mental, emotional and physical activity, is not the start, but the finish; it is not the beginning, but the end. It is the arena wherein what is seen is placed into action and played out; it is not the arena where such matters are generated.

There will be little discussion here on the matter of maintaining good health, for it would seem that such a need is so obvious as to obviate any undue attention. However, there is one aspect of physical health which is important to see.

Inevitable consequences play out through the physical. As one opens, the process of the playing out of these inevitable consequences is accelerated, and hence one may actually experience physical discomfort or illness as the waves of consequences rise to the surface of physical existence to play out in one way or another. Later we will see how one can, from within, actually cause the seeds of inevitable consequences to be exposed and then neutralised or converted to items of back-pressure against which one can place creative action. We will also see how one can, from within, perceive the existence and nature of these seeds, and deal with them earlier in one's own time spectrum – much as one can make decisions earlier in time than one is perhaps accustomed to doing. In doing so, one is actually beginning to take responsibility for one's own destiny, and one can begin to shape the events which one faces.

Just now, however, we will examine another aspect of physical existence: the effect of certain actions upon physiological functions, and the interplay with certain mental processes and emotions. We are here interested to see how one cares for and lubricates those portals and the system of channels wherein the corporeal blends and interplays with the incorporeal. Here, one stands on the brink of a new personal reality.

40 Relating to the Aphenomenal

Where the incorporeal becomes corporeal

The point at which the incorporeal becomes corporeal is at best vague and elusive – sometimes almost indefinable. And in the extreme, it is virtually invisible. This point is a relative place, and can best be described as that grey area where idea becomes fact, where feeling becomes emotion, and impulse becomes action. It is also where aphenomenal becomes phenomenal, where spirit becomes soul, and where soul becomes matter.

Self-determination enables one to be at ease as one moves in and among the corridors of the inner structure. The more one becomes familiar with the inner structure and with the principles, patterns and procedures of moving within that inner structure, the more one does in fact become self-determining, and the more one can then bring the life flow and the life force into balance with one's own contractual destiny, one's real purpose.

Before one's awareness begins to open and expand, the focus of one's consciousness is centred in the grosser regions of one's being, the lower physical regions: the regions of reaction and inevitable consequence. Even after the awareness begins to open, the focus still can remain so centred for some time, and even later, it occasionally centres in those regions in order to deal with certain occurrences of mundane activity.

For someone whose awareness is not open beyond the baser activities and desires of human existence, the juncture where the relatively subtle areas of one's personal existence meet the more tangible is more clearly discernable. For such a one, there is little experience of insight and there are very few instances of enquiry. Here, life is closely controlled by inevitable consequences and instinctive reaction. There is no discrimination, and one's thought is devoid of any concept of responsibility or self-determination.

For such a one, there is little or no distance on either side of the line which traverses this juncture for one to deliberate the worth or advisability of action, or to contemplate the subtle implications of one's actions – past, present or future.

For one whose awareness is opening, all of this begins to change. The effects of this opening and of this change in one's daily life have been widely discussed in other parts of this Material. What we are concerned with just now

Our New Human Consciousness

is an examination of the effect of becoming aware of this juncture where one's awareness of the subtle meets the awareness of that which can be perceived. We are concerned with the structure of that point and with some of the implications of becoming aware of its existence.

As the awareness begins to open, not only does the focus of one's consciousness begin to rise out of the grosser regions and into the finer, but also the depth and width of awareness both above and below this point begin to expand; that is, one begins to have some moments or instances of waking perception, both of the existence of this region and of the activities which transpire there.

It is due to this perception that one begins to have an increasing opportunity to deliberate those things which formerly occurred out of one's waking awareness.

It is due to this perception that one has increased opportunity to act on what one now begins to see in this expanded region of awareness.

One who faces this new awareness with inner trust and fearlessness will wish to see and pursue all that is now becoming newly available.

The nature of the enquiry

The enquiry which one is now beginning to pursue happens largely, in the Western mind, on the plane or level of waking awareness. Our tendency to enquire into the 'why' of everything we face has constructed, over the generations, a circuited mechanism that seeks to answer by referring to conditioned responses within the mind, and these responses cannot answer the new questions in that old way.

Accordingly, while the enquiry still continues to be asked in waking consciousness, the answers must begin to come from another place within, and in a different form, and with a different substance, and built of a different material. If the old way is adhered to, the new questions are of the present and future while the answers are of the past.

As the awareness begins to expand, then, a new process begins to emerge. The questions are still asked in the only way we know how to ask them. This is acceptable, for what is important at this point is not the form of the question, but the asking of it; and what is more important is the form and substance of the answer, and the receiving of it.

This process of asking old questions and receiving new answers is part of the time of transition towards a time when even the questions will be new.

It is evident that this enquiry cannot and does not proceed in the old way – the way by which one has gone about things in the past. Further, it is not enough just to alter the form of the question or the answer. Something major must change – *really* change.

The endocrine glands

To enable this change to occur, or even begin to occur, certain physiological processes are called into play in the physical bodies; certain processes which affect the way in which one functions physically, emotionally and mentally.

The effect on these functions is dramatic and is brought about and facilitated largely by alterations in one's blood chemistry, and the changes in blood chemistry are brought about by activities in the endocrine glands and their functions.

There are several endocrine glands in the body. Anatomically and physiologically, their function is to produce certain secretions which enter directly into the bloodstream and produce certain effects, mostly in the fleshly physical body.

Current medical knowledge contains very little concerning the functions of these endocrine glands. In most persons, they lie dormant or perform some perfunctory services to the physical body with which we are not concerned here.

As evolution brings one to the threshold of voluntary aspiration towards higher knowledge, the latent activities of these glands are awakened, and the secretions which are forthcoming enable consciousness to expand as well as allowing certain physical tools to become implemented.

These tools are necessary for one to be able to perceive those matters which are becoming available to one as a result of the expansion of that zone on either side of the line which traverses the point where the corporeal blends with the incorporeal.

Expanding the zone of awareness

This entire combination of events and activities is a very dynamic phenomenon; that is, this expansion of this zone of awareness, the effect of the awakening of the latent functions of the endocrine glands, and the approach of personal evolutionary readiness to enquire into the matters which have thus far been hidden from view.

In the beginning, and until this combination of events begins to take place, the enquiry, most of which initially transpires at the waking conscious level, can elicit only those reactions which exist in the realm of waking consciousness. Even these responses are limited by the configurations of a mental or reasoning process which is not only circuitous and self-serving but also incapable of perceiving anything outside of the confines of its own operational parameters. They are also undermined by the involuntary activation of a repertoire of terribly base emotional reactions, over which most persons have almost no control and which arise to blind any perception which might begin to become available.

This new interplay of new events begins to enable one to transform all of this. The enquiry, while still conducted largely at the level of waking consciousness, begins to have infeed from other levels of consciousness; that is, the horizons of perception begin to widen and there is access to new material previously unavailable.

All of this does not simply mean that one will see more things, nor that one will see new things; both of these will happen. But additionally, it also means that one will see *other things*.

Perception of these 'other things' requires an accelerated maturing of emotional reactions and a transformation of one's thinking process, for by perceiving these other things one has the responsibility to accept what one sees and perhaps to take some action on it. This requires a constant and continuous update of one's thought processes and emotional and behaviour patterns.

A new balance

In short, what is required is a balance – a new balance in which one perceives something which *is* different in a *way* which is different. All of this produces a result which is different and virtually unimaginable and inconceivable from the position occupied before, perhaps only moments before.

This new balance must be maintained and it can be maintained largely due to the awakening of the latent tendencies of the endocrine glands and the effects which occur on one's consciousness as a result of the secretion of these glands.

The importance of a new Attitude

But even the new activity of these glands is not enough in itself to enable one to maintain that new balance. The real overriding key to the maintenance of that balance is *attitude*. The physiological factors mentioned merely provide one with some of the tools which are necessary. It is up to one to implement these new tools on one's own by the process of an attitude of self-determination and all that it implies.

Each soul who enters an earthly incarnation does so with and for a unique purpose. This purpose belongs uniquely to that soul. So does the responsibility to fulfil that purpose and, at least to some extent, the way in which that purpose will be fulfilled. The latitude in and by which one fulfils that purpose expands concurrently with the expansion of this new horizon of enquiry and perception.

All of this brings one to the brink of a new personal reality, and it is the nature of this new reality that it too is unique to each individual experiences it. It is shaped by the vast and unique trove of inevitable consequences which each one carries and by the unique combination of potential capabilities, desires, dreams and talents.

Since each individual possesses a unique combination of these factors, there can be few if any hard and fast rules which apply to all beyond those rules which have become manifest to govern and maintain an orderly universe in which expression takes place. One who stands of the brink on self determination must obey those rules, but beyond that, there is little which can be said to apply to all except for certain principles and guidelines.

One of these guidelines is the nurturing of a new and different attitude. We will have much to say on this matter of attitude in later notes and in other parts of this Material. Perhaps at this point, however, the most concise and pertinent description of this attitude is that it is one of 'openness'. Lest this sound glib, let it be said that one is cautioned against attaching any definition of any description to this concept of 'openness', for this too will evolve and change as one opens in awareness.

The enquiry in which one is involved necessitates that one be able to enter into alternative dimensions, tapping into information which one needs to fulfil one's own unique purpose – that is, one's contractual destiny. To some extent, each person enters these alternative dimensions in sleep or in subconscious mentation of which one is not generally aware at the waking level. It is, however, impossible for one to enter these dimensions consciously without the aid of the enhanced function of the endocrine glands. This enhanced functioning enables one to see: it is one's *attitude* which enables one to handle what one sees.

And it is discrimination and discipline which enable one to place into action that which one sees.

41   Educating the Life Vehicles

The bridge between Discrimination and Discipline

The activities in which one engages to become self-determining must be carefully coordinated in a concerted effort so that all parts of one's being share in a new awareness.

Discipline in the physical bodies is an empty gesture if there is no discrimination present in the application of such discipline. Similarly, if one has finely honed the ability to discriminate, the forthcoming wisdom is lost if there is no discipline present to place resolve into action.

To coordinate discipline on the one hand and discrimination on the other, a bridge between them is needed. The middle ground, spanned by this bridge, is the fine and subtle area of emotion. The bridge itself is control of this emotional middle ground, and the emotional extremes of desire and disdain. These are matters of which Western psychology really knows very little.

As we have seen in our cursory examination of the mental processes of the Western mind, the obsolete reasoning process is largely activated and controlled by the automatic implementation of circuited reactions. When these circuits are activated, they can lead one on erroneous flights of mental fantasy which often terminate in erroneous conclusions.

Dispelling emotional ignorance

When we leave the realm of reason and thought and descend into the realm of emotion, we find that it too is largely governed by a repertoire of reactions that are often of a very primitive nature. In the present state of emotional immaturity, those living in a Western culture are virtual slaves to emotional reactions over which they have almost no control. This lack of control is a result of the lack of effort – in the right direction – to dispel this emotional ignorance.

Thus far, efforts by Western psychology have been unsuccessful in dealing with, let alone understanding, the emotional process which governs human conduct and behaviour. The specifics of this allegation are explored elsewhere in this Material. For this particular treatise on self-determination, we are concerned specifically with the implications of a lack of control and a lack of understanding of the emotional process for one opening in spiritual awareness who seeks and aspires to voluntarily and consciously become familiar with and explore the inner structure of human being.

Control of emotional reactions is not accomplished by suppression, that is, attempts to forcibly relegate those reactions to a state of contained inactivity. Such an attempt merely energises these reactions and adds to the enervation which they will explosively express when they are catalysed and break the bonds of their confinement. Nor are they controlled by release and expression. Once again, such indulgence, often the essential practice of Western psychological therapy, merely grants a false legitimacy to a very basic and immature pleasure which tries to explain and justify its own existence through excessive expression and supposed release.

Such indulgence also energises not only the primary emotion with which one seeks to deal but also various ancillary reactions which evidence their existence by indulging in their own self-expression at inopportune moments.

Attempts to deal with obsolete and immature emotional reactions in these ways may ostensibly grant temporary relief, but what is in fact occurring is merely a release of a pressure which exists in items on the surface of an emotional ocean at the expense of the further creation of the pressure in the depths of the ocean itself, and in all the other obsolete and undesirable emotional reactions which reside there awaiting the opportunity to express themselves.

Dissolving emotional interference

What we are concerned with here is the frustration which results from knowing something within the Self, and then experiencing the inability to place it into manifested action because of the interference of these unwanted and unwelcome emotional reactions which arise to overrule disciplined action and undermine discrimination.

Spiritual progress is unavoidably subject to the barriers of a circuitous mental process which cannot rationalise itself out of its own confines. It is also subject to a physical sluggishness which is virtually incapable of self-correction or self-motivation, and it is subject to the emotional barriers of desire and disdain. These emotional barriers are often so strong that they defy any attempt to reason with them. Additionally, they can cause an aversion to some intended activity. In spiritual matters, in moving within the inner corridors and structure, one cannot afford the luxury of indulging such emotional obstacles.

The principal problem of concern arises when one is facing an opportunity, most importantly an opportunity within. When one has mustered the needed resolve and determination, there can then arise feelings of desire or disdain which distractingly interfere with the opportunity presented. Especially in the early stages of opening awareness, these distracting signals arise to interfere at most inopportune moments. In the more advanced stages of expanded consciousness, it is imperative that desire, on the one end of the emotional spectrum, and disdain on the other end, be subject to control.

Fear and change

This control is accomplished through education of the lower bodies. To some degree, it is accomplished through experience. The commonest primary emotional barrier which one encounters is, of course, fear. Fear cannot be overcome or conquered; but it can be dissolved by education of the lower bodies and by the inculcation of a confidence instilled by this education.

Ironically, fear thrives on the one thing in the universe which is absolutely inevitable: constant change. So too do desire and disdain derive their sustenance from change – desire being the emotion which seeks to retain some experience from the past or hasten an anticipated experience of the future, and disdain being the emotion which seeks to retain an aversion to some such past experience or avert an experience which looms in the future.

It is the nature of the unique trove of inevitable consequences carried by each of us that it is impossible to precisely anticipate or accurately predict the exact nature of each experience which awaits us in the future.

Some physical experiences, especially ones which recur regularly, are highly predictable, and if they do elicit feelings of fear, desire or disdain, we can often find the wherewithal to overcome them by reference to past experience. It is different with experiences of a mental or emotional nature. It is impossible to predict these until one begins to go within in strength and see the seeds of these consequences which are waiting to sprout into experiences. It is the unpredictable experiences, whether mental, emotional and even physical experiences not previously encountered, which elicit these emotional reactions.

Emotions and the 'spiritual experience'

As one evolves within and begins to open, really open, there is another kind of new and different experience which arises which is unpredictable and totally inexplicable in terms of any past experience. This is an experience of a 'spiritual nature'. Experiences of this nature come by Grace from within, and they may happen only once.

If there is fear, desire or disdain – that is, fear of the unknown, desire to return to the past, or disdain of new experiences – there is the unfortunate possibility that one may deprive oneself of a unique and golden opportunity to go through an enlightening experience.

This is truly tragic, since it is just for the opportunity of such experiences to occur that the consciousness opens and the awareness expands. One cannot prepare for these experiences in the way one attempts to prepare for other experiences. Even if they are described by a teacher, or in something which one has read, such a description, even if it is grasped, is insufficient to adequately prepare one for the actual experience.

Neither are sheer determination, courage, or emotional suppression or control sufficient to ensure that one can navigate this narrow channel of inner experience. Preparation for these experiences by one who wishes to be self-determining must be accomplished through education of the lower bodies.

Educating the lower bodies

This education is not a process which seeks to accumulate a catalogue of experiences which are gleaned from the past and anticipated in the future so that preparations can be made to meet them when they arise. This education is more thorough: it is intended to develop an Inner Discipline, trust and confidence which permeate all levels of one's being, dispelling the darkness of fear, desire and disdain so that one can approach the experiences of outer life or be approached by the experiences of inner life free of these distracting and intrusive emotional influences.

This education is accomplished by patient, gradual and gentle persistence. Rather than teaching the bodies about certain experiences, it teaches them how to go through any experience, pleasant or unpleasant, new or old, adjusting to the changes it brings and manifesting whatever is needed in the moment to complete the experience.

This education teaches the bodies not only of new tasks but also to do old tasks in new ways. More importantly, it teaches one to do all tasks presented with a different attitude and a different approach which eliminate fear and dissolve desire and disdain in favour of this inner confidence. It also encourages one to apply a new formula of action to all situations, problems and experiences.

One can then be prepared for all events, whether or not one can foresee them, anticipate their implications, or analyse their effects.

It must be remembered that this education proceeds from an ability to act – to move – without asking 'why'. This is a training which, when perfected, is very effective in matters of daily life, but in matters of the inner life it is more than that: it is absolutely essential. When an opportunity is presented within, one who stops long enough to ask 'why' will surely lose the moment. And if another new opportunity then presents itself on the heels of the first (which often happens), there is no time to dwell on the first experience which is now in the past and which may, through desire, attract one's attention away from the experience newly forming in the moment.

This education enables the lower bodies to initiate a transformation, and one begins to learn of one's own limitations and capabilities. By this self-transformation, the various parts of one's being begin to co-operate and work together. Thus, when an experience presents itself, that part of the being which is principally negotiating the experience – be it physical, emotional, or mental or spiritual – knows that there will be a diminishing amount of intrusive interference from other parts of one's being which previously felt threatened, frightened or deprived, and then expressed such emotion through disdain, fear or desire.

This education takes time. In some cases, it may take a great deal of time, but it begins to work immediately as soon as one commits oneself to it. The benefits of its application and practice are observable – sometimes instantaneously – for its application begins to broaden one's viewing spectrum in relation to seeing in time, and it begins to shorten the experiential spectrum in relation to being in time. This means that one will begin to see the forthcoming occurrences which must play out as a result of inevitable consequences earlier than one is perhaps accustomed to seeing them, and it means that the time span is shortened between action and inevitable consequence.

To be able to do this, all parts of the being must always be ready for whatever it is that is coming next. This process of self-determination is complete and thorough and the education involved affects all of one's activities. The benefits of an expanding awareness accrue to all parts of one's being, and to everything with which and everyone with whom one comes into contact in any way.

We have already discussed some of the elements of this education, and we will now turn our attention to its further and finer elements: the development of an ability to enter a *new reality*, and the development of an attitude through which one can manifest that new reality.

42   Facing an Alternative Reality

The pressure of change increases

The primary elements of this educational process which we have discussed thus far are essential for one opening to become self-determining. Although there may have been a great deal of effort and activity expended thus far, that which one has done may have been spontaneous and spasmodic; it may have been of an unpremeditated nature. One may have found that inner growth was fortuitous and irregular. One may, in other words, have experienced a gentle introduction to what is about to unfold.

If such has been the nature thus far of the relationship between one who is opening and this new knowingness felt and occasionally seen within, then there is now due an alteration of this relationship; it will begin to undergo a natural transformation in preparation for the training which is now to follow. One may be feeling impatience in sensing the inevitability of that which would appear to be coming next, for one is coming face to face with the recognition that a change of lifestyle and thought style is underway.

It is possible that one has voluntarily entered this time and programme of transformation. In such case, one is willingly attempting to submit to the alternatives one is facing. On the other hand, it is possible that the changes one feels are unsolicited, and it may seem that one is being involuntarily swept along on a wave of change over which one has no control.

Whatever the case, and whether or not any changes have yet been experienced, in all probability some changes are now imminent, and it can be at this time that some resistance will begin to be experienced. This is a critical time for one manifesting this path of self-determination.

Thus far, the pressure for change may have been gentle. As well, the changes which one may have undergone have perhaps, for the most part, been gentle – changes which only slightly taxed ability and which have not yet really taxed credibility. In this time of transition, one may still have been able to retain the ability to rationalise the changes which one has experienced; that is, to explain them to one's mind in terms which the mind understands and in concepts in which the mind is still working comfortably for the most part. In such case, there is still some separation, some divergence and contradiction in the coexistence of these two realms of experience.

Integrating two realms of existence

Certainly these realms have not yet been integrated. There will be items from one realm of experience which cannot be explained in terms of the other. This period of transitionally experiencing the divergence and separation and learning to accept this coexistence may have lasted for months – even years.

Now the two realms of this bifurcated existence will begin to converge. It is the nature of awareness and the state of one's consciousness at this time – namely, when this convergence begins to occur – that the focus of awareness will be placed in the world of physical existence; that is, in the world which has thus far been real, familiar and comfortable.

As this time of convergence and conciliation approaches, then, events will be viewed, as they always are in a time of upheaval, crisis, trauma and change, from the point of view where rationalisation occurs. This is the place within our being where defence resides, and it is the place within us which is ruled and controlled by the ultimate desire, the ultimate need: this instinct of survival. The strength remaining in this instinct – the tenacity of its grip on the focus of awareness – will be determined by how effectively one has placed into practice the elements of self-determination – how effectively one has thus far educated the circuits of the mind, emotions and body in the practice of accepting change.

At this time of convergence of two seemingly irreconcilable realms of existence, the focus of awareness is necessarily placed and rooted firmly in the realm which has thus far been at least seemingly oblivious of the other. The predicament now begins to change. Now one is approaching a juncture at which a decision will be presented. Perhaps more than a time of decision, it is a time of recognition. One may feel some resistance as this time approaches: resistance, first, against the pressure and responsibility of making any decision at all; and, second, resistance to the alternatives presented. This predicament is one which bears some examination, for it is one which will appear and reappear until one masters and assimilates both the attitude and the ability to do that which we are about to examine.

Dealing with resistance to change

Let us just now briefly review this predicament. It occurs when change is imminent, when one feels that a change is inevitable, and when the focus of awareness is still vulnerable to the attack and grip of the instinct of survival. The circuits of the body, emotions and mind have not yet been fully educated and transformed.

It is this lack of education, this ignorance and immaturity of mind, emotion and body which give rise to the fear of change. It is this fear which locks the focus of awareness in the lower circuits as change begins to appear imminent. This syndrome will continue so long as the ignorance remains. This circuitous syndrome itself can produce fear – fear of its own recurrence. Since, by becoming more aware, one opening is reducing the time differential between act and consequence, and seeing and experience, the changes will begin to happen faster and faster. Unless one takes some action, makes some voluntary move within, some shift, in order to be able to accept, cope with and move into these changes, the pressure of change can become unbearable.

It is just such a shift which now presents itself. To make this shift, one must first analyse one's present condition and decide if it is acceptable. In doing so, one must remember, if possible, that this examination and decision are being made in a condition of imbalance – in a time when the focus of awareness is in the circuits – at a time when one may be feeling confusion, disorientation and loss of direction. This is as it should be; the decision which we will describe here must be made in that condition and with the awareness so focused. This is a decision which must be made in and on behalf of that part of one's being which does become confused, experiences fear, and, in desperation, clings to its own ignorance. If one faces one's present condition and knows – and feels – that it is unacceptable, one can then move; one can shift.

To do so, one must be prepared to express a vocal commitment to this change.

In preparing for this shift, and in preparing to express this commitment, one is fully justified in harbouring the suspicion that one may suffer an attack upon every foundation which has, up until now, formed a basis for one's personal concept of existence: one's personal concept of what is real.

Firstly, recognition of the possibility of an alternative reality

It is now that one is called upon to recognise that things are not the way one believed them to be. To make this shift, one must, then, acknowledge, perhaps for the first time, that there truly may be a possibility that there does exist an alternative to what one has heretofore considered to be reality.

This may be the first time that one has faced this possibility – in this way – full on – with full awareness of making this acknowledgement. It will not be the last time it happens. Until one masters the ability to maintain a constant attitude which continuously expresses this acknowledgement, then the need to make the acknowledgement, at varying but regular intervals, will reappear with its attendant traumas and recur with nightmarish regularity. As the need for acknowledgement recurs, it will once again, each time, challenge one's effort and ability to adjust and readjust, not only to the concept of but also the acceptance of the perplexing, auspicious and disturbing possibility that there is, in fact, another, and alternative reality.

When the need for this acknowledgement arises, it will seem that one must decide to pursue a course of action which appears to be virtually self-destructive, and understandably so. It will also appear that one has a choice; but, in fact, this is not the case. One may erroneously believe, in ignorance, that it is still possible to allow this recognition to go away, to die a natural death. One may erroneously believe that one will be free to return to the security of confines and concepts which one has formerly found to be comfortable and familiar.

Self-determination does not have room for the luxury of such self-imposed ignorance. To dispel this ignorance, this illusion, requires effort – self-determined effort – which includes two steps which one may be reluctant to take.

- The first is to seek and accept some assistance from one who can help.
- The second is to proceed to action from Inner Discipline.

The first step can be undermined by the fiction of self-sufficiency, and the second can be undermined by the tendency of the mind to rationalise the action before it is taken.

Both of these two steps must be taken, and they must be taken voluntarily. Even though there may be some external assistance, both of these steps must be taken from within – there will be no imposition of change or action from without. This is the principal element of self-determination.

The prospect of taking these steps may cause apprehension, but this apprehension is minor alongside the more frightening prospect of remaining in the limbo of an unreal reality, replete with the stagnation of inertia and ignorance. It may appear that one was forced into this unreal reality through an involuntary birth and unkind circumstance, but as one grows from within and can see more of one's true situation, one realises that it is rather one's own contractual destiny which has, by Grace, brought one to this important juncture.

Here one has the opportunity to take an enormous leap on one's own personal cosmic evolutionary path. Certainly one will see, if one looks, that this step of recognition and movement, perplexing as it may appear, is the only manner in and through which one can possibly make any attempt to determine what it is that one knows within.

First encounter with the 'ego'

If one can successfully negotiate this step, one will have completed the first of a series of conscious but subtle encounters with that part of one's being which we will call the *ego*; but this term is employed here only because of the lack of any other term in our language which sufficiently or correctly identifies that part of our being which one now has the opportunity to glimpse, objectively recognise, and subtly challenge.

As one moves on this path of self-determination, there are some extremely important guidelines which one is encouraged to heed and follow. It is now time to examine one of those guidelines. It concerns this step of acknowledging the possible existence of an alternative to what one may have heretofore considered to be reality, and it also concerns what one may have seen as a result of that acknowledgement. More importantly, it concerns what one may believe one has seen as a result of taking this step.

The important guideline to see at this present juncture is this: any attempt to define or describe in any way this term 'ego' at this time is not only spurious and delusive but also self-serving to the ego itself.

This problem of defining and successfully describing the ego, let alone dealing with it, is compounded in our culture both by the grandiose proportions to which it has grown both collectively and individually, by the gross errors made by modern psychology in attempting to manipulate it, and by the dangers introduced by many so-called 'spiritual' disciplines and practices in an attempt to crush and destroy it.

If one who is opening now attempts to define what one has seen as a result of this important step which one has taken, one will further compound these enormous follies already perpetrated on our culture by those who should have known better. Any attempt, then, to define this term now, and any attempt to describe that which it defines, can be extremely perilous to the further activities of self-determination which will now follow. It is more than sufficient now for one to recognise and acknowledge the probable existence of an alternative to what one has previously considered to be reality, to assimilate that recognition, and to refrain from any attempt to define, describe or draw conclusions about what one has experienced.

In other chapters of this book, we explore and examine a new and different way to approach this matter of 'ego', and some positive steps which one can take to begin to manifest this new and beautiful alternative reality.

43 *Manifesting a New Personal Reality*

When one acknowledges the possibility of the existence of an alternative to what one has previously considered to be reality, one has then, for the first time, the opportunity of manifesting that new reality.

In this discussion, we will look at just how one can go about making this new possibility a new reality.

Acknowledging the possibility of a new reality

It is very important that one take this step very slowly and carefully, for it is tempting to move too quickly, to take some of the steps too fast, and hence to deprive oneself of the helpful and beneficial effects which can accrue when one moves slowly enough to experience each step in depth.

It is also very important not to be self-deceived by the appearance of this acknowledgement. Although this acknowledgement is made only once for the first time, it is not made only once. The important factor in this acknowledgement is not that there is another reality, but that one has acknowledged the possibility of its existence. The emphasis of importance is on the acknowledgement of the possibility rather than the alternative reality itself. It is the process of making the acknowledgement of the possibility that is crucial, and it is this process which is set in motion by this first acknowledgement.

The first time that one makes this acknowledgement it is an event, an occurrence. What one should now do, after making this first acknowledgement, is to practise this event so as to make it, first, a series of events, and then a process.

The conversion of this event into a process takes time. It is this conversion which is the essence of self-determination, and it must be done slowly, and it must be done alone. It can be coached and sometimes guided by one who can help, but in the final analysis it must be done alone.

When the acknowledgement of the possibility of another reality is first made, one may feel a great relief. By making that acknowledgement, one can reduce a great pressure which has been building up over a long period of time. This pressure was created as one tried to rationalise, confirm and justify certain events being introduced and experienced in one's life in the terms of a reality in which one had been accustomed to living and working. In other words, one may have tried to reconcile things in one's life in terms of the way one believed things to be.

Now, with the pressure which has grown from the impossibility of making this reconciliation, simply making the acknowledgement of the possibility of another reality enables one to breathe a sigh of relief. Now there is no longer any need to attempt to define or interpret events, feelings or thoughts in terms which do not fit those events, feelings or thoughts.

Again, this is a time for caution. It should be borne in mind that what is important here is not the new reality but the acknowledgement of the possibility of its existence. If one attempts to speculate on the nature of this new reality, one may become deluded and confused. One will be tempted to draw conclusions concerning something about which one really knows very little.

It is understandable for one to wonder where this is all going. Where is it taking us? One may ask, 'How is this going to affect my life? How will this new reality make things different?'

Where is this all going?

Perhaps we can have a brief look at just what one is entering by making this acknowledgement. As we have said, the acknowledgement of the possibility of a new and different reality opens up a new and different way of thinking. This acknowledgement does not simply imply the recognition of the existence of other levels of life and other planes of consciousness. It is not too difficult to acknowledge that possibility while holding on to one's present concept of reality as one has come to define that term to oneself – that is, as one has come to know life in a human body. Here we are talking of much much more; we are here dealing with the first acknowledgement of an alternative reality. To the intellect, this may mean something apart, something 'out there', so to speak. So long as this other reality stays 'out there', one feels safe; there is no need to do anything about it.

This may be true enough for the moment. If the possibility looms that something must be done about it, then the mind may begin to feel pressured to define that new reality and to attempt to determine what must be done about it. This approach is incorrect and will lead to massive confusion. Again, what is important is the acknowledgement of the existence of an alternative: the first acknowledgement. This, of course, implies that there will be another, second, acknowledgement. And this is true. Then a third, and so forth; for each time one makes this acknowledgement, one is doing so from a position which was not only inconceivable but non-existent before the previous acknowledgement was made.

Moving into the 'process'

In other words, each time such an acknowledgement is made, there is a little bit of that new reality which creeps into the present old reality, and everything changes. The change may be almost imperceptible, but it is there. If one is able to see within, one may be able to perceive the change. But even that perception will not last very long, for as that new little bit of a new reality is assimilated in one's consciousness, the entire being is affected and changed. A little bit of the old reality is lost.

Just as the new reality was non-existent before it manifested in one's consciousness, so too then does this little bit of old reality become non-existent as it is disintegrated into oblivion by the forces of reduction, which work in the phenomenal universe to dispose of old bits of existence which are no longer needed.

So, now we have two elements to be considered: the old reality and the possibility of a new one. Perhaps we have even moved on to another second acknowledgement. When the second and third and other acknowledgements are made, they are not considering the same alternative reality which was acknowledged in the first instance; for with the change which has occurred, the present acknowledgement is considering something into which one will move from one's present position, not from where one was when one first made the first acknowledgement.

Now it is time to add a third element of this process, and this is that part of one's being which we have referred to as the ego. Although it is dangerous and self-serving to the ego to attempt to define it, we can observe it and perceive some of what it does.

The ego works within a point of consciousness fixed in time and space. It defines its own reality at any given moment, mostly with reference to the past. More important than the actual definition which it concocts at any given moment, is its inclination to cling to and defend that present definition, whatever it may be. To accomplish this end, it deludes one into believing that the present definition of reality is the way things are and that the definition has actually been determined by the True Self. It is when the time comes for a new acknowledgement to be made that a searing inner conflict can be felt, as the previously amalgamated reality begins to divide.

The ego at this point does not know what to do or how to cope. At this point, there is no denying that things are not as one believed them to be, and the longer the ego attempts to cling to the old belief, the more agonising becomes the inner turmoil.

If one can embark on a gentle series of acknowledgements of the possibility of an alternative to what one has previously considered to be reality, this process begins to break down. The conflict created by the acknowledgement actually will be *less* each time one is made. This is the essence of the education of the lower bodies, for that is where the ego resides and where it clings to its concept of reality.

This is not an easy process. It takes time and it takes effort. Most probably, if one is engaged in this process of self-determination, one is living in the world, dealing with everyday matters of life, and it is easy to believe that with things changing so often, with a new reality presenting itself so often, that one is at a loss to determine a course of action. This is not necessarily so. This process of acknowledging the possibility of a new and different reality can actually make it easier to make decisions, for what one is doing each time one makes the acknowledgement is to open to the possibility of a new way of doing things.

Moving towards a constant and continuous acknowledgement

Contrary to popular belief, it is not a new way of doing things which creates problems; it is the clinging to an old way of doing things when it is time for a change. If one is able to place into motion this process of acknowledging the possibility of a different reality, then one eventually will find that rather than a series of such acknowledgements, there is a constant and continuous acknowledgement of such a possibility.

It may appear that this is easy to do, and of course it should be easy to do. In fact, nothing should be easier; it is a very simple process which says that things are the way they are at any given moment in time. The difficulty arises as the ego fastens its focus on a particular given moment in time – either one in the past, or one now in the present and moving into the past – and attempts to retain it. In doing so, it loses its fluidity, its motion, its ability to adapt to the changing present. It attempts to define a present reality according to past experience. It fixes its focus on the present moment, distorting it according to that definition, and then drifts into the past with the point on which the focus is fixed.

Thus a conflict is created. Not only does the pressure of conflict increase as the point of focus drifts into the past, but the pressure increases also on the ego to attempt to defend the old reality which is fast becoming non-existent. Something has to happen; something has to give. Either the ego must admit it was wrong in its conception of the way things are, and acknowledge the possibility of a new reality, or that new reality will be forced upon it by external change.

The former is far preferable to the latter. It is far better to begin to educate the ego and the bodies early to continuously and constantly acknowledge the possibility of an adaptation to a new and changing reality than to have that possibility become real through an abrupt and traumatic break with the past.

New tools to reconcile the future and the past

How is one to go about this? How is one to anticipate a future which is fast becoming the present? How is one to reconcile the changes of that future-cum-present with an old present soon to become the past? It is difficult if not impossible to reconcile the two with the tools which one has – with reference to the way in which one has gone about things in the past. A new element must be injected. Some new and different personal chemistry must happen so that one can adapt to and manifest this new reality. And that is exactly what is happening.

The bodies, with the increased functions of the endocrine glands, are already well into the physiological changes needed for this new reality to be accepted. The process by which this new reality is accepted is in itself a new and different reality, for it is assimilated in a way which, as we have said many times, is not learned. It is accepted in a way which is not yet in evidence in one's lifestyle and thought style.

This process of acceptance is not learned and cannot be learned. It must be experienced, and the nature of it is that each new bit of reality and each new acceptance of that new bit of reality cannot be anticipated or predicted.

There is one part of this process which can effectively be predicted, and that is that it is going to happen. It is going to happen again and again, and it is going to happen faster and faster until the string of events does in fact become a process – a continuous and constant process.

It is helpful if one can grasp the fact that this string of events is a stream of activity which consists of incidents, each of which have little in common except for their very occurrence. This means that when the time comes for another acknowledgement, there will be very little or perhaps nothing which enables one to say 'that same event which happened before is happening again' – that is, the old way in which one recognised forthcoming change. Since one is now moving from a position which has incorporated and is made up of a part of a new and different reality which may have been assimilated only moments before, there is no event or occurrence which will be just like one experienced before – except the experience itself.

That experience itself can be recognised if one trains oneself to watch for the earmarks of its approach; and that experience as it continuously presents itself, each time in a different form, can gradually be traversed with greater ease if one trains and educates the bodies, the mind, the emotions and the ego to approach this event in a certain way.

We will now look at how to develop this watchfulness and this new approach.

44 Rejecting, Dismantling and Discarding the Old

The true essence of human nature is True Growth rather than stagnation; peace rather than turmoil; serenity rather than struggle. As one begins to become self-determining, one begins to become that which one has always been rather than something which one imagines one should become but can never be. The new reality which one seeks to manifest is thus something which one *is* rather than something which one is to become. It would be naive for us to say that what one is becoming is the full manifestation of the essence of our nature, for that is the full purpose of evolution; but we can say that this new development is the next step in the eventual full manifestation of that essential reality.

Developing an inner trust

This next step then is to be taken with confidence, and from that confidence can develop an inner trust. This step must be taken from where one stands as it begins; one cannot project to where one would like to be when one starts, nor can one await the time when one would supposedly be in that state where one would like to be before presenting oneself at the point where one would start this step. This step is taken now, where one is, as one is when it begins.

As if in a dream, one watches the mind define its predicament and attempt to define its past and its future. It feels as if it knows what is ahead, and, in truth, in some ways it does. But it vacillates back and forth, surging forward to catch a glimpse of a new reality, and then falling back, a victim of the grip and pull of the attachment to thoughts, emotions, habits, actions and objects of the past.

As each step in the manifestation presents itself through each acknowledgement of the possibility of a new and different reality, relationships begin to alter and fade. Relationships with everything – human, material, mental and emotional – are changing, moving and dying as the prospect of acknowledging the possibility of a new and different reality looms now, not only in the future, but now – right now – in the ominous present.

Obviously, this is a time of change. Each time the acknowledgement of the possibility of a new and different reality is made, it is time for a change, and each time this happens, the change as well as the new reality presents itself in a different form. The precarious equilibrium of one's mental and emotional balance can now depend on one's ability to move – to put into practice the resolve and the action of which we have spoken so fully – for to remain in a state of inaction and indecision increases the pressure already weighing so heavily.

Just what is one to do now? How is one to go about even knowing what to practice, let alone putting it into action?

The groundwork has been laid in the effort which one has put forth thus far: that is, the effort to develop the discipline to move; the effort to develop the ability to discriminate in the moment; and the effort to bring into reality the resolve to become self-determining. This groundwork is essential now for one to take the next steps.

As we have mentioned, the changes which have been arising thus far have perhaps appeared to happen fortuitously and unpredictably. This may be true from where one has viewed the events to this point. Now that can change, for one can begin to develop a new and different kind of watchfulness and awareness, so as to be more prepared as the next move or change approaches.

There are essentially two parts to being able to anticipate the time when another acknowledgement is to be made.

- **The first** is to become constantly cognisant of moments and instances when one is employing an old approach to the analysis of one's predicament. This first part also includes the conscious repudiation and rejection of that old approach as soon as its use is recognised.
- **The second** part is, so far as it is possible, the conscious and intentional use of a new watchfulness, a *new awareness*; that is, the becoming aware of the time when one must open to the possibility of another, new and different reality once again.

Being watchful in this new way requires one to constantly *put* forth effort to subjugate the temptation to anticipate new events based on old earmarks. But even subjugation of that temptation is not enough: one must dissolve it as it happens. As soon as one is cognisant of falling into the spiral of an ir-resoluble circuitous mental or emotional conundrum, it is not that particular circumstance or predicament which causes concern, but rather the system of thought processes or automatic emotional reactions with which one must deal.

What one must now expect from oneself is essentially another and more sophisticated form of something which one was expected to develop very early in the time of one's opening of awareness: an act of repudiation or rejection of some item. This time, the item is not a material object but rather it is a thought process or an automatic emotional pattern of reaction. There is another difference now as well. Previously the item which one rejected was not only of a physical or material nature, but it was probably personally obsolete: perhaps even so personally obsolete that one had developed a reprehension for it. At least there was an element of neutrality of feeling concerning it.

Rejecting that which is near and dear

Now the item to be rejected is something which is held near and dear; something which one sees as a 'given', something which one sees or has seen as a 'non-negotiable'.

How is one now to know when this is to be done without reference to events of the past, memories of how it was last time, and how one handled this (or at least what looked like this) the last time it happened?

This is a time of personal transition – a transition from one mode of personal operation to another. It is a time of changing the way one operates in the mind and the emotions, and it is a time of changing the way the mental and emotional operations play themselves out through the physical body. There is little in one's mental or emotional repertoire to which one can make reference in order to determine what one should do now.

But there is one thing which one can watch for: it is a signpost, a signal which can alert one to the possibility of the approaching time when one is to make that all-important acknowledgement that there may now be another, new and different way of going about things. This signal is not something which can be given an ironclad definition or description, but it can be felt, and if one practises it regularly, the feeling which comes with its approach can eventually be recognised.

Watching for the signals

Rather than attempting just now to describe the signal itself, let us have a look at what it signals, and then we will have a look at how to recognise it and what to do about it.

When it is recognised that it is time to dissolve some personal mode or system of operation and to acknowledge that there is a new and different way approaching, this signal actually says that it is time to sort out the new from the old, the viable from the obsolete; it is time to discriminate.

In times past, the decision made in discrimination was perhaps made on the basis of attraction or non-attraction, and it probably related to some physical item. The decision may have been made, and made easily, when applied to something which one felt that one no longer needed, and it may have been difficult when made with reference to something for which one felt a fondness or with which one felt an affinity.

Applying Discrimination to the 'near and dear'

The items to which discrimination is to be applied now are not so easily discernible. In fact, their shape and form may be so nebulous and their employment by one's physical body, emotions, and mind may be so ingrained and deeply rooted that they are erroneously considered to be part of one's self. When discrimination is to be applied to such items, to say one is fond of them or to say that one may feel an affinity for them grossly understates one's attachments to such items, which in such a state are not items at all but processes or concepts.

These processes which are to be dissolved, dismantled and discarded are by their very nature so strongly entrenched that they are not easily even recognised, let alone removed. It does little good to say that one should watch for this or that emotion, or this or that way of thinking. Further, it is only superficially effective to attempt to deal with such emotions by violent or explosive therapies or by circuitous intellectual exercises.

Here we are talking about the way of emoting or thinking that is the way one goes about things. This entrenched way of living is dismantled piece by piece, and it takes time. One will be unable to recognise what should be discarded by watching for the appearance of the item itself, but one can recognise the feeling that arises when it is time to discard something, even though one will not know what it may be.

This is the important thing to watch for: the feeling that it is time for something to change or for something to be discarded. It is a strangely simple feeling, so simple in fact that it is most often overlooked. It can arise at the most unexpected times stimulated by the most benign remark or event. It could be described as a feeling of a sudden sinking or emptiness; a feeling that something is wrong or that something has changed.

In fact, this feeling or recognition is common to all of us, but it is most often glossed over or ignored, or it may be attributed to some minor external circumstance. Its occurrence is suppressed in the mind, and its significance is intellectually dismissed. By ignoring these signals, we bury the feeling and the opportunity to make some small move to dismiss some small item in our intellectual or emotional repertoire, the absence of which would enable our life to run on more smoothly. It is this tendency to accumulate and retain these items and then to ignore the signal to release them which is our undoing.

In the 'busy-ness' of everyday life, it is very easy to gloss over such signals. In fact, when our contact with the world is exclusively external – that is, when our daily activities are so physically engrossing and demanding – the inner feelings become so subtle as to become essentially non-existent as far as our external consciousness is concerned. In order for these signals to be recognised and acted upon, this must change, and it is relatively easy to change. In many cases, it entails merely the small effort of stopping to look, or at least stopping to create an inner antenna which listens and watches for these subtle signals.

The signals will appear even if one is not listening and watching. It may be that one does not have the time to stop and pay attention to them when they appear or occur, but this can be remedied by setting aside a time every day to examine them. It is as if they are stored away temporarily and then retrieved. When retrieved, they can be contemplated, and if one will but look, one will see what needs to be done.

Concocted consequences can generate fear

Even as one develops the ability to see these signals, however, there is then a further tendency to ignore them. The fear generated by the imagined or concocted consequences is often too great to overcome. This fear is merely the result of speculation of the consequences imagined. It is a result of a speculation which projects too far into the future, compounding consequence upon further speculation until a reprehensible result is conjured up by a conspiracy of a circuitous and unreliable rationalisation process and a defensive, immature set of emotions. It is this conspiracy and all that it stands for and stands on which one is now beginning to dismantle. And it is the appearance of these little signals which can show one, from within, the steps to take to begin that dismantling process.

But the mind is very fast, and it has two strong allies: the defensive emotional structure and the ego. The mind can conveniently overlook these factors which will, in fact, intervene and occur to prevent the happening of the very thing which the mind has decided will happen. When the emotions see the scenario created by the imagination, they too mount their defence, and then the effects are seen and felt in the physical body. The ego, ever believing that it is self-sufficient and self-contained, further exacerbates the problems by attempting to block out and ignore the possibility that there may be any alternative to what it has determined is reality.

These are indeed fearsome adversaries. They are strong, and they are powerful, and they cannot be overcome by force. But they can be transformed: not by attacking them, not by arguing with them, nor even by trying to understand them. They can be transformed; if one engages them with the right stance, the right attitude.

It is this attitude, the development of this stance, the creation of a different approach through a new awareness which we will examine now.

45   *Attitude in Transition*

When the awareness opens and begins to perceive the subtle signals which herald individual change, the precise definitions of a previously well-structured reality begin to become blurred around the edges, and the mental, emotional and physical components of one's being will begin to express their concern and consternation about the changes which are occurring.

Attitude: the controlling factor

Although action is important now, actually essential, it is not the factor which is controlling. The controlling factor is attitude, but even attitude is now to become only another phase of transition. A new attitude, a new stance, will become an inaugurating mental state for the emergence of an entirely new state of consciousness. It is from within this new consciousness that one will be able to construct an entirely new position from which to view not only the concepts, ideals and standards which now come under scrutiny, but also to view every item of mental, emotional and physical process in which one has previously been engaged. Each of these processes will now, eventually, be brought forth for examination and disposal. These include the ancillary processes, below the surface – processes which are in fact ramifications of behaviour at the waking level of consciousness, and which most often escape examination.

It is at that later stage that the consciousness, then not only experiencing change, but also beginning to intentionally incorporate change into one's behavioural repertoire, begins to turn in upon itself. It is then that the process of true self-determination begins.

Developing a transitional attitude

This matter of developing a transitional attitude is one of some importance. The word or concept of attitude is often associated in our minds and in our lives with a value judgement of behaviour. That is not the matter which we are considering here.

Attitude in the way we are concerned with it in this Material and for the process of self-determination is a step in the establishment of a state of consciousness. It could be defined as the aggregate or overall condition of consciousness which one maintains or from which one views that which happens during this time of transition. It is attitude which enables one to maintain mental, emotional, and physical balance during this time of transition.

At this early stage of considering attitude, it is not possible to define or describe the particular attitude which is suggested to be most beneficial. In fact, it is not necessary to do so at the beginning or at any stage. What is important is the ability to grasp the concept of 'attitude' itself: that is, first, just what attitude is; and secondly, the fact that it can be changed and adjusted. Once this concept is grasped, this adjustment can be accomplished at will.

What attitude is not and what it is

To begin to establish the ability to alter, adjust or activate an attitude, one must first see what *attitude*, as it is used in this context, is not. It is not a reaction.

It is not how one reacts to that which happens; that is, it does not mean a good attitude or a bad attitude towards that. Nor is it the way one views things; that is, it is not the conglomeration of ideas, emotions and feelings which causes us to react in a certain way. Nor is it the reaction itself to the things which are viewed; that is, it is not what we do as a result of harbouring the personality traits we have. Nor is it the factors themselves which affect, colour and manipulate the prejudices which interact with the interpretation of the things we see and experience.

The attitude with which we are here working is rather the position or condition from which things are seen and in which events are experienced. It is, so to speak, one step back from the ordinary definition of attitude. It is from a position or attitude that we can constantly correct the pitch or the angle which we assume as we move through the events and consequences which comprise what we call 'life'.

This position or condition of angle, approach or attitude is something which can be itself adjusted and manipulated. The purpose of being able to adjust it is to be able to maintain a balance which is essential if one is to become self-determining; for it is only from a position of balance that one can perceive for oneself, from within, the relative truth of any given moment, the discrimination necessary to be able to assume a proper stance for action and the discipline necessary to be able to implement that action.

This position, angle, approach or attitude is the condition in which one can allow a flow to move through the consciousness, so that whatever happens is relegated to its appropriate position of importance in the repertoire of experience. It affects the way we think, the feelings we have, and the physical reactions which arise as a result of experiences.

When the concept of attitude is understood, and when one has developed the ability to effectively assess the difference between present and desirable attitude, and when one has refined the ability to instantly adjust the attitude to the appropriate angle, then one is able to move into the application of this concept of attitude.

How attitude affects our reality

The ability to constantly remain open to the possibility of a new and different personal reality is dependent on the ability to release or dismiss at any given moment anything which impedes or inhibits one's ability to remain so open. The application of adjustment of attitude enables one at any given moment to release or dismiss such items. Self-determination is grounded on one's ability to do this.

Self-determination is based on the principle of creative evolution even in the life of each of us personally. It is based on the principle of movement, flow, change and balance. Its antithesis is possession, retention, and protection of anything, including emotions and mental processes, which have become personally obsolete or anachronistic.

This principle can be applied at any and every level of consciousness, from the determination of action to be taken at the very most basic activities which we encounter in our daily lives to the very most elevated and refined activities which we wish to enter in the deepest states of our inner awareness. It is the application of this principle which will bring success in either of these extremes and in all activities which lie between them.

When one can constantly and continuously apply this principle, there is, of course, no longer any need to think about it or try to apply it, for it has then become part of one's being – a way of life, so to speak. It will have then contributed to and become a large part of a new and different consciousness. The adoption of and adaptation to this new state of consciousness is relatively easy after one applies even a minimal amount of enquiry into, and consideration of, the way in which one relates to any item of possession. This enquiry also forms a major part of the ability to become self-determining. The principles and guidelines can be imparted, but the operation must be done on one's own from within. As with other activities which we have discussed, it must be done alone.

The items of possession spoken of here include everything from items of a physical nature to those of the most refined mental nature. Such items, no matter where they stand on our personal possessive scale, were at one time created in thought through perception, conceived into action through desire, and manifested into form for enjoyment. The form of such items then ramified further into physical diversity precipitated by a reflection of the creative process: that is, further desire and further enjoyment.

For our purposes, when we are speaking of physical items here, we mean not merely those which have taken tangible physical form, but those items which exist in our emotional repertoire and in our mental activities, for emotions and thoughts are things as well. They exist; they can be seen; they can be felt; they can be experienced; they can be enjoyed. They were all created for this purpose. And they can be uncreated, as it were. They can be released, dismantled, dismissed, discarded – though they seldom are.

It most often does not occur to us to discard, dismiss or dismantle something which we have created or something which, perhaps created by someone else, has come into our possession. We tend to accumulate; we tend to retain. When we do discard something, it is generally an item which we have decided that we no longer need, and it is generally something which has form; that is, something which exists physically, as physical matter. And too often, when we do discard something, we do so only with the intent and on the condition that it be replaced by something of equal value, equal utility – and it must provide equal, if not superior, comfort and security.

Further, if we do discard something in this way, we most often demand the right to examine that which is being offered to replace the item we are faced with discarding or dismantling. We further demand the right to be able to decide for ourselves whether the new replacement meets the requirements which we have established to define our own standard of security and comfort. If the replacement item falls below the standard, we are not only reluctant to accept it, but we are also adamant in our refusal to release and discard the item under consideration.

If this were all there were to the present syndrome of possession, which is characteristic of the human psyche, it could be corrected fairly easily; but there is more. The items which we have acquired, accumulated, and which are considered essential to our comfort, security, and even our existence, are not merely possessed for those purposes; they are actively defended and their relative worth is rarely, if ever, examined.

Items of a purely physical nature, that is, material possessions which one can see, handle and touch, can be assessed in worth, for they are easily assigned a relative monetary value. But even when this is done, a dichotomy arises in that the relative monetary value for many of us bears little relation to the true worth which any item has to us *personally* – that is, in terms of the essence of life.

As one moves from items of a purely physical nature to those items which occupy space in the other realms of activity in our life, that is, emotional experiences and thought processes, even this common, but inadequate, system of evaluation does not exist. We have no system for the evaluation of such experiences, except the comfort and security they provide or the rationalisation that they are simply a part of our make-up. It rarely occurs to us to question their worth, let alone their necessity.

Examining the value of non-physical items

Hence, we virtually never examine the essence of such possessions – and possessions they are. With the tendency to misidentify with what we *have* rather than with what we *are*, the result is the faulty conclusion that what we possess is what we have become. This, of course, leads to the further erroneous belief that we cannot part with such items of possession. Once the true nature of such things is seen, there is an entirely new and different process available to us. Before we can examine this process, however, we must examine how to dismantle some of the obstacles which stand in our way to applying this process.

Defending 'defence'

Let us first examine the assumption of the necessity of defence: that is, the assumption of the necessity of defence based merely on the platform of prior possession. When something is possessed, it is assumed to be worth retaining – and hence, of course, worth defending. All such positions are assumed: that is, they are taken to be essential without examination; and all such positions, if so taken and assumed, become vestiges of an antiquated consciousness. It is a consciousness and way of thought whose time itself has come for review and examination.

Defence of items for comfort and security is a very basic human characteristic; so basic, in fact, that we could define it as an instinct. Unless it becomes subject to review and examination, it cannot be elevated beyond that primitive state. It should be observed, however, that such defence can be so deeply implanted experientially that it is virtually impossible for one to examine the assumption of its necessity and the innate tendency to defend it in the extreme. This is the condition for those who occupy two states of existence.

The first are those of an extremely primitive nature whose very being is infused only with states of mind, emotion and body that are sufficiently evolved and developed to be able to be concerned with sustenance, maintenance and survival itself.

The second are those who are more evolved, but who have perpetuated an assumption of the necessity of defence of possessions because their condition or belief was born of deep economic depression or deprivity. These persons live as if it is virtually impossible even to question the need for such defence, because of the strength of the memory of the experience and the attendant depth of the beliefs which resulted from the experience.

Too often, after this condition is alleviated, those who have been subject to this experience refuse to accept that the experience is past and there is no longer any need for the obsessive paranoia which accompanied the experience and remained after it was finished. In short, they refuse to acknowledge that things have changed.

We will now look at how an appropriate attitude can help to correct this.

46   Dismantling an Obsolete Belief System

Those whose very nature is such that they can think of nothing other than the simple matters of sustenance and survival itself are expected to defend their possessions, for their concern is for nothing more than comfort and security.

An obsolete defence

But those who retain this posture of defence of possession even after the time of danger has passed must largely bear the responsibility for a widespread belief which manifests in the accumulation, protection of, and active and sometimes vehement defence of, not only physical chattels but also of outmoded emotional actions and ways of thinking. These include antiquated ideals, standards and concepts. This responsibility for the creation of this obsolete approach to life rests with those who cling to such obsolete beliefs. They are also responsible for inculcating such beliefs, through the educational system and the instructional devices of our society, into those who have come into the world since their own beliefs were crystallised.

If those who have experienced depression and depravity continue to cling to such beliefs, they must also bear some of the responsibility for widespread and pervading beliefs which, now ingrained in our very thinking, impede our mental and emotional progress and evolution. These obstacles also stand in the way of the emergence of a viable and indigenous spiritual ethic which each culture, including our own, must manifest as part of its own growth.

But they do not bear this responsibility alone. Those who have come into life since the time of danger to economic survival has passed and who have had the antiquated customs, ideals and standards thrust upon them now bear the responsibility of examining those values and ways of life and, if necessary, changing them.

Pride in possession and belief

The practices of accumulation and defence of possessions – physical, emotional, and mental – have been perpetuated in our world by a spirit of something which goes beyond even the fear of deprivation. The accumulation, possession and defence, born of necessity, grew into pride: social pride, economic pride and patriotic pride, which exhibits itself in the extreme when those displaying it to exaggerate the defence of an item, possession or belief that *defence becomes offence* – an offence designed to foist its acceptance upon others to guarantee or ensure not only its continued existence but a virtual demand for its further necessity.

A belief can have its roots in two places which will sustain it

The first of these is in those who have formulated that belief, and the second is in those who have had such a belief inculcated into them by those who have formulated it. This is true of all systems of teaching, be they intellectual, social, religious or spiritual.

The first group, that is those who formulated the belief, often cannot question the belief, for that would be to question the very foundation of their reality. The second group, that is those who have received the belief from the first, must question the belief, for not to question it denies them the evolutionary right to develop the very foundation for their own reality.

Beliefs from past generations

When generation after generation accepts a belief or beliefs which have been formulated in the past, and the strength of such beliefs has its foundation mainly in the memories and teachings of a culture, a pressure begins to build. This pressure is due to a conflict which grows between the desire to sustain a belief for comfort and security and the need to question such a belief for the implementation of change.

One who is engaged in the perpetuation of the belief for comfort and security must develop strategies and tactics so that the belief will be ramified and proliferated by the offence. To accomplish this – that is, the acceptance of the belief by others – there must then be designed tools and implements deemed necessary for such an endeavour. Then the tools and implements must also be exported, in order to enable those who have blindly accepted the previously formulated belief to export it by offence onto still yet others who, it is hoped, will form a root foundation for the continuation of the belief.

Soon, one becomes hopelessly mired in the process itself. Any ability, or even any tendency, at all to stop and examine the relative worth, importance, or necessity of the belief or item being so defended and exported, is abandoned. The processive circle is thus completed as further accumulation then becomes necessary to continue the defence, offence, and so on.

The main obstacles to question and change are the delusive belief in the superiority of the goods which have been accumulated, the pride in the accomplishment of their accumulation, and the assumption of their continued relative contemporary worth. The reluctance to approach these obstacles and question them is justified with the rationalisation that these actions and beliefs are required for economic and social progress. The motive is ostensibly laudable and would be justified if the worth of the goods were reassessed periodically; but, sadly, that relative worth is too often taken for granted without question.

Regaining the ability to question

We can see then where we have lost the ability to question the relative worth of an item which we have previously believed to be essential. It now falls on the generation of change to at least stop and re-evaluate the worth of the goods which have been previously determined to be indispensable. This includes everything from the tools and weapons which enforce the export right back to the elements of the physical items being exported, and beyond to the emotional bases for our behaviour, and the beliefs upon which our present activities are based.

Again, it is important to remember that this principle applies to everything from the events of daily life to the most sublime and superluminal experiences which are now arising to be manifested into the waking consciousness of humankind. Without the ability to release and move on, the flow of personal as well as cultural evolution becomes so clogged that there can be no room for anything truly new. True Growth then comes to a standstill, but it cannot be impeded for very long at a time of rapidly accelerating change.

Before we can attempt to dismantle this undesirable state of affairs, we might have a look at the attitude which supports it. This attitude is actually a state or process of mind, and it refers to the concept of attitude which we must grasp before we can begin to make any changes intentionally. The condition of affairs has degenerated to the level it has, both in our culture and society and in the individual minds of its members, largely because of this inability to intentionally change the attitude which supports all of these antiquated beliefs.

It is now time to change this attitude, but it would be ineffectual to attempt to define the old attitude and the new one before we define just what attitude is. That we have attempted to do in the last few paragraphs: it is the position, posture or angle from which one views things. Such a position, posture or angle can be changed if one is aware that it can be changed. Many are not aware that this is possible.

Now let us look at the attitude which has supported and perpetuated the antiquated beliefs which are now so obsolete as to be erroneous. These beliefs, while borne of physical, economic or social conditions, have now so permeated our psyche as to be insurmountable when one wishes to introduce new or different beliefs into one's own mental or emotional environment. And the force which such obsolescent beliefs has gathered over the last few generations certainly precludes the consideration, let alone the introduction, of the possibility of a new and different reality.

The attitude which has prevailed over the past few generations began with a belief in the necessity for accumulation for the maintenance of one's needs. This, of course, in turn had its roots in the primitive and basic foundations of the *need for survival* which we previously discussed. The emergent attitude was one which eventually became anachronistic. It led, for instance, to hoarding in a time of plenty; it led to the export of concepts in an attempt to preclude any change precipitated by import.

So long as a belief remains intact and unchallenged, one continues to exist in the relative comfort and security of that which one believes to be a relatively stable and unchanging reality. In fact, it is only the belief which is unchanging, and a static belief does not inhibit the changes taking place in the environment. This is a prime example of belief being out of synchronisation with reality. It becomes fairly obvious which must make the change.

Bliss based on erroneous belief

This state of relative bliss based on erroneous belief which is not in harmony with reality can be challenged by another defending or perpetrating their own concept of a desirable state, concept or condition. If one can harbour the belief in the superiority of one's accumulated goods (physical, emotional or mental), then someone else can do so as well. One who has fought so desperately to develop the security and the comfort which accompanies that security becomes very threatened by the clash of either weapons or ideologies.

The pain or fear which ensues is not in fact attributable to the clash. It proceeds directly from the refusal or inability to release any hold on any item which in any way supports or forms a part of the bases for such security and comfort. One so attached to the security which one believes is provided by items, ideas, emotions, concepts or standards, which in fact have become obsolete and which are really no longer of any personal worth, is deluded by this false security.

Certainly, one so attached to this nebulous security has lost the tendency, let alone the ability, to examine any of these items themselves, including their current necessity, obsolescence and present relative value.

Challenging the worth of that accumulated

Although one being so threatened cannot untangle the quagmire which has resulted from this intricate syndrome, it can become fairly clear what has happened when viewed from the outside or from a distance. If these items of security – be they physical, emotional or mental – form and determine the literal foundations upon which one rests one's conduct and one's security, it is not difficult to perceive that if the relative worth of these items is challenged by another exporting their own items of worth, what is really being threatened is one's grasp on one's concept of reality.

It is further fairly easy to perceive that in such circumstance, this very attachment to these items and concepts is what prohibits one from even considering the remotest possibility that there might be an alternative to that which one has previously considered to be reality.

The change of attitude which is required here is almost impossible to make intentionally unless one has grasped an understanding of the process as a whole.

The first step in such a change would be to perceive that the real pain, fear and threat come in the challenge to the relative worth of the items which are the very underpinnings of a present belief, which may just possibly be out of harmony with *the way things really are*. Unless one can see that such an examination is necessary and that such a challenge inhibits that examination, then there is little possibility that one will be able to alter or adjust the attitude so as to undertake the necessary examination.

So, the position which one must now assume to inaugurate the transition towards a new consciousness is one which enables one to see things in a different way. There are some basic steps one can take to do this. If one takes these steps, one effectively begins a reversal of the process which has led to such massive confusion in the collective and individual psyche of our culture. This reversal begins, then, to lead to the acceptance of a new personal reality and the establishment of a basis from which to implement this new reality.

These steps we will consider in the next part of the self-determination series.

47   Questioning the Basic Assumption

The process which one must undertake to reverse this deplorable condition is so dynamic in effect that it can be metamorphic and so simple in application that it can be overlooked.

How does one reverse this process?

One considering this Material who wishes to engage in that which is described in this final instalment on self-determination should be aware that what is now to be described, while apparently simple in form and nature, if applied, can, and will, have monumental effects on the emotional and mental composition of the individual personality. One should approach the following material with due respect and apprehension, but likewise, with courage and confidence.

The process begins with the ability to discard something which is no longer of use. This is something each of us does every day. It is a relatively easy process when it is applied to items of a material nature for which we no longer have any need or affection. Even a child can reject and discard a toy which it has outgrown.

There are two problems which arise when we begin to apply this to items beyond and other than childhood toys.

- **First**, the items to be examined are not of a material nature.
- **Second**, the items to be discarded are often mistakenly assumed to be essential.

The ability to apply this process, then, requires us to undertake to learn two things:

- **First**, how to identify items which are not of a material nature and whose relative worth is to be reassessed; and
- **Second**, how to redefine our threshold as to what is essential and what is not.

When we consider the objects to be brought under scrutiny, we realise that the items of a material nature – that is, items made of wood, bricks, and mortar – are the easiest to see. They are tangible. They are palpable. They can be picked up. And they can be easily thrown away.

How does one scrutinise items of a more subtle nature?

As we move from items of a material nature, up the scale into consideration of items which are not so tangible, we are looking at emotions, emotional reactions, and feelings. Further up the scale of intangibility come items which are still very real but which are more nebulous and elusive in form. It becomes more difficult to identify them. Here we are talking of thoughts, thought processes, and mental habit patterns.

All of this has been covered and discussed in depth and breadth in this Material, especially in this series on self-determination.

How does one see the items to be discarded?

What we will now consider are the actual steps which one can take to develop the ability to see these items to be examined which lie beyond the purely material spectrum, and then to determine realistically which ones are to be retained and which are to be discarded. This is a simple process; it does not necessarily follow that it is easy. It takes hard work and constant attention.

Redefining the 'threshold of necessity'

We will first discuss the steps taken to begin to redefine and readjust the threshold of necessity. This is the ability to consider some object, any object, and to ask whether it is essential or can be discarded. This requires some action first, and then some agile movement into the right attitude to be able to take some further action.

The first step in this process is to develop the ability to question an assumption already made. This is an objective examination which repeats a question the answer to which has been previously given automatically in the affirmative. In simpler terms, the question asks, 'Is this really essential?' This may be the first time this question has been asked in full open and waking awareness, and it may certainly be the first time that the question has been asked in such a manner about the object now being considered.

The nature of the accumulation process which was described in earlier paragraphs has virtually nullified our ability to discriminate. Generations upon generations of our forebears have automatically answered in the affirmative any question which arose as to the essentiality of almost any item of any nature beyond those of a purely material nature, and most material items as well. The process of discrimination, the ability to question, has thus been lost to us. The assumptions of necessity and essentiality are so ingrained in us that we do not even question. This ability to discriminate and to question must be re-established.

This first step, then, is the ability to examine a conclusion previously drawn as to the essentiality of a possession. In all likelihood, the question has not been previously asked. The values, the emotions, the concepts, the mental processes which we as a culture have accepted and engaged in for generations have been automatically assimilated by each new generation. This worked perfectly well for many centuries. With the advent of a change of consciousness now before us, it is time to re-establish this ability to examine and question, and to change. It is only through such a process that we will be able to undergo, individually and as a culture, the immense changes which we face.

The first occasion upon which this action is performed, that is, the first time this question is asked, initiates a reversal of the process of automatic and unquestioned acceptance and accumulation of unnecessary and burdensome emotion and mental superfluity.

This first step is not to be taken lightly. It is to be taken with serious contemplation, and it is to be taken slowly. Its effect can be dynamic. Since we are first considering how to go about making this change rather than on what it operates, it would be best perhaps if this first step were applied first to an item of low materiality, which is no longer used and which is known to be no longer essential.

How to question an assumption

To be able to apply this question to items of a subtler nature will first require the application of the question at all, and it is most easily applied first to some obsolete material item. The essential action is action itself, and practice. It is important that one not underestimate the significance of actually performing the action of asking this question. It is not enough to simply think through it and then attempt to mentally contemplate the conjectured implications. The end result through practice will be, as we will see, an attitude from which one can move towards application of the question to items of an emotional and mental nature – items which form the very basis for one's concept of reality and which are so ingrained that they literally control our every action and stifle our innate ability to ask questions of real importance and to receive answers which we know inherently carry the ring of genuineness. Such answers are not accepted on faith; they are assimilated because they are known to be true.

The first time this question is asked and applied to some item initiates the reversal of the accumulative process and inaugurates the ability to discriminate. We can now have a glimpse of the significance of this process in regard to the items to which it is applied. It is the process itself which is important. The form, structure, or nature of the items to which it is applied is really of little concern, for it is relatively easy to see that, from the standpoint of the one asking the question, it is only a matter of degree which distinguishes the items one from another. It is only a matter of degree from items of a palpable material nature to those on the other end of the spectrum: that is, those of an intangible emotional or mental nature. Although it is easier to see and identify items of a material nature, the process of the application of the question is the same.

Dismantling the 'subconscious process'

Material items are accumulated and retained, as we have seen earlier, because a decision is made as to their necessity. The intricate ramifications of the process which have led us to accumulate these items have so refined and developed the process that the decision as to their necessity is often now not even a conscious one. It is made so automatically that we do not even know that it has been done. This is truer of items of an emotional and mental nature. Here we are speaking of the most basic emotional reactions which we experience and the most basic mental processes which control and govern our thought processes and which inhibit our ability to engage in *true reason*.

The delusion of 'deductive reasoning'

The process which has gradually undermined our innate ability to engage in truly creative mentation is the process of deductive reasoning. The deductive reasoning process is largely responsible for decisions made wherein there is a consideration of a set or number of apparently similar sets of circumstances. This set of circumstances gives rise to a decision or conclusion which gains acceptance in the human mind under the guise of what is commonly termed 'rationalisation'. This is a process which, through consideration of a number of factors which have been demonstrated and are considered 'known' or 'given', concocts a plausible reason for results, conduct or consequences. The reason offered through this process is often apparently acceptable, but it may or may not be true.

This one process could be charged with most of the delusion and deception which the human mind has perpetrated upon itself. In spite of the fact that it seems to serve adequately for the making of decisions and drawing conclusions of an elementary nature in terms of the necessities of daily life, its use and application on matters beyond those basic necessities should be regarded with the greatest apprehension and suspicion. The misguiding conclusions drawn according to the application of this process are to be considered virtually reprehensible, and inimical to the sincere search for truth and the expression of real creative thinking.

Dismantling the deductive reasoning process

On the first occasion when one asks the question of the necessity of any item, as we have outlined above, one sets in motion the process by which the automatic application of this delusive deductive reasoning process can be dismantled. If we examine the deductive reasoning process, we can see the bases for its acceptance and use, and how it has ramified in and through the minds of countless generations of our ancestors. It will be remembered that the accumulation, possession, and retention of many of the material items which we have are justified by the comfort or security they provide and the fear that would arise if they were lost. So it is with emotional reactions and mental processes and concepts. Their necessity is a foregone conclusion which is so deeply entrenched below the level of conscious sight and waking awareness that we never have the opportunity nor inclination to question it. They are a part of our make-up. They are virtually a part of our being – at least part of that which we believe our being to be.

Such a conclusion of necessity, if it can be seen in operation, happens at the termination of a deductive reasoning process which began with an accepted decision, conclusion or concept. This given concept incorporated a series of ancillary or succeeding similarly accepted decisions, concepts, givens or postulates. These ancillary given and accepted matters, coupled with the first or beginning decision, led to a further concept or conclusion which was generally accepted without further concern with the truth of, or even reasonable enquiry into, the relative credibility of the conclusions with which one began and which were employed by this process itself to propel one's naïve and unquestioning mind forward to the deluding final conclusion. The only claim to the right of existence by this final conclusion was that it was born of and based on a series of assumptions, the validity of which were never questioned.

This whole process becomes so insidiously delusive and self-perpetuating that anyone who sincerely wishes to engage in any kind of real creative thinking becomes hopelessly misguided and mired. The deception grows and grows until one resolves to undertake its attempted exposure and questions the entire process.

Reversing a centuries-old thinking process

To question the entire process at once can be very dangerous; in fact, it can be devastating. It must be done slowly, deliberately and intentionally. And it begins with one question, 'Is this particular item necessary?' When one asks this simple question for the first time, one initiates a reversal of the previously well-entrenched process which has circuitously deceived the human mind for centuries. The development of the process then becomes one of asking the question again... and then again... slowly... of items of an increasingly subtler nature.

Eventually the process itself begins to ask the questions. It will begin to bring forth the items for examination and present them to a freshly enquiring mind, which by then is beginning to ask, discriminate, and believe what it sees.

We will now look at how one goes about further developing the attitude which enables one to handle the answers one finds.

48   It's Time for a Change

The process of deductive reasoning, and all these ancillary processes of reaching conclusions on which to base action, are deeply entrenched in Western thinking. They are so foundational as to be considered inviolable and almost sacred. It is this process, of course, on which the entire foundation of Western scientific thinking and investigation is based. To question the system, to ask even the first question, is considered by some to be personally, socially, and certainly scientifically at least indiscreet if not almost blasphemous.

The purpose of Self-determination

The whole purpose of becoming self-determining is to be able to find answers for oneself: to be able to place into action new insights which emerge from what is known within without reference to external sources, external authorities or past experiences. The answers which one seeks must, then, be able to carry the ring of truth. These answers come forth in response to questions. These questions begin with one question, 'Is this necessary?'

Self-determination itself is for the purpose of one to effectively search for answers. In the search for answers, there are many obstacles, and the asking of this one question is the essential primary step in the development of a conscious systematic rejection of disposable and insignificant emotional and mental trivia which were previously considered to be foundational before they were questioned.

When this process of questioning is set in motion within the mind, within the self, one has set one's feet upon a road by which one can effectively perceive and at least objectively observe the various states of consciousness through which one must pass as the awareness opens. Through a timeless existence, we have entered countless states of consciousness, lived in them, and then moved on to enter another state of consciousness. In the earlier part of our existence, this process, of course, is evolutionarily automatic. We have virtually no choice in the matter.

The onus shifts

When the awareness begins to open, the onus shifts. It becomes not only our opportunity but our evolutionary duty to move from one state of consciousness to another, both individually and collectively. We have the opportunity to move and to grow voluntarily; we have the duty to move and grow, full stop. If we rush, we are restrained, but if we hesitate, we are nudged; if we wait, we are pushed; if we refuse, we are changed.

When we are opening in awareness, we must constantly be ready to assess the timing, for timing is all important. Even when we ask the essential question, 'Is this necessary?', its timing must be carefully considered. If it is asked at the proper time, the answer will be forthcoming. If it is premature, then we must wait patiently for the answer. If we ask the question belatedly, the answer may already be upon us – or within us – or even all around us. It is then that we must be able to change very quickly. It is then that we must be able to accept, very quickly, the possibility of a new and different reality.

Such a time is now upon us individually as well as collectively. We have hesitated. We have waited. We have refused to acknowledge the need for change, and the change is now upon us, and it will soon be all around us. This change is a change of consciousness, and it carries with it not only the possibility of a new and different reality, but also the essence of a reality which is so new and different that we will marvel at its innovation.

We are being called upon to move very quickly to assimilate this change of consciousness. The transformation which it carries is so deep and so widely consequential that its implications cannot be grasped from where we stand at the moment. There are many steps which we must take to move into it. There are many states of consciousness which we must experience before the new change of consciousness is fully manifested.

We do not now have the luxury to carry with us as we travel through these various interim states the burdensome emotional and mental baggage which we should have jettisoned long ago. There is a pressure and an urgency to dispense with those items which would hold us back and bend us over under the weight of change.

We must begin to dispense with these items of antiquated thinking and behaviour which are holding us back, and we must begin to do it fairly quickly. They cannot be effectively discarded until they are seen and seen for what they are: things that served well in their time and place but which have now become obsolete, superfluous, and unnecessary.

Disposing of transitional states of consciousness

As we traverse this time of transition, the opportunities and the obligations to look, see, question and reject will come faster and faster for all of us, individually and collectively. The process is much the same whether it is one individual undergoing the transformation or a culture which must effectively transform itself. The experience of this transformation can bring one to the precipice of emotional and mental turmoil.

Only the cultivation of an appropriate state of mind – an attitude – a posture which enables one (individual or culture) to accept change, to accept change quickly, and to accept change completely enables us to maintain the proper balance. This means quickly assessing and rejecting anything at any given moment which is in disharmony with that which has only just appeared as a speck of speculation on the horizon of our experiential spectrum, but which will in only a short time be accepted as fact. An attempt to retain anything which conflicts with the changes which are coming will place the opposite ends of this existential spectrum in antagonism to each other. There is no question as to which end will triumph in the final analysis.

The proper state of mind, the appropriate attitude which must be assumed in order to accept this change of consciousness which is imminent, is one which is always open to the possibility of a new and different reality, for reality will begin to be new and different at each possible turn. The process of change, once one opens to it, accelerates, and then accelerates at an increasing rate. There is little time for rationalisation in order to attempt to understand what is happening. In the first place, there is no time; and in the second place, the experiences, decisions, or assumptions are from the past.

Maintaining individual and cultural sanity in a time of change

There is an absolute necessity to maintain individual and cultural sanity as the change of consciousness descends. It is a relative sanity in the midst of 'unsanity'. This state of sanity is maintained by constantly assessing and discarding anything which is unnecessary. The process of this assessment and discard operates continuously and completely. It eventually operates on every possible possession: physical, emotional, and mental, even into and including that core of present existence which is considered to be *identity*.

This process is evaluative not conclusive. By this, we mean that there are many items which come under scrutiny which will be retained because they are still useful. Some of these will be seen, in assessment, to be things which eventually must be discarded, but which, for the moment, serve a good and useful purpose. On occasion, it may be advisable to discard something, but the trauma would be too great to proceed with the rejection.

There is a time of Grace for the action. One can evaluate its presence only through practice and constant application of the essential question. The application of this question eventually becomes itself a process, and the question is not so much asked as it is presented. And eventually, it is not only presented, it is simply present.

The need for orderliness in a time of urgency

Although there is an urgency, there is also the need for orderliness. Chaotic rejection and disruption are as damaging as the change imposed when one refuses to move.

But the process itself is thorough and complete; nothing is exempt. Everything is subject to its cleansing sweep, and in the end, in the final condition, only consciousness itself will remain, pure and untainted, free from both foreign substance and foreign attitude.

The cleansing sweep of this change of consciousness is inevitable. Only the manner in which it is received and undertaken is subject to individual regulation; the only thing we can intentionally and voluntarily adjust is the attitude with which we receive and experience it.

Once underway, the question of whether and when the process will operate is answered by its inevitability. The only question remaining is how it will operate, and this is determined solely by the attitude assumed by the one experiencing it. It is in the assumption of this attitude that we have one of the few opportunities thus far to exercise what we might call 'free will'.

Two transactional ingredients in the process

Although the process of release and rejection are essential and inevitable, there are two essential transactional ingredients in the application of the ability to change quickly by discarding what is no longer essential.

- **The first** of these is the recognition of when it is to be applied.
- **The second** is the ability to instantaneously assume the proper state of mind for its immediate application.

As one is able to recognise more readily when the process is to be applied, one also becomes more adept in the assumption of the attitude to be assumed. When the time of application arrives, one will increasingly recognise a feeling which one has perhaps for a long time overlooked. It is a feeling that something is wrong, that something has changed, or that something is about to change. It is a feeling which says it is probably time to ask the essential question again. The attitude to be quickly assumed, then, is one which readily accepts that change is once again imminent and that it is time for something to be set aside.

In the beginning, it is tempting for one to believe that the item to be discarded is something material, something purely physical. One who is too quick to draw such a conclusion may find that after the irrevocable discard of something material the feeling of change still remains. Eventually, one will begin to see that it is not necessarily the item itself which must be discarded, but the way one thinks about that item, or the way one feels about that item – or items in general. It is perhaps the attitude which one has towards items of possession.

The key to the orderly acceptance of the change of consciousness is *balance*. We must have what we need to maintain order in a time of transition, and the blending of the new with the old must be done carefully – in an orderly manner.

It is the maintenance of this balance in this time of transition which will enable us to change – gently and effectively, but also completely.

Our New Human Consciousness

Last Times, First Times:
The Work of the Pathfinder

It is time for us to find a path for a *new human consciousness* to move out of the jungle of our confused and tired world. If you are one who can help, you will know this within yourself; you are probably a pathfinder for this new human consciousness.

Hence, I am going to go straight into the task as I see it, and describe some of the things I can offer for you to use in your work if you relate to what I am saying.

But first, let's look at some of the basic principles that I have described in the Material that apply to the implementation of the new human consciousness; then we will see how we can apply some of these principles and guidelines.

Who is the pathfinder?

One who can help find the path must have worked through a few things within to be able to accept the task at hand. As you would know by now, these include the recognition that there is something 'known' – a **'knowingness'** – within the self that you have not learned: it is innate; it is 'being there'.

Then, you must recognise that knowingness; you must acknowledge it. Next you will recognise the need to *discriminate*; that is, apply a constant process of determining what is real – still real – each moment, and discard that which is no longer relevant.

Then there is the acceptance of *responsibility*. This entails the mature decision to acknowledge that you have made your own history, you will make your own future, and you are responsible for your own present. With this responsibility comes the inherent move towards being of help to others… but only if they ask you for help:

the onus is on you to go forward and do what you have to do, but it is on the one who wants help to ask for it.

Following these steps, you will begin to develop a new *communication*, both within yourself, within your Spiritual Self, and among those with whom you work. This is all well and good until the time comes to do something.

The next steps involve your own assessment of your own personal *discipline*, how well you have developed it and how it must be developed further.

Once you have developed some discipline, then you must begin to apply that discipline – and all of the other steps that went before – to a new kind of *action*. And as you become able to move with that action, you will then begin to develop an appropriate *attitude* for you to do your work.

Now that's just for starters.

One of the principles I mentioned in the early Material is very important here.

There are no rules.

This might sound strange when you consider that this whole activity is to develop and apply a new spiritual path and a new spiritual discipline. But if you consider this precept – that there are no rules – in light of the new human consciousness being generated by this new path of self-discovery, you can see that if there are any rules they must apply to everyone, and every part of this new path is unique to the individual.

Of course, this precept of 'no rules' does not apply to anything that is illegal, or immoral behaviour, or anything that would harm another. These are basic considerations that we assume when we embark on the path of self-discovery.

Rather, 'no rules' means that you must decide *for yourself* what you must do to unfold your own path of self-discovery, and you must further decide for yourself how you can, if you choose, help others find their path through the wilderness of this difficult time of change.

In other times and other disciplines, there have been rules. Many disciplines and paths tell you what you can eat, what you must wear, whether or not you can have a sexual relationship, how you must act, and how you must practise your spiritual discipline. It is a characteristic of this new path of self-discovery that each of us must find our way to our own LightSource, and we must each look for ourselves and apply what we see when the light begins to shine for us. True, we need help to get started. I had help – lots of help – and I am one who can help you if you want me to. I will help facilitate the project, but you will manage your own process.

Now just what is the 'project'?

There are so many aspects to this new path and the new human consciousness that it will take many years to unfold. In fact, it has been unfolding for many years already, and we still have some time to go. If you have related to what I have said thus far, you will probably already have recognised what I am going to describe now.

There is a precept to help get us started.

There is a last time for everything, and there is a first time for everything.

This may sound simple – even simplistic. But it carries something for those of us who wish to unfold the path within ourselves and to help unfold it for others as well. This has very broad and far-reaching implications, for it means that everything in our life, that is, everything in each of our lives as individuals and everything in our life as a collective human family – will be transformed by the new human consciousness.

Please ponder this for a moment.

Do not dismiss it as a glib statement of an obvious truth.

What I am saying here is that *everything* – everything – we do will be done differently with the new human consciousness: how we butter our toast, how we walk down the street, how we make love, how we speak, how we wash our clothes, how we pay our bills, how we relate to one another, and certainly how we relate to our self as we discover our Self and apply that which we see and know within.

Now what does this mean to us in our everyday life?

If you consider the finer points of discrimination, it means that something you did yesterday may not be appropriate for you to do today. And if you add the element of service, it means that it might be appropriate again tomorrow.

By this I mean that as you grow, you will recognise that there is a last time for everything. You have heard the old saying that when I was a child I played with a child's toys, and when I grew up I left those toys behind.

As you grow in awareness, you will find that there are things you do every day, things you think, things you say, that you perhaps should let go of. If your awareness is open and you have tapped the LightSource within you, you will see these items as you go through your day.

But if your awareness is pulled by an anchor down into the ego that indulges in the fiction of self-sufficiency, you will not see the signal that comes from the Self.

The essential process is one of constant discrimination along with every other aspect of the steps I described above in the first few paragraphs. When you see something that has to 'go', you must ask yourself,

'Do I have the discipline to act on it, release it, and let it go?'

In other words, can you discard it with the proper attitude?

For instance, let's look at some little everyday behaviour like anger.

Many people consider anger to be a natural human emotion. In fact, there is a view in psychology that says you must express your anger rather than keep it pent up inside you, because you might explode – or implode, as the case may be. But there comes a time when we must let go of the activity of anger; anger simply is not appropriate, and if you indulge in it, it becomes an anchor, and it will pull you down.

Our New Human Consciousness

More correctly, it will pull your point of focus down – down from the Point of Becoming (that point at the top of the head) which you have worked so hard to find. As an anchor pulls you down, you are then fair prey for the other anchors that lurk in the dark spaces of that lower realm of focus. As we all know, it is at times like these, when we are pulled down by an anchor, that we lose contact with the LightSource, and we then literally stumble in the dark and are subject to all kinds of dark experiences.

To say that you must not be angry would be to state a 'rule', and there are no rules. If you choose to be angry, that is your business, but I mention it here because it would seem doubtful if anger has a place in the new human consciousness, which has as its hallmarks the development of tolerance, compassion, patience and gentleness.

Is this all just so many nice little platitudes?

Perhaps, and that is why the rejection of anger cannot be a rule. If you disagree with what I am saying, and you wish to retain anger in your repertoire of emotions, then please do so. I have used anger here as an example. But if you agree that anger – and many other emotions, actions and behavioural syndromes – are vestiges of an antiquated culture which are best left behind, then with some thought, you will probably see that sometime along the way there will be a last time that you get angry.

'OK, all well and good,' I hear you say. 'If that happens, and anger falls away, then so be it. If I don't get angry anymore, then that's OK with me, because I really don't like to be angry; but sometimes I can't help it.'

It is true that the obsolete practices will fall away, but there is an effort and action needed here in this new path and in the new human consciousness that is absent in the other philosophies that say it will just wither away. At some point, there needs to be a recognition that the old way, the old behaviour, the old thought or thinking pattern, must be rejected – rejected consciously, with full awareness and with some gesture or statement of rejection and dismissal.

Often when it is time to discard something, we do it with disdain – or even anger. We throw it away as if its presence irritates us. Often what we are really saying is that we are irritated with ourselves for hanging onto something for so long when we knew we should have gotten rid of it. It may be that we have been addicted to this old behaviour or thought pattern. That is not the fault of the behaviour; it is our own fault – if fault there be – and it is our own responsibility to deal with it. But the rejection or dismissal must be done in a new way.

So, how do we reject something that is obsolete?

The rejection itself must be done with objectivity. When it is time to lay something aside, it is best done with detachment and with a statement of acknowledgement that this has happened. You might say inside,

'It is time to let this go, and I am now releasing it.'

There is also something you can do inside to help this happen.

First, it is helpful for you to recognise that you have probably put a lot of energy into building your attachment to this behaviour. If we can continue with the bit about anger, you may have even worked out how you are going to behave when you are angry, what you are going to say, and how loudly you will yell. Now it is time to reverse that process. In your personal self-reflection when you go within, picture this behaviour or item that you wish to discard. As you take a deep breath, withdraw all of the energy from that item or behaviour. Remember that the energy you have put into this behaviour is the phenomenal – or negative – energy. It is the same energy that enables you to speak, to run, to yell, to eat and to fart.

It is not the positive energy that gives you the light to see what you want to discard. So, pull the energy out of it, and what remains will be the empty shell of the behaviour.

Good job! Now, do you reckon it is over? Is the behaviour gone? Don't believe it! You took years or lifetimes to build up that energy, and it may take months or years for that framework of behaviour to disintegrate and for you to be free of it. Its echoes will reverberate within you for a long time, and each time you drop your focus or have it pulled down by an anchor, that old echo will be there to grab you and try to get you to revive it, because that is part of what keeps your emotional body going: it loves excitement and wild vibrations.

The emotional body will eventually be transformed by the light from your LightSource and from your application of what you see within yourself just as every other part of you will be transformed. You will be successful, but it will take time.

Each time the echo of the old anchor tries to pull you down, it will have less force. If your inner sight is twenty-twenty, you will be able to see the difference between the nature of an anchor itself and the echo left when you have pulled the energy out of it.

Now what does this have to do with pathfinding?

Here is another precept for implementing the new human consciousness:

*One who can help must **do to learn it**,*

*So that one who needs help can **learn to do it**.*

This may sound cryptic, but it is really a very practical application of the elements of the new path of self-discovery and the implementation of a new human consciousness.

Let's take it that you are well focused and you are cruising through your life bringing down your own New Human Consciousness.

Things are going right for you, and you are going right with things. All of a sudden you see something inside: it is a gem.

'Wow! I didn't know that!' you say. (Of course you didn't know it; it's new.) And you say, 'This is for me – this is what I am going to do.' (Go on – this happens to you every day. Think of one that happened today, and you can work with it right now.)

With self-determination, you decide that you are going to implement this new thing into your life. How do you do it? Well, there is no way you could know how to do it, because it is new. You could not have learned how to do it, because it has not happened before.

So you just have to do it.

First, so you can *do* to *learn it*.

This is where the disciplined action comes in. You must act without reason; at least, your actions may seem irrational, because you cannot justify them in logic.

And second, so that others can *learn* to *do* it.

Well, you can probably see the punchline already.

There is a last time for everything, and there is a first time for everything.

What so many people do not see – or do not wish to see – is that each of us, every day, does something for the first time.

But many people think that everything that has any value must come from some external authority or expert and be done first by someone else – for the first time. Many refuse to accept that they can do something for the first time. They feel that they are not good enough to invent something or do something for the first time. We really have a diminished view of our own uniqueness.

So, it is important to perceive that we can do something not only for the first time for ourselves,

but for the first time ever.

'Who, me?' (I hear you say).

'Why me?'

And I call this the old

> *'who-me-why-me-whammy'.*

Why not you?

Now let's go back to one of the matters we discussed a couple of pages ago. Everything we do – everything – is going to be transformed by the new human consciousness, with the new awareness, with the Presence from the top of your head.

So if someone asks you, 'How do you eat breakfast off the top of your head?', you tell them, 'Very carefully, so as not to spill the orange juice.'

The point is that if you are going to take this seriously and implement your own personal new human consciousness, you can also do it for others.

Here is another principle that we will explore in depth elsewhere:

> *Once you do to learn it, then others can learn to do it.*

In other words, you can establish the vibrations for a new activity: a rejection of something it is time to let go of, a new emotion, a new way of talking or thinking. If you get it right, then, by its nature, you can make it available to others.

It can be very satisfying to work hard to reject something or build something new with the energy from the fourth creative dimension and then say,

'There, I've got that right. You can have it, realm. This is my gift.'

Sounds arrogant? Not at all. Really, what we are doing is something that has been going on already ever since time began, but many have not been aware of it:

We are inventing!

Now it is time to do it with awareness…

'…awarely!'

(How's that?)

Now before you cry, 'This is too much!' – a word of comfort. You do not have to make all of the changes yourself. But you can, if you wish to accept this mission that seems sometimes impossible, take some of them on, and change them, and then give them on for the benefit of others.

Which ones are yours?

That is up to you to find out.

And this is interwoven with two things that we mention elsewhere:

- **First** is that rare opportunity – this chance for us to clean some of the consequences out of our bag and to offer some service as well – for each of us to accept this work and make great strides in our own personal evolution;
- **Second** is that your own bag of inevitable consequences holds many of the items that you can work with. But as with all consequences, the one that will provide the back-pressure for you to do something for the last time or the first time will probably, as usual, pop out of your bag without warning at the most inopportune time.

'Surprise, surprise!'

says the little voice in the consequence bag.

'Here is another chance for you to:

make history, present, and future all in one go;

erase some of your own karma;

teach the world something new;

transform part of your emotional body;

change some of your thinking patterns or paradigms;

improve your love life;

lose some weight;

help your digestion, and

get rid of your pimples all at the same time.'

Grab it! **You may not get another chance!**

Our New Human Consciousness

Epilogue:
'Why Me, and What Should I Do?'

If you relate to this Material, after you have asked the initial question of 'Who am I, and why am I here?', one of the first questions that may present itself is, 'Why me, and what should I do?'

Let's have a look at some basic foundational elements that affect those of us who find this question relevant. See if they make some sense to you.

The Basic Assumptions

First, let's look at some of the basic assumptions:

> A change of consciousness is imminent on our planet;
>
> This change of consciousness will totally change the way we live our life;
>
> The transition towards this change is already here and is manifesting;
>
> This transition manifests through individual persons;
>
> Many who are manifesting the change know who they are;
>
> If you don't yet know whether you are to manifest this change, still, you may suspect that you have something to do;
>
> Whether you participate in the manifestation of this transition and this change is somewhat a matter of choice, but the stronger the inclination to do the 'work', the stronger the urge to make the *'only'* choice;
>
> When you make the 'choice', you probably won't know what you are getting into;
>
> Once you make the choice – *the commitment* – there is no turning back;
>
> Once you have rounded the point of 'no return', your life will begin to change.

At this point, you may start asking questions like:

- *Why is this happening to me?*
- *What am I supposed to do?*
- *How am I supposed to do it?*
- *Is there anyone else who feels and thinks the way I do?*
- *Why do I feel so all alone?*
- *Is there anywhere I can get some* **Help?**

If you relate to these questions, you are probably on the 'path' already, and you have probably explored many facets of the path; thus, you have probably asked, and perhaps answered, questions like:

- Where can I search to find the path that is right for me?
- Why do some of the teachings that are supposed to be 'truth' seem so empty?
- Is there someone who can help me, and where can I find them?
- Who will teach me about the things that are important to me?
- Why can't I voice the things that seem important to me?

Now let's look at some of the principles that are fairly well established:

A change is indeed happening.

This change is 'new', really new; that means that it carries **something that was not here before.**

The change has certain characteristics:

- It is 'collective' and will lead to

a 'collective identity'.

- It manifests from introspection rather than extrospection.

Each person who makes the commitment has a unique piece of the puzzle or aspect of the change.

Each of us who makes the commitment and accepts

The Responsibility

to manifest our part of the puzzle must do so *on our own*.

We are each
TOTALLY independent in our work:

Your piece of the puzzle is 'yours' and you are most suited to place it into

THE BIG PICTURE

because of your unique configuration of consequences and foresequential possibilities.

However, if you don't pick up your piece of the responsibility, someone else will.

Epilogue: 'Why Me, and What Should I Do?'

If you don't pick up your piece of the puzzle, you have lost your chance to:

- Contribute to the change;
- Share the benefit of your personal evolutionary experience from lifetimes of consequences and growth; and
- Vastly accelerate your own personal spiritual and evolutionary growth.

Now let's look at some of the theory, practices, methods and techniques that you can use if you have made the commitment, accepted the responsibility and are ready to start or wish to continue in the 'work'.

The Theory and Philosophy

First the 'Theory'

> ***The way things are*** up to this point, is a culmination of events, consequences, and evolution.
>
> Where our present condition has evolved from is the ***manifested universe***: the key word is 'manifested'.
>
> Real change is the introduction of something 'new' – that is, something that is not yet manifested.
>
> This new element comes from outside the manifested universe.
>
> This can apply to every level of manifestation and creation.
>
> There is a point where this ***something new*** comes into the manifested universe;
>
> ***This point exists in each of us.***
>
> Evolution is supported by a 'drip feed' of this 'newness' all the time.
>
> As this 'newness' comes in, the manifested universe gobbles it up and lives on it.
>
> For the most part, the manifested universe uses this drip feed for its own purposes: that is, to perpetuate its own existence.
>
> Periodically, there is an increased inflow of this 'newness': let's call it
>
>
>
> **The Positive Presence.**
>
>
>
> **It is a Presence rather than an energy or force.**
>
> Periodically, this Presence manifests more strongly than a drip feed so that

it can make a major change in the manifested universe;

Sometimes this manifestation is *a Great Teacher.*
This time it is

OUR NEW HUMAN CONSCIOUSNESS

This time, the change is coming not through one great teacher but through lots of people who are in a way like lots of *little great teachers and hard workers.*

It is these people who 'suspect' that they have something to do.

Some of them have already made the commitment.

Some of them are only beginning to suspect that they have something to do and that there is a commitment to make.

Some are already well into what they know they should do; they are well into their work.

No matter at which stage of their development, each person who is truly committed is literally 'crying out' *to do* what they should do: that is, to fulfil their 'contract'.

You may ask, *'Who, me? Why me?'*

Those who have either made the commitment or those who want to 'try it on' and see how it fits.

NOW THE METHODS

These methods are described here.

> **These are the steps you can take. These are practical exercises for you, to help you gauge your own position, your commitment, and your 'contract'.**

First, recognise that you *can* open yourself to this Positive Presence.

When you open to the Positive Presence, your own consciousness will begin to change.

Begin to develop an

objective trust.

The key here *is whether you can develop a trust in something before you know what that something is. The key is not whether you can trust by deciding first whether it is trustworthy.*

The test is *whether you can trust in something remote, something that you don't know about yet, that you haven't seen:*

TO DO THIS

Ask yourself if you have any choice:

If you do have a choice,

then don't read any further.

If you don't have a choice, then place this trust and see how it goes.

Take on board a new practice and try it out. This new practice is something like a yoga asana or a t'ai chi movement or a transcendental meditation mantra, in that it is something that someone says, '*If you will do this, it will have an effect on you.*'
Try this practice for a while.

This practice is to:

- **First**, determine that you can move the focus of your awareness around;
- **Second**, when you can move your focus around, move it to a point just above the top of your head.

This will open a 'valve' at the top of your head, and the Positive Presence will begin to flow by more than a drip feed.
When this presence is flowing into your manifested vehicles, it will mix with your own bag of consequences – your own 'evolutionary contract'.
(This contract is not available to those who have an elementary consciousness and who are not yet ready to reach an evolutionary state where they can begin to contribute to manifested evolution.)

Once you reach a state where you have an evolutionary contract,
you have the opportunity to:

1. Learn from your own cosmic consequences and evolutionary experiences of past incarnations;
2. Offer to others that which you have learned through many lifetimes;
3. Begin to accept a share of the responsibility for the state of things as they are ***now*** due to your own consequences and the collective consequences of your fellow humans;
4. Accept the responsibility to manifest a part of ***the overall plan, the overall change...***

Our New Human Consciousness

That is

your own little contract – for the future evolution of where things are going.

Several things will begin to happen when this Presence becomes active and you accept *the opportunity/privilege* to work with it.

The elements of your contract will begin to unfold and help determine what parts of your consequences 'we' (the whole project) can use to move things along.

Certain things will begin to drop away; in particular, those parts of your inevitable consequences that are either irrelevant to your own part of the project or have already been picked up by someone else who is more suited to manifest something about them from *their* consequences and *their* contractual elements.

When these items begin to drop away, **they will begin to fall out of your memory.** That means that you will not be able to remember them.

If you have made the commitment, **you won't care if you forget these things or not.**

If you have not made the commitment and are merely 'trying it on', you will find out part of how the whole thing works so you can decide if you want to make the commitment.

As you begin to place more **'objective trust'**, you will find that you remember the things that you need to remember.

If you wonder why things are so hard, you are probably retaining some of your consequences and using them as an *evolutionary engineer or scientist* – to create a laboratory for you to get as much out of them as you can, so that you can contribute what you are learning to the 'project'.

If you don't want to do this,

get out of the project!

NOW FOR SOME OF THE TECHNIQUES

When you focus at the point where The Presence enters and you maintain the awareness there, the flow of presence increases, and the following phenomena will probably occur:

At first, your mind will play tricks on you. It will give you an idea and tell you it is new;

it's just trying to get you to do something it wants you to do either for its own pleasure, so it can control you, or for its own survival in its present state.

It may be very disorienting if you try to figure out what is going on.

After a while, *you will be able to distinguish whether a new idea is coming from your mind (as mentioned above) or whether it is* **a new insight inspired by and filled with the Positive Presence;** *something that you can do to help your own evolutionary growth and contribute to the project as well.*

It will be very exhilarating if you accept what is going on and…

flow with it.

As the flow increases, you will begin to 'join' a

Collective Identity

which is co-ordinating the project and manifesting it into the *manifested universe*.

This creates **a 'paradox' – a contradiction.** This paradox or contradiction can be described as follows:

On the one hand, you are part of a big 'whole' project – a collective identity responsible for implementing the project;

On the other hand, you are totally independent and totally responsible for what you do.

Further, as the flow increases, your 'past' will begin to fall away, *your memory into the past will shorten; yes, you may be able to remember events way back in your childhood, but you may not be able to remember what you had for breakfast three days ago (unless, for instance, you eat the same thing for breakfast every day);*

And, as the flow increases, you will be less and less able to project what you are going to do in the future. This is due not only to your loss of irrelevant memory and memories but also the inapplicability of your conjecture and speculation about:

What you should do in the future and

How you should go about doing it.

As the flow increases, and as you place more **objective trust** in what is happening to you (even though you don't yet know where it is coming from), you will find that you are increasingly unable to project even the present into the future. If you have made the commitment and accepted the responsibility mentioned above, this is perfectly understandable in that:

- what you ***should do*** changes constantly because there are a lot of people like you who are doing exactly what you are doing;
- In the ***collective identity,*** all of our decisions and actions are mixed up in a big bowl and then each of us gets a spoonful of the new mixture whenever we tap into the point where the Presence enters;
- even the decisions you made a few seconds ago went into the bowl and the decisions you make tomorrow had better be based on what is in the bowl ***then***.

The way you find out what you are supposed to do is to 'look into the bowl' and find out what the state of the mixture is *then*.

As you tap into the flow of the Presence, your commitment will increase and you will accept even more responsibility for a bigger share of the project.

And this means that:

That is when you must decide what to do; ***you*** will have to make bigger decisions.

Many of the people around you may disagree with what you are doing because either:

- if they are *switched on and into the project*, they have forgotten that you have your own combination of Presence/consequences/contractual foresequences; *or*
- if they are not 'switched on', they don't have any idea what you are doing anyway, because *you are not making decisions and deciding what to do* **the way they do, which is:**

- based on the past;
- based on the desire to survive intact;
- based on the desire to control others in order to survive intact;
- based on the wish to keep the status quo without change so that they don't have to think about what they will do next;
- based on the urge to retain some kind of pleasure or comfort zone.

And they will not understand how you could want to hold onto something that may give you pain (a consequence that provides you with back-pressure to work through something for both your own evolutionary growth and for something that you can share to the project).

As the flow of the Positive Presence increases, you will find that you are sharing common or similar problems of others; that is, you and many others in the project may have a little aspect of the same or similar 'problem' in your spoonful that you got from the mixture.

Although it looks like the same problem, your aspect of it is unique **if you work with it**. If you don't work with it and don't take the responsibility to work with it, it will end up on someone else's spoon for them to work with;

- at this point, as you move further into the project, you will have the privilege of rejecting certain aspects of work that are offered to you, but this is based on
- your development and refinement of discrimination so that you can **decide** what you can do in the time you have with the talents you have; and

how much pain of *original thought* that you can bear, and even then, even when you think you cannot handle it.

Sometimes the *collective project* still says:

Please Do It Anyway.

As the flow increases, you will increasingly have the ability/right to make decisions that affect not only you but also the project, others around you,

and the whole human family.

These decisions are often *evolutionary* such that **you can decide** (based on the state of the 'mixture' when you look into the bowl)…

> **That** *'we' are finished with a certain kind of activity and that you are now deciding to withdraw energy from it, dismantle it, and return it to its elements in the manifested universal energy.*

When you do this, you begin to countermand the efforts of those who wish to perpetuate the activity. You don't have to join a movement to do this; you can do it mentally as you accept more Presence and work with the Presence in a certain direction.

That *'we' could do with a new way of doing something: for example,*

- *a new way of relating to each other, or*
- *a new way of making decisions, and*
- *you decide that you will put some of the Presence flowing into you into that new way.*

This looks hard at first, but remember you are not alone in this: the elements of **how** a new something is to be done are available to you if you look into the bowl of the collective work, and chances are someone else has at least *wondered* how we might do something differently, and their *wonderings* provide you with at least some elementary ideas of how you might work out this new way.

As the flow increases, and you begin to work more with it, remember then that

the decisions you make go into the bowl.

You should also know that when you put something into the bowl, *you* change the make-up of the mixture *right then*, and it will for ever be changed. Even if you *know* the effect you have had and the state of the mixture then and there, it is a mistake to assume that it will be the same **tomorrow** or even in **a few seconds,**

because the process is dynamic.

This means that

it is *ever-changing*, and it will never be the same *again*.

This whole process goes contrary to the way we make decisions now; that is, by saying, 'Oh, this worked in the past, so we'll try it again,' or 'It seems to be working now, so it will probably work again tomorrow.'

Those others who are working on the project are in the same condition as you are in: they too have to keep up day-to-day and minute-to-minute, and it is just as hard for them as it is for you.

But one thing is comforting:

Even though you are on your own,

YOU ARE NOT ALONE.

Printed in Great Britain
by Amazon